Critical Muslim 24

Populism

Critical Muslim is published quarterly by C. Hurst & Co. (Publishers) Ltd. on behalf of and in conjunction with Critical Muslim Ltd. and the Muslim Institute, London. *Critical Muslim* acknowledges the support of the Aziz Foundation, London.

All correspondence to Muslim Institute, CAN Mezzanine, 49-51 East Road, London N1 6AH, United Kingdom

e-mail for editorial: editorial@criticalmuslim.com

The editors do not necessarily agree with the opinions expressed by the contributors. We reserve the right to make such editorial changes as may be necessary to make submissions to *Critical Muslim* suitable for publication.

C. Hurst & Co (Publishers) Ltd.,41 Great Russell Street, London WC1B 3PL

ISBN: 978-1-84904-899-6 ISSN: 2048-8475

To subscribe or place an order by credit/debit card or cheque (pounds sterling only) please contact Kathleen May at the Hurst address above or e-mail kathleen@hurstpub.co.uk

Tel: 020 7255 2201

A one year subscription, inclusive of postage (four issues), costs £50 (UK), £65 (Europe) and £75 (rest of the world).

The right of Ziauddin Sardar and the Contributors to be identified as the authors of this publication is asserted by them in accordance with the Copyright, Designs and Patents Act, 1988.

A Cataloguing-in-Publication data record for this book is available from the British Library

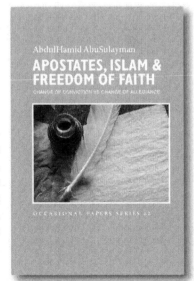

Critical Muslim

Subscribe to Critical Muslim

Now in its sixth year in print, Hurst is pleased to announce that *Critical Muslim* is also available online. Users can access the site for just £3.30 per month – or for those with a print subscription it is included as part of the package. In return, you'll get access to everything in the series (including our entire archive), and a clean, accessible reading experience for desktop computers and handheld devices — entirely free of advertising.

Full subscription

The print edition of *Critical Muslim* is published quarterly in January, April, July and October. As a subscriber to the print edition, you'll receive new issues directly to your door, as well as full access to our digital archive.

United Kingdom £50/year
Europe £65/year
Rest of the World £75/year

Digital Only

Immediate online access to *Critical Muslim*

Browse the full *Critical Muslim* archive

Cancel any time

£3.30 per month

www.criticalmuslim.io

CM24

October–December 2017

CONTENTS

POPULISM

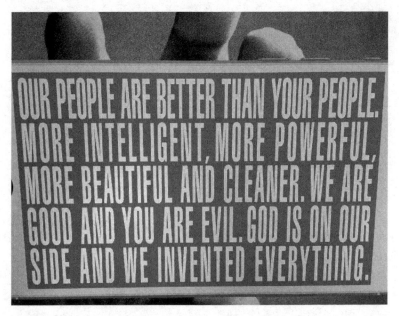

Barbara Kruger, *Untitled (Surrounded)* 2017, Installation, 'Space Force Construction'
V-A-C Foundation, Palazzo delle Zattere, Venice

ARTS AND LETTERS

REVIEWS

ET CETERA

This issue of *Critical Muslim* is dedicated to Ashis Nandy: friend, intellectual companion and champion of life enhancing traditions, who celebrates his 80th birthday this year.

POPULISM

INTRODUCTION:
FIBS AND FIBBERS

Ziauddin Sardar

'This is a true story.' Every episode of FX's black comedy and crime drama *Fargo* begins with this superimposed text. Gradually the word 'true' evaporates and we are left with 'this is a story'. After we are informed of the time and place the alleged true story is set, we are told: 'at the request of the survivors, the names have been changed. Out of respect for the dead, the rest has been told exactly as it occurred'. Of course, it is all fiction. But the deliberate interplay between 'true' and 'story' suggests that we often regard the narratives we imagine and create about ourselves, no matter how preposterous, as true. The delectable dubious villain of season three, V A Varga asks the protagonist Emmit Stussy, 'Do you think that if you believe honestly that a Lie is true, it is true?' 'I don't know,' replies Stussy. 'It's your story.'

Fibs projected as true stories. That is what populism is all about. Like all stories it has elements of truth. And like all stories it is fiction in the true sense of the word, involving falsehood, lies, misrepresentation, untruth. But the stories are enticing and emotionally charged. They are held to be totally true by those entranced by populism.

The word itself can be applied to all variety of political and ideological positions. It has been applied to movements and their leaders, policies and manifestos, on the Right as well as the Left. Always used as a finger of accusation, it implies that the accused is manipulative, corrupt, and high-handed. The emergence of both Trump in the US and Brexit in Britain is seen as populist. But it cuts both ways. Right-leaning media commentators have, in turn, characterised the rise of the Labour Party's Jeremy Corbyn or Bernie Sanders of the US as alarming examples of populism, albeit of the socialist variety. So, is populism merely in the eye of the beholder? Does the label carry an undertone of political sour grapes or scaremongering? If Trump is a populist, then what about India's Narendra Modi, Turkey's Recep Tayyip Erdogan, Russia's Vladimir Putin, or Venezuela's Nicolas Maduro (and Hugo Chavez before him)?

In everyday usage, 'populist' seems to apply to any person, movement, or regime that tries to appeal to 'ordinary' or 'little' people. In the 1980s, however, scholars became perplexed by a new breed of Latin American politicians who mobilised incredible public support while implementing neoliberal policies that, on paper, should have been anathema to 'ordinary people'. This is when the term 'neopopulism' made its debut in academic debate. And, for a while, Latin America seemed to be the natural focus for commentaries on populism in academia, journalism and popular culture – remember *Evita*? Now with the rise of the far Right in Europe and America, when it has spread worldwide with the devastating speed of stage 4 cancer, populism has gained much wider currency.

The consensual definition comes from political scientists Cas Mudde and Cristóbal Rovira Kaltwasser who present populism as an equation with two sides. Populism, they suggest, is a form of politics that pits 'a morally virtuous people against a corrupt elite'. Let's leave morality and virtue aside for a moment and focus on the other side of the equation: corrupt elite. Well, there is no limit to their corruption. The ruling elite almost everywhere are on the whole corrupt. In America, the Congress and Senate do the bidding of corporate lobbies. In Britain, there is a revolving door that takes politicians to well-paid jobs in the city, the media and corporations. Look at the lucrative post-politics careers of former Labour Prime Minister Tony Blair and Conservative Chancellor George Osborne. Russia is ruled by an oligarchy of criminals. India is awash with corrupt political elite at all levels. In Pakistan, a populist movement led by former cricketer turned politician, Imran Khan, has ousted the incumbent Prime Minister, Nawaz Sharif, on allegations of corruption – to be replaced by someone who is just as corrupt. Indeed, it will be easier to discover the proverbial pin in a haystack than to find a politician in Pakistan who does not face allegations of corruption. In South Korea, two prime ministers have resigned in quick succession due to corruption charges: Lee Wan-koo and Sung Wan-jong. In Indonesia, the popularly elected man of the people, President Joko Widodo, is knee deep in corruption charges. Ditto Jacob Zuma of South Africa, Rodrigo Roa Duterte of the Philippines, and most political leaders in Eastern Europe.

But it is not just the politicians who are unprincipled. Consider the ability of CEOs to award themselves obscene salaries and vast bonuses regardless of performance and make absurd profits from company liquidations. The gall of pharmaceutical corporations to implement profit margins of thousands of per cent. The transformation of universities into covetous corporations. The insatiable greed of Wall Street and City of London. As Paul Wilmot and David Orrell show in *The Money Formula*, the financial markets are a big fraud. We have recently learned that the London Interbank Offered Rate (LIBOR), the framework for trillions of dollars of daily transactions that has operated for decades, is a fiction! It is not just that banks manipulate LIBOR. No. They make it up – like a story. As a group of bright economics students at Manchester University discovered, much of what they were being taught was made-up stories. No wonder they rebelled. What we are being taught, they declared in their guarded language, is 'econocracy': economics that is 'disproportionate to our state of knowledge', 'too narrow in its technical focus and too broad in its social impact', and places 'excessive degree of policy power in the hands of technocrats wielding them'. In other words, mostly junk. That science has been steadily corrupted over recent decades is now well established. Way back in 1972, in his seminal work, *Scientific Knowledge and Its Social Problems*, my friend and mentor Jerry Ravetz argued that the industrialisation of science was corrupting it from inside. Since then he has been charting the continuous expansion of this corruption. Even mathematics, that symbol of objective purity, has now been corrupted: big data, artificial intelligence, algorithms are all, in the words of Cathy O'Neil, *Weapons of Math Destruction*. When human behaviour, performance and potential is reduced to mathematical formulae, they tend to reinforce discrimination, reduce the accountability of those in power and create 'a toxic cocktail for democracy'. Soon racist bots and algorithms will take over the whole world making most human beings surplus to need. And there is no redemption from art, the secular foundation of redemption, which is essentially a highbrow and banal market-driven commodity. Marjorie Allthorpe-Guyton finds the 2017 Venice Biennale to be little more than 'monuments to hubris'. From being the Olympics of the art world it has now become *Game of Thrones*. The media too is drenched in corruption. The salary controversy at the BBC is just the tip of the iceberg. The so-called public service broadcaster, seen by many as the doyen of impartiality, was revealed to pay vast salaries to its 'talent' (and executives) while discriminating against women and ethnic minorities. On the whole, producers and researchers at the BBC are badly paid; and journalists for the World Service, who often risk their lives to do their job, are at the bottom of the pile. As Jon Snow, presenter of Channel 4 News notes, 'the echelons from which our media are drawn do not, for the most part, fully reflect the population among whom we live and to whom we seek to transmit information and ideas'. The media 'are comfortably with the elite, with little awareness, contact or connection with those not of the elite'.

A few years ago, my friend Ashis Nandy, the celebrated Indian public intellectual, got into trouble by merely pointing out that corruption has been democratised in India. It is not just the conventional elite who are corrupt but the emerging elite amongst the *dalits*, the marginalised and oppressed untouchables, are similarly disreputable. The *dalits* took great offence and tried to take Nandy to court. But the democratisation of corruption is now a universal phenomenon. However, it is not just that corruption has now reached all levels of society and has become an integral part of the system. The point is that corruption *is* the system. It manifests itself in the inherent inequities of capitalism, the sleaze of the global financial infrastructures, the bankruptcy of socialism (*vide* Venezuela), the tyranny of the majority in electoral democracy, the ineptitude of governance, the cynicism and unaccountability of those in power, the increasing irrelevance of some academic disciplines, the wholesale marginalisation of populations including working class communities, and alienation of youth who have no prospects and hence no hope. So the 'morally virtuous people' are totally justified in standing up to both: the corrupt elite and the inherent corruption of the system that sustains the world; they are, in fact, the same. The challenge is to change the system without the 'hatred for the traitors and the corrupt'. As Nandy notes, 'once you let loose this other form of populism, political institutions have little control over it. For the vigilante groups operating as mobs behave as if they have been left free to define sedition and moral corruption'.

The other side of the equation is all about hope. The 'morally virtuous' find themselves in a position where they have nothing – not even hope. Populism, in its different disguise, becomes a source of optimism and a vehicle of expectation. The problem is not so much populism *per se* but the subject of hope – what exactly the populist movements desire. The populist movements led by Jeremy Corbyn in Britain and Bernie Saunders in the US place their faith in accountability and democratic reform – the hope is that this would lead to a more just and equitable society. The populist alt-right, white supremacists and Nazi movements in the US place their hope on racial purity – they believe that blacks are inferior and should be, in the words of Ibram X Kendi, the author of a notable history of racist ideas in America, 'segregated, incarcerated, enslaved and eliminated'. They hold similar views about Muslims, Jews and immigrants. So we cannot equate these two types of Left and Right populism. To treat them under the general rubric of 'populism' would be as absurd as denouncing, as Trump did, both the torch-wielding far right marchers shouting 'blood and soil', 'white lives matter' and 'Jews will not replace us' and the counter protesters who gathered to oppose them at the University of Virginia in Charlottesville on 11 August 2017. Similarly, the populism that swept Emmanuel Macron into power in France created a new political party in just over a year, marginalised the conventional Conservative and Socialist parties, and brought numerous fresh faces into the Senate and National Assembly cannot be compared to the populism enjoyed over the years by the far right *Front National*. Neither can the populism of Imran Khan in Pakistan, discussed by Raza Ali, be equated with the populism of Frauke Petry, the smiling face of

Germany's fascism that frightens Leyla Jagiella. To bundle all variety of populisms into one lump, under a single definition, is, in my opinion, a category mistake.

A good example of an all-embracing definition is offered by Gordon Steffey via Ernesto Laclau who argued that 'populism is defined not by ideological contents but by a "logic of articulation" or formulary for the promulgation of any contents whatsoever. It is a logic with no specific commitments or, if you prefer, is open to any specific commitments, left, right, and centre. This is why it has been possible to describe Le Pen, Thatcher, Chávez, and Perón as populists, and why too our sitting US President now joins this merry band. What defines populist logic is its embrace of diverse ideological demands and its homogenisation of their diversity in a shared antagonism to power'. I am not sure whether such a broad definition is useful as an analytical tool. Thatcher may have been populist but she was not a white supremacist like Le Pen (Père); and the ideals and goals of the followers of the two were/are distinctively different even when some of the rhetoric may appear to be similar. Thatcher was very specific in her ideology, her commitments, and her precise goals. 'The pestiferous Leaderene', as Merryl Wyn Davies describes her, 'laid waste to swathes of Britain and the lives of large numbers of ordinary people' in her quest for 'the ideological purity of market forces'. Both Thatcher's populism and the populism that brought the Ayatollah Khomeini to power and turned Iran into a theocracy are right wing yet quite distinctively different. Steffey reminds us of Laclau's observation that 'there is no populism without discursive construction of an enemy: the Ancien Régime, the oligarchy, the Establishment or whatever'. That's probably one of the two common elements in all varieties of populism. For Thatcher the enemy was the welfare state; for Le Pen it was anyone who was not French as he defined it; for Khomeini it was excesses of modernity as exemplified by the Shah of Iran. The other common element is the construction of the popular: in Laclau's words, 'populist discourse does not simply express some kind of original popular identity; it actually constitutes the latter.'

An alternative approach to populism is to explain it in terms of propositions. This is what Bart Bonikowski, in a much cited paper, tries to do. Populism, he argues, is a discursive frame, not limited to the Right, not new and is (primarily) not an ideology. Certainly, right-wing populism is hardly new in the US: fascism has deep roots in American soil going back to the Silver Shirts movements in the 1930s, when it was comfortably embraced in the shape of eugenics by highly respected academic institutions. In the 1980s, it re-emerged as *Friendly Fascism*, the title of Bertram Gross's insightful 1980 book, when Big Business and Republican administrations came together to manage society in the interests of a rich and powerful elite. Trump is a direct beneficiary of that manoeuvre. Europe too is not a stranger to populism. The far right movements in Europe are building on a well-established history. Sindre Bangstad, in his contribution to this issue of *Critical Muslim*, presents three propositions on right wing populism in Europe: the 'people' in populism is neither any people, nor your people; it's not (only) the economy; and for all their talk of 'religion', the faith of populist right-wingers is largely faithless. I would suggest that in certain types of populism, the economy does play an important part. The 'people' often become fodder for the factories that sustain neoliberal economies. When the factories move elsewhere in search of cheaper labour, the people are left abandoned. They do not have skills, resources, the ability or motivation to leave their communities and move away in search of employment. Not surprisingly, they turn to those who claim to represent their interests – the tub-thumping, Bible chanting demagogue of the far right, who is, in the words of Barnaby Rogerson, 'a bewitchingly brilliant speaker-leader, who achieves absolute mastery over his people through his evil genius and then like some mad self-selected Demi-God leads them off towards their ultimate destruction'. But, Rogerson tells us, the demagogue 'was initially just a leader of the people drawn from the people'.

The people? There is a strange category for you. For one thing, people get blamed for everything. Both Brexit and Trump have been blamed on white working class people. Even the fact that they suffer from unemployment and poverty is their fault. But while constantly decried and neglected, they are invoked whenever it is politically expedient. As Bangstad notes, 'much scholarly ink has in recent years been spilt on figuring out exactly who "the people" to which right-wing populists every so often refer actually are'. And the populists, both of left and right, claim that they and only they exclusively represent the people. The Urdu word for the people is *awaam*. In Pakistan, writes Raza Ali, 'politicians, political commentators and religious leaders all routinely use the term *Awaam* to refer to an entity which harbours the same emotions, hopes and opinions as themselves'. But, Ali says, he has never met this 'mythical group'.

What would 'the people' look like when you actually come face to face with one of their members? The answer is provided by the French intellectual Didier Eribon in *Returning to Reims*. Eribon is a historian and social critic who happens to be gay. He left his working class home in Reims, largely because of his father's homophobic views, to pursue an academic career in Paris. And he never looked back: he hated his father who becomes a symbol of loathing for his working class background, which he worked hard to hide, a price of admission to the elite intellectual circles of Paris. Decades later, he is forced to return home to the 'garden city', which was basically 'a reservation for the poor', at the pleading of his mother, who drives daily twenty kilometres to the nursing home where his father is dying. He never had a conversation with his father: 'he was not capable of it'. His mother, 'slave to motherhood', was violent; and spent most of her life cleaning houses. Eribon is shocked by the fact that both his father and mother, who were staunch communists, now support the *Front National*. Eribon traces the history of his parents and grandparents and is astonished at the grinding poverty of their lives, the education system that is designed to dump them on the scrap heap, their isolation and loneliness, and the abandonment of the entire working class by the European left in its embrace of neoliberal rhetoric and policies – 'the naked violence of exploitation'. 'When people write about the working class world', Eribon says, 'which they rarely do, it is most often because they have left it behind. They therefore contribute to the social illegitimacy of the people they are speaking of in the very moment of speaking about them'. Why would these 'working class people' abandon their left leaning politics to embrace an extreme right-wing party?

There comes a moment when, being spat upon, you turn the spit into roses; you turn the verbal attacks into garlands of flowers, into rays of light. There is, in short, a moment when shame turns into pride. This pride is political through and through because it defines the deepest workings of normality and of normativity.

Much the same can be said about those living impoverished and isolated lives in the *banlieues*, the ghettoes outside Paris.

So populism is based on a string of long and deeply established trends. Ashis Nandy traces it back to the French Revolution. Now, it has brought us to a moment when, to use the word of James Ball, the former specialist project editor of the *Guardian*, 'bullshit' has become ubiquitous. Evan Davis, presenter of BBC's *Newsnight*, suggests the bullshit is wrapped in a dual mystery: 'why would anyone be taken in by the stuff if it is blatant nonsense' and 'why on earth is so much breath wasted on producing it'. What all this bullshit means is that we are entering the era of 'declining value of truth as society's reserve currency' with the simultaneous and infectious spread of 'pernicious relativism as legitimate scepticism', says Matthew d'Ancona, columnist and former editor of conservative weekly *Spectator*. A 'post-truth' panic amongst journalists has led some to produce instant tomes to defend their corner. (One ought to point out that these are the very chaps who, according to Jon Snow, got almost everything wrong in the past year: 'The Brexit referendum: we got it wrong. Trump defied so-called experts, pundits and journalists alike. Theresa May's general election: we got it wrong'. Even the June 2017 Grenfell Tower inferno, which killed at least 80 people, could not be reported with due consideration for the victims, Snow anguishes). Indeed, books on post-truth have become a small cottage industry.

Like populism, bullshit – half-truths, lies, damn lies and manipulation by statistics – is also not new. The West has been selling bullshit as History to the rest of the world for at least two centuries. Orientalism, as constructed lies, has an even longer history. We live in a culture saturated with advertisements, which are basically lies, often blatant lies. Popular press and certain television channels constantly publish lies with impunity. As Ari Rabin-Havt and Media Matters for America show in *Lies,*

Incorporated, mega corporations sell lies on a mega scale and fight and suppress anyone who stands against them: tobacco companies, oil giants, health insurers, arms manufacturers – it is quite a list. And there is an industry that is dedicated to the promotion and dissemination of these lies: the lobbyists and the PR goliaths. The case of Bell Pottinger who are accused of inflaming racial tensions in South Africa is the most recent example. The PR firm promoted its pernicious narrative by incorporating it into speeches of politicians, press releases, broadcasts, websites as well as slogans. Given the extent of such activities, it is not surprising that we have reached a 'double-bind' that Ashis Nandy analyses with evident skill. One segment of 'the people' fully believes these lies to be true. Climate change deniers did not emerge overnight; they were produced, curated and nourished for decades. The other segments had had enough of such lies and have lost all trust in politicians as well as public institutions, including the media.

D'Ancona's 'pernicious relativism' also has history that goes back several decades: it is called postmodernism. In fact, we can pinpoint the date when postmodernism emerged as an all-encompassing trend: the publication of Jean-Francois Lyotard's *The Postmodern Condition: A Report on Knowledge* in 1979. Postmodernism triumphantly declared that 'grand narratives' are meaningless, that all truths, whether based on science, religion, history, tradition, or ideology, whatever their source, are totally relative and, as such, as bad as each other. This philosophy, which became an arch ideology, fuelled academia, architecture, philosophy, fiction, cinema, television, fashion and even shopping malls. The arrival of Trump, the iconic face of Post-Truth, is hardly surprising given that we have been systematically, and quite comprehensively, nudged towards accepting the fallacy that all truths are relative.

What is really new is that a number of deeply embedded trends – from postmodern relativism to the isolation and marginalisation of whole swathes of society, from cavernous inequities of capitalism to the eager embrace of neoliberalism by the Left, from globalisation to the rapid growth of technology – have crashed together. The end-product is a globalised, networked society where things happen rapidly, often simultaneously and globally. Complex networks have a tendency towards chaotic behaviour. Accelerating change and contradictions enhance complexity, generate positive feedback, and regularly take us to the edge of chaos. We call it postnormal times, where social media makes it possible for insignificant groups who operated on the margins to connect with fellow travellers instantly, to transform themselves into complex, ever changing networks, and create chaos. Such groups can not only shape the centre from the periphery but actually occupy the centre. Paranoia, to use the words of d'Ancona, takes centre stage.

Under such circumstances, it is easy to be overwhelmed. Abdelwahab El-Affendi sees the Muslim world in the grip of a triple plague: populism, corrupt despotism and terrorism, 'each is its own worst enemy'. 'Populism', El-Affendi writes, 'is an attack on Western societies and values, before being an attack on minorities and foreigners. Despotism is a war on the people, just like terrorism. Groups like ISIS come with a self-destruct mechanism, but not before devastating the communities they infect. The evil alliance between terrorists, Islamophobic populism and despotism will usher in a dark age of experimentation with old-style colonialism, as Europe goes back home to its Islamophobic dark ages'. Richard Appignanesi sees populism as an 'existential condition' without a cure, leading us toward 'an immense, tragic and ineluctable *loss of world*'.

While there are reasons to be pessimistic, it is perhaps not the best prescription. Postnormal times are a call to arms: an invitation to challenge our assumptions and biases about the contemporary world and possibilities for the future. It demands that we interrogate our sense of what we have accepted, and continue to accept, as 'normal' and 'conventional'. The important point to note about all varieties of populism is that each tells lies about the other and believes its own lies, particularly about itself. But it is not just the populist we need to stand up to. We also need to interrogate the lies we tell about ourselves.

In the third season of *Fargo*, the villainous V A Varga makes a key observation: 'the problem is not that there is evil. The problem is that there is good. Someone who cares'. We don't need heroes. Just good people. There is hope as long as there are 'morally virtuous people' who care; and embody the old-fashioned virtues of human dignity and worth, equality and social justice, compassion and forgiveness, humility and patience, sincerity and thankfulness, courage and self-control. This is the moral compass we need to navigate a system that is at the edge of chaos, when a hasty move can have serious, unintended consequences which can tip the system into collapse. A modicum of imagination and creativity would not go amiss either.

THE NETHERWORLD

Ashis Nandy

Until recently, populism hid a double-bind. For it carried with it two perfectly contradictory sets of associations. Both sets had direct connections with the French Revolution, the mother of all revolutions that can still be called the paradigmatic revolution. However hard Karl Marx might have tried to scientise history, by giving it a social-evolutionary thrust and by linking it to a brand-new concept of revolution with a clearer modern connection and a new scientific and moral status, his theory of revolution remains tied in public imagination to the romance and adventure of the revolution of 1789.

Some of the popular sayings and beliefs about the French Revolution – sayings such as 'a revolution always consumes its own children' and beliefs such as 'virtue is helpless without terror' – were applied to the October Revolution verbatim. Either to condemn or to justify the terror associated with the Russian version of the game. The Soviet regime also sired less colourful but more ambitious versions of Maximilien Robespierre in several parts of the world to 'normalise' the large-scale killings in the name of revolution in the Soviet Union. Yet, the slogans of liberty, equality and fraternity survived such instrumental use of 'surplus violence' and managed to inspire numerous struggles for freedom and dignity all over the world. Even in far off India, Ram Mohan Roy (1772–1833), the first social and religious reformer of modern times in South Asia and the representative of the Mughal Emperor in the British court, invoked the values of the French Revolution in some of his correspondence with French authorities.

The French revolution was a spontaneous, popular rebellion that changed our world irrevocably. To millions of its admirers all over the world, for all its excesses, the French Revolution was arguably populism's grandest, most creative moment. This brings us to the other avatar of populism associated with 1789, which entered the world stage at around the same time. It, too, has shown its resilience by intermittently becoming the dominant presence in many societies, over the last two hundred years – sometimes as a political strategy, sometimes as a major strand in the culture of democratic politics. This populism is associated with the fear of the mob setting the pace of politics and sometimes running amuck in spontaneous, one-sided violence, as in lynch-mobs, witch hunts, kangaroo courts and other similar instances of instant justice. In *A Tale of Two Cities*, Charles Dickens neatly captures this split heritage of the French Revolution in the very first sentence of the novel.

In Gustave Le Bon's *The Crowd*, a pioneering effort, there is the presumption that the simplified ideology or idea that holds a crowd together comes from its leader. This now needs qualification, to accommodate the growing role that mass media has begun to play in mass violence. The role of state controlled media and mass-based political parties in mobilising 'de-individuated' mobs through appeals that enter the homes and the private lives of the citizens with their simplified ideological messages is now a part of normal politics in many countries. A mob now may not need a crafty demagogue of the calibre of Mark Antony in Shakespeare's *Julius Caesar*.

Perhaps the best example of this is the Rwandan genocide in 1994 and the role a humble medium – state controlled radio – played in that genocide. It was probably the most momentous use of radio since Orson Welles in 1938 triggered panic in the United States through a documentary-style radio play based on the novel *War of the Worlds* by H.G. Wells. (That unintended 'experiment' in mass behaviour is now routinely taught in courses of social psychology and in communications. There is controversy about the seriousness of the impact and the element of premeditation in Wells, but there is little doubt that the event has remained a milestone in the social psychology of mass behaviour and mass psychology. The Rwandan experience, at one level, took the early 'experiment' to its logical conclusion.) In Rwanda, a small country of about 7 million, four-fifths of a million were killed in record time, probably most of them within ten days. There were cases of even husbands killing their wives belonging to other ethnic groups.

This darker version of populism, of course, breaks out not only in epidemics of instant violence or mob justice, but also in shrill appeals made to the potential vigilante groups to endorse policy choices that promise to disempower the elite and the ultra-elite, or at least clip their wings. Either in the name of nationalism or as an attack on their moral bankruptcy. Such appeals now ritually invoke not love for the nation or financial probity but hatred for the traitors and the corrupt. Once you let loose this other form of populism, political institutions have little control over it. For the vigilante groups operating as mobs behave as if they have been left free to define sedition and moral corruption.

Such freedom to define enemies is now seen as a necessary part of mass mobilisation and, in its humdrum version, as a necessary ingredient of a decentralised electoral campaign. An atmosphere of fear is created and it silences everyone who disagrees with the killers and their patrons within the law-and-order machinery and in the higher rungs of politics. It *is* psychologically easier to mobilise people on grounds of hatred—fear has a subsidiary role in that hatred—exactly as dystopias in literature touch us more deeply than do utopias.

Both President Trump of the United States and Prime Minister Narendra Modi of India came to power riding the crest of this version of populism. Both hate the sharper edges of their own campaigning style when that style is deployed against them, to discredit their regimes or to bring them 'undeserved' infamy. Both subtly communicate to their minions and constituencies that excesses may not be tolerated but their right to 'legitimate hatred' will be fully protected. This bifocal communication is handled so deftly that it seems to be a major strength of this strand of populism.

Unknown to its practitioners and protagonists, this double-think has a systemic impact. On the one hand, it works as an angry populism that addresses the frustrations, rage and sense of betrayal of the dispossessed and the displaced, seeking to assign responsibility and identify targets. During the French Revolution, the rebellious mobs found clear targets in the aristocracy and the clergy to give their uprising its distinctive character and its paradigmatic status. Pankaj Mishra's *The Age of Anger* is an excellent comprehensive account of this part of the story.

Today, despite such attempts to assign responsibility and locate targets, a part of the task remains incomplete. For, often, the other side of the anger is the confused, uncomfortable feeling that its targets are invisible because they are impersonal, vaguely defined and can only be glimpsed through a complex maze of institutions. When Donald Trump speaks about Washington politicians or vendors of fake news, it is a generic condemnation, not a specific accusation. No genuine debate can take place on the subject, for the only thing real is Trump's contempt for his enemies and his free-floating anger. It is that anger that seals the bond between the mob and a much larger political constituency in the form of a transient 'pseudo-community' of the lost, the marginalised and the excluded.

Such generic anger gives its sponsors distinct political advantages. It allows local leadership to instigate or organise local vigilantes to find local targets based on local grievances. You bypass the problem of educating the vigilantes in complex ideological issues and, yet, give them the feeling that they are participating not in a local feud but in a much larger national or global mission. Let me give an example.

The last time lynching broke out in the United States was in the 1950s in the wake of the civil rights movement. It made global news. Now, after nearly seventy years, it has broken out in India on a larger scale. And, unlike in the United States in the 1950s, the Indian state does not give the impression of being an impartial ruler; the ruling regime is ambivalent towards the lynch mobs. If anything, the regime would like to dismiss the instances of lynching as stray criminal acts that the police can handle, but it also knows that the perpetrators are supporters of the regime and expect some degree of impunity, despite what the Prime Minister might publicly say.

Two other forces underwrite the long life of the lynching epidemic in India. First, there is the attempt, deliberate or incidental, to reduce the citizenry to a mass of passive receivers of messages from the mass media and consumers of centralised propaganda. Mass communications through television and social media have come to India relatively late and those exposed to them are yet to develop a healthy scepticism towards the fare dished out for their consumption. Like Trump's constituency, Modi's too is willing to trust only its leader; the rest of the world, it believes, has ganged up against him.

Second, in Western Europe and North America, at the beginning of the twentieth century, one-way communications – books, newspapers, radio, public lectures, sermons, TV, cinema, etc. – were only a small part of all communications. The rest were bilateral or multilateral. By the end of the century, one-way communication had grown enormously and in many sectors occupy more than 90 per cent of an individual's available time. This growth is accompanied by the spread, popularity and reach of what could be called 'total media', the forms of media where, little or no scope is left for the imagination of the audience to work on; the audience is reduced to being passive consumers of messages. Almost all its sense organs are engaged in ensuring total immersion in someone else's imagination. A novel or a short story allows you to imagine on your own the looks and voices of its various characters, the landscape and homes where the events take place. Depending on the way the novelist has entered your mind, *you* can enter the story in different ways – as a passive observer or as a direct, active, participant observer. Even a staged play, though it may sometimes come close to being total media, forces you to re-imagine the context and the location, by not allowing you to be fully immersed in the experience of seeing and hearing. When the surgeon general of the United States advises you to restrict television viewing to 45 minutes a day, he or she probably has in mind the run-of-the-mill movies and shows.

Total media is habit-forming. Once you allow it to seduce you into a virtual world that gives you the feeling of belonging, there is much less space for the world in which you otherwise live. It has been estimated that an hour's television news covers roughly only the news on one page of a newspaper. Yet, it gives you the feeling that the hour you have spent in front of the TV has equipped you to understand, comment upon, and judge the flow of global events of the day. That you are ready to vote, be politically active, and decide the future of your country on the basis of that exposure. The narrowness and superficiality of such media exposure is lost on you because you are not alert to the political design behind the message.

The dominance of one-way communication in our interpersonal world is also facilitating the emergence of a new kind of citizen. David Riesman in his book *The Lonely Crowd* called them the other-directed ones, products of a mass society where many forms of sociality, family and community ties have weakened. He had in mind a society that had shed many of its primary ties and is increasingly peopled not by inner-directed persons guided by personal values and choices but by mass media, advertisement and peer-driven choices.

Today, in some societies, this other-directedness may have acquired a more sinister dimension. Authoritarianism is not only imposed from above. There is also demand from below for a more controlled, militarised democracy, some form of 'developmental authoritarianism', theocracy or, for that matter, an ideological state fulfilling its promise outside its democratic mandate. This is a theme that has been explored at different times by Wilhelm Reich in *The Mass Psychology of Fascism* and in Woody Allen in his movie *Zelig*.

The archetypal presence of the French Revolution would not have been possible without the spread and the reach of mass media in our public life. Elections in major democracies are becoming like advertisement wars and election campaigns have increasingly come under the control of media experts and media tycoons who determine the tone and the postures of candidates according to the preferences of the electorates culled from opinion polls. Ideological differences and visions of a desirable society no longer have any role in an election. Nor have ethical concerns and critical awareness of the way voters are controlled and manipulated.

Thus, democracy in plural, mass societies is facing dangers it has never previously faced. Because democratic choices have themselves begun to throw up leaders who would have been considered morally unworthy in earlier times. Many political parties now have 'fixers' who can give you designer riots and customised demonstrations to ensure your electoral success or the defeat of your rivals. Such interventions are no longer considered aberrations, but normal ploys of politics. But there are other less ominous implications of the return of populism in the electoral arena.

First, given the expanding capability of media technology and the spectacular growth in the destructive power of modern wars, populism may not perhaps remain a sustainable political strategy. Populism's shrill, chest-thumping foot soldiers have always wanted to live with the risk of war, but now that walk on the margins has become more perilous. And even the most inept populist leaders can quickly figure out that surviving in a partially open politics requires something more than tall promises, gifted media consultants, and a docile press.

Second, populism presumes a certain innocence in the consumers of populism to be truly effective. If you are vending stereotypes about an ethnic community, floating rumours about a conspiracy being hatched by an enemy country or promising prosperity to everyone within five years flat, there has to be a gullible public not eager to be sceptical towards its chosen leaders. I have already mentioned that complicity between the rulers and the ruled.

A functioning, open, democratic order is an unheroic affair. Populism, in whatever form, distorts or negates that basic premise and advances a heroic, dramatic solution to a country's problems. It does so by 'temporarily' abridging civil rights, introducing a militarised version of nationalism and a garrison-state mentality, and by altering the political culture of a country to host some form of 'developmental authoritarianism'.

Fortunately, most populist leaders, once they come to power, soon reveal their iron fists and rule not by the spirit of the Constitution but through various desperate measures that would sustain their regimes. These measures further expose the weak, insecure persons behind the mask of hyper-masculine, theatrical heroes fighting the enemies of the country outside and within its borders. When their regimes finally collapse – yes, they do finally collapse without exception – their supporters are crest-fallen to discover that the number of the country's enemies has suddenly shrunk dramatically, but not the number of the country's problems.

BACK HOME TO A DARKER AGE

Abdelwahab El-Affendi

I blame Paul Berman, Christopher Hitchens and, of course, Tony Blair. They became the enemy within: the intrepid jihadists parachuted behind the lines into the citadels of the liberal left and proceeded to disseminate 'kosher' Islamophobia using the rhetoric of defending 'liberalism' against 'illiberal' outsiders. They would wrap the language of Jean-Marie Le Pen into fresh, halal, packaging of left-wing radicalism. One could add Fareed Zakaria for good measure, although it has always been a chore to distinguish him from his neo-con friends. Or we could have started with Salman Rushdie, the Orientalist from the Orient, the man who blurred, if not obliterated, the lines of distinction between Marx and Jerry Falwell. And why not Netanyahu, the first politician to make Fascism respectable in Jewish circles. But why don't I start with Matti Bunzl, an Austrian anthropologist who worked for a while in Chicago, before moving to head the Wien Museum in Vienna, the city's main museum.

Bunzl made a brave attempt to distinguish Islamophobia from anti-Semitism. This was interesting, since the term Islamophobia was coined by a commission set up in 1992 by the UK-based Runnymede Trust to study the worrying reappearance of anti-Semitism in Britain. The commission produced its powerful report, *A Very Light Sleeper: The Persistence and Dangers of Antisemitism*, in January 1994 and noted that its research:

> has thrown up a separate and equally alarming new example of active prejudice against a religious minority. British Muslims too have found themselves in the firing line. The Commission has recommended that the Runnymede Trust undertake further study into the phenomenon known as Islamophobia.

This was the proverbial coining of a term: a phenomenon was identified and named for the first time. It was stumbled upon by a group which was not searching for it, but for a revived anti-Semitism. The Trust eventually obliged, setting up in 1996 the Commission on British Muslims and Islamophobia, under the chairmanship of Professor Gordon Conway. Its report, *Islamophobia, a Challenge to us All*, was published in 1997. Bunzl, however, wanted to prove, against this strong evidence, that the two pathologies were indeed quite distinct, originating in two 'different projects of exclusion'. While anti-Semitism emerged in the nineteenth century 'to police the ethnically pure nation-state', Islamophobia reflects attempts 'to safeguard a supranational Europe.'

Bunzl starts by identifying two opposing views on the resurgence of anti-Semitism in Europe. The first was that of the 'alarmists', who often belong on the political right and support Israel's right-wing governments. For them, anti-Semitism is a constant of the European scene, and has only been in remission. It has found a new pretext in criticism of Israeli policies, and received a boost from the increased Muslim presence in Europe. Governments and official circles avoid confronting this surge in order not to antagonise Muslims. The other view, which Bunzl terms the 'deniers', dismisses these fears, arguing that the resurgence of anti-Semitism is a function of a general right-wing resurgence, of which both Jews and Muslims are victims. Both sides miss the point about the 'radical historical transformations in the status and function of European anti-Semitism'. One mistake is to consider religion as the relevant marker for exclusion in both cases, overlooking its actual marginality, as both processes depend on secular foundations. Anti-Semitism emanated from a focus on the modern secular concept of race, which 'gave Jews an immutable biological destiny'. It is consequently linked to fantasies of the ethnically pure nation-state, where the 'racially alien' Jew can never fit in, no matter how culturally assimilated he may become. In contrast, Islamophobia emerged over a century later, when the focus was no longer national identity, but 'civilisation' and European identity. Here Muslims are not seen as a threat to the nation-state, but to Western civilisation as a whole.

Interestingly, while some vestiges of the old anti-Semitism exist within the right, the new anti-Semitism, especially when it is a phenomenon among Muslim youth in Europe or the radical left, does not target Jews

because they are alien outsiders. Quite the reverse, in fact: Jews are
targeted precisely by Muslim youth in France, for example, because they
are seen as an integral part of a European hegemony 'that not only
marginalises Muslims in France but, from their point of view, also accounts
for the suffering of the Palestinians.' In this regard, anti-Semitism in this
form is the ultimate recognition that the Jews are now fully integrated in
Europe. In fact, even the new right has transformed its outlook to be more
accepting of Jews and Israel.

Bunzl's is a rather subtle, and more empirically grounded, version of the
'clash of civilisations' thesis marketed more crudely by Samuel P
Huntington, following Bernard Lewis. In both cases, 'civilisational'
identities are granted a concrete reality, and used as explanatory variables.
Lewis uses the 'civilisational' label to explain the presumed Muslim
hostility to the West, in an attempt to arbitrarily eliminate the factor of
actual Western aggression against Muslims. Thus it is not actually
colonialism or the Israeli displacement of the Palestinians which is the
problem, but the feeling of inadequacy of Muslim men in the face of the
more advanced Western civilisation, which is the source of the 'Muslim
rage' against the colonial powers. Huntington widens the explanatory
scope and posits 'civilisational' identity as the independent explanatory
variable of international politics. Without citing either, Bunzl tells us that
Islamophobia *and* Muslim anti-Semitism are both reflective of
'civilisational' identities in action: right-wing Islamophobes foreground a
pan-European identity and pose as defenders of the European civilisation
threatened by Islam; while Muslim anti-Semites rise in defence of
persecuted Muslims against Jews who are seen as part of the European
hegemonic enterprise.

Paul Berman, a prominent convert from left-wing politics to what
amounts to neo-con partisanship, did not mention civilisation, but he all
but equated Arab-Islamic culture with barbarism. In his *Terror and
Liberalism* (2003), he made the case for a perpetual war against 'Islamic
terrorism', which he depicts as the new incarnation of European fascism.
The latter is, in turn, a new incarnation of the biblical Apocalypse, where
an evil infection of society needs to be exorcised by a phenomenal
amount of violence. In this regard, 'Islamic terrorism' is an irrational
hostility to liberalism that has little to do with real facts such as the

dispossession of the Palestinians or other colonial assaults on the Middle East. It is merely liberal naïveté which seeks such 'rational' justification for Muslim anger.

Rather than seeing Tony Blair as a leftist politician who had converted to neo-liberalism, it might be more accurate to describe him as a neo-liberal who had infiltrated the ranks of the left, and led a whole movement into the other side. Like Berman, he decries the naïveté of gullible liberals who do not see 'Islamic terrorism' for what it is, and are too timid to call it 'Islamic' lest they offend Muslims. Blair lambasts the 'plain stupidity' of what he terms the 'majority view of a large part of Western opinion', which blames the US-British invasion of Iraq for the chaos there. Unlike Berman, he mentions civilisation, a lot. In a major speech he gave in March 2006, to mark the third anniversary of the invasion in Iraq, he attempts to convince us that the evolving Iraq debacle was the ultimate defence line of civilisation. Again, the core idea is that Muslims are virtually irrational, if not outright insane. All conflicts involving Muslims, from South East Asia to the Caucasus to the Middle East and Africa, are related to a warped Islamic ideology, and are virtually the same worldwide struggle against liberalism and civilisation. There is no alternative to fighting them with violent interventionism, like the one in Iraq.

Fighting 'Islamo-fascism' with 'Populism'

As Tony Blair continued to harp in many of his interventions on the classic populist theme of being a Jeremiah preaching to the blind at heart, his prayers were answered in more than one miraculous way. The ascendancy of right-wing populism in Europe and America heartily embraced the mantra of fighting 'Islamo-fascism' by the more civilised Western variety. This surge has now culminated in the arrival of Donald Trump at the White House, with a cohort of assorted Islamophobes, White Supremacists, and a host of other allied hate-mongers. The rise of the 'Islamic State in Syria and Iraq' (ISIS), a ragtag outfit of assorted Islamic militants, sought to actualise Blair's thesis in the reverse: that all the struggles involving Muslims from Chechnya to Mindanao and Mali, should be made into one conflict.

In addition (the man is really in luck) another source of support fell into his lap. Just as he was kicked out of Downing Street in the summer of 2007

– for more than one good reason – he was appointed as the envoy of the so-called Quartet, an ad hoc body made up of the United Nations, United States, Russia and the EU. Founded to oversee the peace process in Palestine, it was a cruel irony that the man who has helped ignite the Middle East's most devastating war was put in charge of peace! And it was no surprise that, after seven years of work, the region is farther from peace than ever, thanks in no little measure to Blair's machinations. For he was not happy with the fat salary he drew from the Quartet, or the exorbitant fees he charged for his speeches. So he ingratiated himself with assorted Middle Eastern despots with cash to spare, in particular the oligarchs of the United Arab Emirates, which became a major donor to his company, Tony Blair Associates. When the UAE, and its Saudi allies, decided to concoct a rent-a-mob quasi-populist insurrection to topple Egypt's first and only democratically elected president, Blair was there to help. He advised the UAE on policy and how to improve its image (for a fee of $7m a year, according to the *Daily Telegraph*), and also acted as a 'consultant' for the new military regime in Egypt. He would visit Cairo and Tel Aviv almost once a month from July 2013 when the coup took place.

It is not clear what role Blair played in the most recent phase of this process, which culminated in the alliance between Trump populism and the most retrograde Gulf states (complete with a virtual coup in Saudi Arabia, and the current attempts to take over Qatar and shut down the last non-Saudi co-opted media spaces in the region). But it would be a big surprise if his ongoing 'consultancy' had nothing to do with it.

What is not in doubt is that many 'converts' to anti-liberal politics like Blair have played a crucial role in the current resurgence of populism in the West. According to Jens Rydgren, populism's first important European breakthrough in the mid-1980s, with the rise of the French National Front, cannot be explained solely with reference to structural causes. These included economic stagnation, financial crises, loss of confidence in the political elite, decline of class politics and ensuing convergence of left and right. The main cause appears to be the evolving of a new 'master frame – combining ethnonationalist xenophobia, based on the doctrine of ethnopluralism, with anti-political-establishment.' The adoption of 'ethno-pluralism', or more precisely 'cultural racism', including the advocacy of virtual segregation on cultural grounds, helped the new right to evade the stigmatisation and discrediting of fascism and its biological racism. In this context, traditional anti-Semitism was modified or abandoned, even at times transformed into philo-Semitism and admiration of Israel.

The Nature and Trajectories of Populism

In spite of its current ubiquity, populism (described concisely by Cas Mudde as 'an illiberal democratic response to decades of undemocratic liberal policies') remains a difficult concept to pin down. It is at once pejorative (implying demagoguery and rabble-rousing) and euphemistic (stopping short of applying the 'fascist' label to far right groups). Therefore, it is convenient to use, precisely because of its ambiguity. In fact, while many analysts argue that the term has been excessively used to stigmatise otherwise legitimate social and political movements, others have pointed out that the term is being used as a euphemism for outright fascist trends. This makes it important to try to introduce some precision in order to make the analysis more fruitful. A good starting point may be the definition proposed by Albertazzi and McDonnell of populism as 'an ideology which pits a virtuous and homogeneous people against a set of elites and dangerous "others" who are together depicted as depriving (or attempting to deprive) the sovereign people of their rights, values, prosperity, identity and voice.'

There are echoes in this characterisation of Berman's depiction of Islamic and Arab nationalist ideological trends, haunted as he claims by the apocalyptic fear of alien contamination. However, some theoreticians have rejected the very depiction of populism as an ideology, even if it is characterised as a 'thin-centred' ideology. First because the concept of ideology is in itself problematic and contested, and is not suitable to build upon to address another elusive concept. The notion of a thinness is even more elusive. Second, the populist label has been applied on both the left and right, making it compatible with diametrically opposed ideologies. Third, populist discourse lacks the coherence associated with ideologies. There are similar problems with the alternative of treating populism as a political strategy where 'personalistic leaders' try to secure power by mobilising 'direct, unmediated, uninstitutionalised support from large numbers of mostly unorganised followers'. For every political act involves strategic dimensions, making this characterisation only marginally more helpful. The solution, in this view, is to treat populism as 'an *anti-elite discourse in the name of the sovereign People*' (sic). More precisely, it should be looked at as 'discursive frame', according to framing theory, where the problem is framed in terms of a serious crisis involving an elite conspiracy against the will of the people, and the solution is the mobilisation of the people to defend their sovereignty.

Populism is certainly premised on haunting narratives of insecurity: stories about impending doom and awaiting calamities, which necessitate immediate and drastic action. It is an instance of what I have elsewhere called hyper-securitisation: depicting problems in terms of major and drastically threatening crises. However, the discursive framing angle as proposed by Aslanidis does not fully grasp the nature and dimensions of the phenomenon. For populist framing, whether on the left or right (or even among Islamists), is not just about diagnosing a crisis and a threat to popular sovereignty via elite corruption, or even about extreme securitisation. At its core, it is some form of a conspiracy theory: the villains of the piece (the political elite) either deliberately mislead the people for their own benefit, or are too stupid, short-sighted and naïve to see through the machinations of the real enemy. In this regard, their narratives are incapable of falsifiability, since they are premised on the existence of an intricate and impenetrable web of deception. Like Donald Trump's perennial 'fake news', in which all the media are collectively complicit in deliberate deception, any contrary evidence to the populist narrative is by definition planted 'fake evidence' to throw people off the track.

Thus populist narrative starts from an acknowledged crisis: it could be a stagnant economy, financial crisis, general decline in a country's fortunes/status, deteriorating race relations, perceived internal or external threat, etc. The crisis is then depicted as an existential threat to the community, demanding drastic action, even if it calls for the disregard of accepted norms of ethical and legal restraint. One could not – and should not – bother with such niceties as the human rights of refugees or suspects when the nation's very existence is at stake. Simultaneously, the crisis is blamed on a combination of foreign enemies who have infiltrated the community, and on the naïve, incompetent, or criminally complicit elite, unable/unwilling to deal with the problem. Simple and simplistic solutions are then proposed, which the incumbent elite are depicted as too cowardly, incompetent or criminally complicit, to decisively implement.

The threat could thus be Muslim immigration, which is threatening to obliterate Western culture, and 'Islamicise' Europe or America. To confront this threat, Muslim immigration must be totally and immediately halted, and Muslims already in the country thrown out. 'Islamic' terrorism is equally a major existential threat, which calls for drastic action, including barring Muslim immigrants, mass internment, and the invasion and occupation of some Muslim countries.

In spite of nuances and shifts, almost all right-wing populist movements have Nazi and fascist inspirations, in the sense that they would not condemn Nazism outright, if not express sympathies with its ideals and goals. Historically, the new right groups have deliberately sought to evolve a new narrative to replace the discredited Nazi ideology and its association with the Holocaust and other atrocities (which they nevertheless deny or try to minimise), mainly for pragmatic reasons. Thus hate for Jews is replaced by hate for blacks, immigrants or Muslims. Ironically, pro-Israeli lobbies have increasingly allied themselves with these populist trends, or at least tried to use and exploit them. As a 2011 report by Washington-based Center for American Progress has shown, a small industry for purposely fomenting Islamophobia has developed during the first decade of this century, funded by mainly pro-Israeli donors, and manned by activists and intellectuals sympathetic to Israel.

Populist movements thus invariably espouse narratives of irrational blame of designated categories for the concrete problems faced by societies, coupled with varieties of conspiracy theories explaining why the dominant ruling elite do not want to accept these narratives. Immigrants are thus simultaneously blamed for dependence on welfare, and for working for low wages to undercut native workers, even though the economies in ageing Europe would have collapsed without the influx of youthful immigrants. While it has become fashionable to express admiration for Israel in recent right-wing populist narratives, anti-Semitism has not entirely been purged from these narratives. The convergence of anti-Muslim narratives among the now dominant extreme right-wing in Israel and those of various populist movements in Europe may have obscured the tensions between the two trends, but as the case of Donald Trump's former advisor, Steve Bannon would indicate, the tension did not go away completely. American White Supremacists remain vehemently anti-Jewish. The declared love for Israel among some of the American right-wing, especially within the Christian Right, is as benevolent as the interest of the 9/11 hijackers in their fellow-passengers: Israel is where Armageddon will take place. And the more Israel is goaded into a destructive conflict with its neighbours, the quicker the Saviour will return!

Populism is thus a movement based on irrational blame of arbitrarily designated others, assorted conspiracy narratives, simplistic views about the complex political and economic processes, fantasies about magical solutions, and constructed insecurities over the globalised and interconnected world. These narratives are coupled with illusions about turning a clock back to the idyllic rustic world of pre-industrial societies, while enjoying all the benefits of post-industrial bliss. In this regard, it is anti-democratic, anti-liberal, anti-human rights, anti-globalisation and anti-free trade. In short, it is anti-Western and anti-capitalist. It is hostile to the values and processes which has made the West what it is today, and gave it the leading international position it has acquired. It is thus self-destructive of the West, morally, politically, economically and socially.

That is why populism had found it difficult to make a breakthrough into mainstream Western politics. The body politic rejects it instinctively as the human body rejects alien invading bodies. Even when it makes a contingent breakthrough, as happened with the Berlusconi episode in Italy and the current Trump phase in the US, it appears at war with both society and the state. Such a breakthrough comes only in drastic circumstances, at a high cost, and with devastating consequences on the affected societies. That is why Bannon outlined in one of his first media appearances after the Trump 'coup', plans for subverting and commandeering the American state: by purging the judiciary and the bureaucracy from 'liberals', and staffing the state bureaucracy with right-wing extremists.

Islamophobic Right-Wing Populism

As emphasised above, it is not sufficient for a major populist breakthrough, in particular extreme right-wing populist win, to have some of the major structural conditions (major crises, economic frustration, political distrust, narrowing of the political spectrum), or political opportunities charismatic leaders, etc.) in place. It is also essential to evolve a very potent discursive frame to bridge the huge chasm between the totally unacceptable ethos of traditional fascism (or, in the case of left-wing populism, discredited classical Marxism), and the mainstream liberal consensus. That is usually done through a number of moves, chief amongst which is the positing of a very exceptional situation demanding very exceptional measures. Intellectually, an instance of a 'Eureka moment' must present itself: a kind of 'discovery' which suddenly seems to resolve an impossible contradiction.

In this regard, the debates surrounding the 'war on terror' secured all these conditions in a 'miraculous' way. Right-wing populism has managed to achieve an ascendancy in the West from the late 1980s, as seen in the rise of Margaret Thatcher in Britain in 1979, followed shortly by the presidency of Ronald Reagan in America in 1980. But this was a milder form of populism, with a focus on the economy and the promotion of traditional conservative values. However, these 'victories', and the subsequent collapse of the Soviet Union, created the climate for the emergence in more ambitious, not to say more virulent, trends. These included the neo-conservative religious right trends in America, and an assortment of extreme right-wing tendencies in Europe, Israel and Russia. While the neo-conservatives who came to dominate the presidency of George W Bush (2000–2008) had elitist tendencies and remained a fringe movement, even within the Republican party, they did apply populist tactics. This was in particular the case in the form of scurrilous attacks against academia and liberal intellectuals.

However, more overtly populist movements did emerge in the form of the movements spearheaded by the likes of 1992 presidential candidate Ross Perot, and Republican Party leader (and House Speaker from 1995 to 1999) Newt Gingrich. These tendencies were eclipsed from 2009 by the so-called Tea Party movement among the Republican grass roots. The latter in particular adopted tactics of mass protest and street mobilisation, a hallmark of the populist arsenal since the Nazi era, but often ignored by students of the movements in favour of concentration on discourse and rhetoric. However, these mass mobilisation tactics are potent weapons of motivation (and intimidation) that continue to be crucial to boosting the chances of populist movements. Intimidation, even of the rhetorical kind (accusing opponents of betraying the very values the populist leaders trample on) are a key item in the armoury of populist movements.

For the most part, the agenda of these movements appeared to be internal and focused on economic issues (tax cuts, less welfare, lower government spending, anti-abortion, etc.). There are always some implied racist undertones, since attacks on welfare and government spending targeted the poor, who also happened to be black. Opposition to the federal government also has historical connotations (since the Civil War) of opposition to civil rights gains for blacks. It is a supreme irony that Trump's slogan, 'America First', was first coined in 1940 by an isolationist, anti-war group, that was overtly anti-Semitic and militantly right-wing. At a later stage, hostility to Latino immigrants began to figure as a prominent populist theme, usually in the guise of attacks on crime and illegal immigration.

In this regard, the 'war on terror' gave right-wing populism a phenomenal stepping stone, since it became much easier to silence critics by accusations of sympathy with terrorists. As indicated above, it has also become easier to focus hostility to immigrants and 'foreigners' on a clearly identifiable group: the Muslims, who are usually visibly different. Muslims were not only accused of being potential terrorists, but also hostile to 'American values', refusing to integrate, and even trying to 'Islamicise' America. The campaign received another strong boost from the backing of pro-Israeli constituencies, keen to propagate the idea that Israel and America faced an identical challenge of 'terror'. Israel's problem became more acute, with its sharp right-wing turn from the 1970s, and its aggressive wars in Lebanon in 1978 and 1982, severely denting its image in the West as an 'endangered' democratic state in a sea of Arab 'barbarism'. Matters turned again for the worse when Palestinians adopted, with the 1987 *intifada*, tactics of civilian protest reminiscent of the American civil rights movement. The televised brutal suppression of the protests did not make Israel look good. Therefore the pro-Israeli lobbies had to redouble efforts to stigmatise Arabs as terrorists.

The coincidence of the rise of the 'Islamic Resistance Movement' (Hamas) in Gaza in the 1990s, and the rudimentary presence of 'Islamic terrorism' in the US, made that association easier. The latter development was a spillover from internal insurgencies in Egypt and Algeria, where the West was seen as supportive of oppressive regimes at home. The presence of US troops in the 'Land of the Two Holy Mosques' (Saudi Arabia), as a consequence of the war to evict Iraq from Kuwait in 1991, was also a major source of tension. The US, already accused of blind support for Israeli occupation, found itself in the middle of multiple Arab civil wars.

In Europe, the path from racism to Islamophobia was a smoother one, since racism and hostility to immigrants was closely associated with hostility to Arabs and Muslims, given that a large section of immigrants (the majority in countries like France) were Muslim. Thus organisations like the Front National in France found it easy to combine anti-Semitism and hostility to Arab-Muslims (mostly North Africans) in one over-arching narrative of demonisation.

However, the major breakthrough for right-wing populism came when 'liberal' voices from the left and centre began to join in on this demonisation of Muslims. In France this started early, with the 'headscarf' ban of 1989, where young Muslim girls and their families were harassed and excluded from schools in the name of 'freedom' and republican values. It did not help much that this episode coincided with the controversy in Britain over Salman Rushdie's novel, *The Satanic Verses*, which also had 'liberals' up in arms against perceived Muslim illiberalism. It is no wonder that France was – and remains – far ahead of other European countries in the size of support for extreme right-wing populism. For the extremists could very easily draw on mainstream rhetoric on the refusal of Muslims to 'integrate' and accept 'republican' values. That is the origin of the so-called 'cultural racism', which claims not to be racist against *Muslims*, but legitimate hostility to cultural and religious values that are incompatible with liberalism and democracy.

A comparable development occurred in the Netherlands, where former Marxist Pim Fortuyn made a career of calling for a Cold War against Islam. His views were so controversial that the populist party, Livable Netherlands sacked him in February 2002, less than three months after electing him as leader by a large majority. He then proceeded to form his own individual party, the so-called List Pim Fortuyn. Due to his influence, anti-Muslim right-wing populism remains very strong, in spite of his tragic assassination in 2002.

The plethora of 'liberal' and left-wing converts to hostility to Islam, and their use of the language of liberalism in their discourse, has helped advance and naturalise the cause of right-wing populism in America as well. It has made hate respectable, even noble. The Trump campaign managed to mobilise a very broad coalition of assorted negative views, interests and grievances at a time of widespread discontent and distrust of both government and expertise. However, while the accepted wisdom is that the Trump campaign 'tapped into a deep vein of distress and resentment among millions of white working- and middle-class Americans', this may be misleading. Trump and his billionaire friends are not working class, and the language of xenophobia they employed is not indigenous to workers. True, American right-wing populism has deep roots going back to the Ku Klux Klan of the 1920s, and is often spoke in the name of 'working and small farmers'. However, the uniting glue of these disparate groups appears to be hate, mainly of Muslims, but also of Obama, African Americans, and the 'liberals' who believe that these people have rights.

The Dark Age to Come

Populism is essentially a narrative of deep and generalised insecurity, with a readiness to blame others for one's misfortunes, and a yearning for simplistic solutions that usually involve vindictiveness and cruelty towards the less fortunate. The most popular chants during the Trump campaign were 'Lock her up!' (for Hillary Clinton), or 'Build the Wall!' (to bar Latino immigration). On numerous occasions both before and during his campaign, Donald Trump openly made or favourably responded to hateful Islamophobic comments. The current surge in populism in the West incorporates racist and Islamophobic tendencies, 'genetically modified' anti-Semitism, and a high threshold of tolerance for cruelty and injustice. Thus the broad alliance has no qualms about depriving millions of fellow-citizens from medical care to score a political point, and would penalise whole categories of people (Muslims, Latinos) without proven guilt.

It is thus important to put to rest the idea with which we have started this discussion, Bunzl's claim that Islamophobia is somewhat civilisational, and the allied suggestion that populism is distinguishable from Fascism. For in fact, as with Brexit and similar manifestations of deep hostility to European liberalism and its EU embodiment, right-wing populists are more hostile to what the West stands for than Islamic fundamentalists. Europhobia and Islamophobia often go hand in hand.

Of course it is rash to dismiss some of the genuine fears provoked by the brutal terror tactics of groups like ISIS, which have given Islam a bad name. The Muslim response to this menace still leaves a lot to be desired, especially on the intellectual level. It is not enough to condemn and disavow groups like ISIS, which is after all a plague on Islam and Muslims. First, because its victims are primarily Muslims. Second, because its actions 'disarm' Muslim communities morally by painting them as barbaric. Third, because Muslim causes which such groups champion, while just causes, as was the case in Iraq and Syria, automatically become lost causes by this very association. Worse, persecuted Syrians and Iraqis suffer much more under ISIS and because of its wars: they suffer its brutally oppressive rule; they suffer the bombing and devastation of attacks on it, and are more often used as human shields to defend ISIS fighters, rather than receive protection. And they suffer after ISIS defeats with the loss of homes and livelihoods, and demonisation by association. ISIS and similar plagues are thus a Muslim problem before being a Western or American one. And they demand a decisive Muslim solution.

However, the current alliance between Islamophobic American populism of the Trump kind on the one side, and corrupt Muslim despots on the other, is not going to offer a solution for this problem. In fact, they are going to make matters much worse. Any vain hope that murderous tyrannies like that of Egypt's Abdel Fatah el-Sisi and his Gulf and Israeli allies would 'reform Islam', and overcome the current pathologies of Muslim societies, is an insanity with heavy consequences.

Following Trump's multiple pilgrimages to Riyadh and Jerusalem last May, this alliance of misfits came up with the brilliant idea that removing Qatar from the map, and with it the vexatious Al Jazeera, would bring about a Thousand-Year Reich of untroubled despotism and American hegemony in the region. Qatar, they charged, supported Islamism, which in turn generates terrorism. Al Jazeera destabilised the 'good' despots of the Gulf, and introduces Gulf citizens to subversive ideas. It gives airing to Arab sentiments that are not friendly to Israeli occupation and dispossession of the Palestinians. If only Al Jazeera could be silenced, Islamism vanishes, and democracy becomes a dirty world, bliss will reign in the region. There will be peace in Palestine, Sisi and other despots will live in perpetual peace, and no one will notice their corruption and limitless brutalities. Slavery will return to the Middle East, and people will worship dictators instead of Allah.

This is to credit Qatar, Al Jazeera and Islamists with too much influence and power. In fact, the bumbling Islamists remain the despots' greatest assets. These regimes remain in place precisely because they present themselves as bulwarks against Islamists. If the latter were to disappear, they would lose their function. If Hamas were to disband today, Netanyahu would no longer have enough pretexts to continue with his daylight robbery of Palestinian lands and livelihoods. And if Al Jazeera is silenced, the persecuted in the Middle East will stop watching the news and go out to do something about their plight.

The triple plagues of populism, corrupt despotism and terrorism may be allies, but each is its own worst enemy. Populism is an attack on Western societies and values, before being an attack on minorities and foreigners. Despotism is a war on the people, just like terrorism. Groups like ISIS come with a self-destruct mechanism, but not before devastating the communities they infect. The evil alliance between terrorists, Islamophobic populism and despotism will usher in a dark age of experimentation with old-style colonialism, as Europe goes back home to its Islamophobic dark ages, when both Islam and enlightenment were seen as existential threats. It will be phenomenally destructive, but it will be short-lived precisely because of its self-destructive dynamics. For a relatively brief period, a very dark and brutal night of the soul will descend on our world. And then multiple revolutions, probably starting in Washington, DC, will bring copious amounts of fire and light. Those awaiting Armageddon will certainly have a lot to think about then.

LOSS OF WORLD

Richard Appignanesi

The connection between populism and terrorism is not obvious. So let me consider it briefly.

What is understood by populism? It expresses a rankling discontent gestated in the commonalty that can assume strength enough, as we have recently seen in the United States, to fracture the liberal consensus. The mass of ordinary folk, belittled in their beliefs, betrayed in their everyday aspirations by a distant establishment elite, will at last seek justification in their own common denominator politics made intelligible to them by a charismatic leader who voices their grievances. Multitude democracy, as can be said of populism, reckoning itself disenfranchised, will threaten civil war against the 'absentees of privilege', the middle-class and its unrepresentative minority of party-machine professionals who have claimed sole control of mainstream political orthodoxy.

Populism can have a left or right reformation agenda, or a peculiar conflation of the two, and turns naturally to fundamentalism. A mood, if not the reality, of being on a war footing is symptomatic of populism. Is populism revolutionary? In our day – that is to say, in postcultural, or some might prefer, postnormal times – the answer is uncertain, or, pardon the pun, the dark matter of globalisation. In the first place, there is no such Leviathan 'multitude' but socially degenerated class fragmentations, like ice floes adrift and grinding into each other. And in the second place, populism ends by disadvantaging the very people it was supposed to safeguard, their hopes disabused and their ideals tyrannised by populism's fundamentalist purpose of revindication.

Here I step in to ask: are there not elements in this populist scenario that speak of Islamism? Terrorism is so mesmerising in its gravity that we

cannot dare give the least credence to the revolutionary purifying purpose
of Islamist jihad. Think of it this way: *terrorism is militarised populism*. The
finality of Islamism's redeeming purpose assumes a multitude of Muslims
summoned to the grand territorial Caliphate – true home of Dar al-Islam.
But Muslims socially fragmented by class, sect, tribal loyalties, cast abroad
in foreign residence, will gain no advantage but nightmare from Islamism's
populist dream.

Populism, and if I am right, its correlative terrorism, have neither to do
with imagined political gains but with marginality, with an immense, tragic
and ineluctable *loss of world*. This is the aspect of postcultural reality
engaged in these pages.

The question appears to me to be really this: is the terrorist recognised
as the bellwether martyr of postculture – and can we opt out of the
postculture? The choice is reduced to a pair of Shakespeare's contrasting
endgame options.

'Thus bad begins and worse remains behind.'

– Hamlet

'The worst is not.
So long as we can say, "This is the worst".'

– King Lear

What is being prophesied at present by knowledgeable analysts assures
us of entrenched and inescapable terrorism. Terrorism is now systemic, we
are told:

this is, and will be, a multigenerational struggle against an implacable enemy,
and the violence we're dealing with in the Middle East and Africa is not some
unfortunate aberration – it's the new normal…if we fail to face the threat
where it is today – primarily in the Middle East and Africa – we'll suffer the
consequences at home.

'It's the new normal.' Such is the discomfiting forecast of David
Kilcullen, former strategic consultant to the US Presidents Bush and
Obama, and outspokenly critical of both administrations in their inept
pursuance of the 'war on terror'. He does not exaggerate a
'multigenerational struggle' which has been pledged time and again by

Ayman al-Zawahiri, presiding over Al-Qaeda: '...resistance will transfer the popular wrath from one generation to another and keep the desire for revenge alive in the people's souls.'

I should emphasise from the start the frontier difference between militarised terrorism and terrorism organised for clandestine attacks of vengeance. Their fields of tactical operation are distinct but interlinked. The presumptive Islamic State 'caliphate' is not a terrorist organisation but a Sunni sectarian army engaged in regional civil war and additionally sponsors international terrorism. It is a militarised entrepreneur of terror. Destruction of Islamic State on the battlefield will not guarantee riddance of worldwide, sporadic, hit-and-run terrorism. This can be promoted as much by a shadow organisation as by the reality of a military one. There is no confusion if we bear clearly in mind that Islamist organisations have been waging war, precisely *jihad*, in progress ever since September 11. For certain interpretations, terror is a collateral asset of properly conducted Qur'anic war, as Brigadier S.K. Malik made plain in his manual of strategy, a war that will endure in perpetuity so long as infidels endure. Kilcullen acknowledges this when he remarks that the terrorism recently experienced in Western counties is not simply a 'spill over' from our failure to deal with Syria but something other. 'While there is an entity, whether it be Isis, al-Qaeda or any other group, that can attract young people in our societies, preying on their idealism and alienation, the threat will remain.'

The coda of Kilcullen's prediction – of terrorism brought home to us – is what preoccupies me. What does it mean, 'the threat will remain'? Is it the next bidding of worse to come? He appears certain of it:

> Today, people seem to think that Isis is as bad as it gets, but that's far from the case: there are threats out there that make Isis look tame. I'm not talking about a worse version of today's terrorism – I'm talking about things beyond terror altogether.

Christopher Andrew, official historian of MI5, on the lookout for worse, informs us that: 'Looming on the UK horizon, perhaps as early as the next decade, is the terrorism of the nuclear age and of chemical and biological warfare.' Indeed, already in 1998, 'Osama bin Laden declared that acquiring weapons of mass destruction (WMD) was a "religious duty" for his followers'. Andrew cites the Chatham House report of 2015: 'Criminal groups in Moldova are believed to have already smuggled radioactive and nuclear materials to Isis. "Making a radiological weapon", the report concluded, "requires little technical and scientific expertise, and radioactive materials can be used with conventional weaponry (such as dynamite) to make a successful dirty bomb." Demand from terrorist organisations and "lone wolves" seems to be producing a growing black market.'

Predictions of the likely are the stock of news currency, and as such, subject to the unpredictable nature of facts. Terrorism can nevertheless profit by deferral of immediate incidence. I am reminded of Andreas Baader, shortly before his suicide in 1977, warning that his first-generation of Red Army Faction terrorism was but a promise of 'far worse to come'. This seems to me the story of terrorism which, as I have remarked elsewhere, 'is always there and yet always just beginning'. Hamlet and King Lear had long since signalled the fatal relativity that governs the time of saturnine, melancholic *acedia* – nihilism – which sits at the dead centre of all Seven Deadly Virtues governing postculture. Waiting for the worse. On and on. The endless roadside interlude mapped by Samuel Beckett's *Waiting for Godot*.

Late as it might seem, at the ending of this present inquiry, I am drawn to the question first posed by the philosopher Alain Badiou in the immediate aftermath of 9/11 – the fundamental question to ask all over again – '*Who is this "we" facing terrorism?*'

> When 'our societies' are spoken of and it is declared that 'terrorism' wanted to 'strike them in the very heart' or 'destabilise' them, let us agree that what is being referred to is… 'the West' but in a more demure fashion, or it is a material paradigm; a certain state of objective wealth which, in itself, has no kind of value for the philosopher and furthermore which would not be able to ground any kind of consistent solidarity. If this is not the case, then why does the crime of New York affect 'our societies', while neither the millions of AIDS deaths in Africa nor the genocidal disasters in Rwanda affect them in any way? 'Our societies', designating in a faintly obscene manner the completely relative well-being of some of the wealthiest human groups (minorities) on the planet, hardly make for a presentable face-off against the supposed substance of terrorism.

9/11, 'the mass crime of New York', must fit into a formula of consensus to 'neutralise reactions' and 'generate support' among us ('we in the West')

for an avenging American war on terror. The 'excellences' of democracy, it
is agreed, are the grounds of consensus to conduct retaliatory war. Badiou
exercises the heavy hand of scepticism. And I too have poured a number of
scalding questions on those 'excellences' and the 'we' under threat of
terrorism that democracy presumes. But where to next?

I venture this forecast: the mystifying nature of terrorism will in the end
disclose something other than it is…as in a novel. Terrorism has been the
manifest subject of my existential meditations in this book. It was written
in the shadow of another that awaits writing. I would prefer it left
unwritten rather than face the dispiriting trials it demands. What inhibits
me? A scruple? A fear? I have a foreboding of the quagmire that postculture
poses to the exploration of contemporary history. Postculture is not some
catchpenny turn of phrase but a real condition designating historical
entrapment in hyperreality's interminable contemporaneity. A disturbing
account of history underlies Kilcullen's apparently obvious remark on the
generational threat of terrorism which will remain. This and the next
generations of alienated youth, recruited at home or afield, are the
destined body donors to a constant terrorism that menaces 'worse yet to
come'. They are envisaged *as if* already reckoned dead – and history
becomes a grotesque graveyard spectacle of body-snatching ghouls.
Zombies, revenants, vampires – the legendary undead – is it by chance that
this gothic genre appears favoured in teen media, books, movies and TV
serials in the present second decade of chronic terrorism? Pop culture
scuds along the surface of history. But what lies beneath?

One can shrug off terrorism as merely troublesome, upsetting to normal
life, a danger that can at least be contained if not eliminated. I do not
measure terrorism like this, as some irritant tic plaguing postmodern life.
Terrorism is symptomatic – but a symptom of what precise disorder I
believe does not answer to the diagnoses usually offered. What lies beneath
– the undecipherable disorder – can be named *loss of world*. I refer not to
the loss of 'a' world, such as is normally presumed real, but loss of one's
world design. One has been deprived of the means of designing or, so to
speak, of 'worlding' the world, for oneself. Loss of world applies in
particular to the anthropological account of imperilled or vanishing
culture which impacts on individuals' grasp of the world. Existential
psychoanalysis speaks of this as our situation of being-in-the-world which

will anchor individual beings in the real, symbolic and imaginary domains of psychical health or illness. Psychic ill health, such as determines the terrorist's schizoid selfhood, has the consequence of restricting the individual to inescapable captivity within the delimiting spheres of race, milieu and history as the boundaries of available existential options. Concern for the well-being of the human entity – the critical condition of its world-structuring design – is not only a matter for existential psychoanalysis and anthropology but, surprisingly perhaps, the philosophy of literary criticism.

I have found an enlightening focus for these three channels of psychiatry, anthropology and literary criticism in an expression used by writer and film-maker Pier Paolo Pasolini in his condemnation of Italian society in the 1970s, *anthropological genocide*. Terms of grim finality which refer to the extermination of a race, from the Greek, *genos*, correlate of *gens*, *gentes*, 'family', and *gene*, 'heredity', combined with anthropology understood as involving 'total culture'. Pasolini is not describing the annihilation of a specific race, such as for instance Nazism attempted on Jewry, but of a certain hereditary way of being, that is, the wiping out of an entire cultural species of existence. To be clear, then, genocide of the anthropological type deprives its victims of their culture but not necessarily of their lives. It does perhaps worse by being a discountable crime against humanity executed in the name of progress. The majority of its victims who do not perish in this genocidal progress undergo what Pasolini also terms 'anthropological mutation', or historically speaking, they are 're-classed'. Pasolini's source for this radical 'cultural cleansing' is Karl Marx and Friedrich Engels' *Communist Manifesto* of 1848 in which the revolutionary role of the bourgeoisie is outlined in brief, bold and memorable strokes. 'Wherever the capitalistic bourgeoisie has got the upper hand...[it] has left remaining no other nexus between man and man than naked self-interest, than callous "cash payment".' 'All fixed, fast-frozen relations, with their train of ancient and venerable prejudices and opinions are swept away, all new-formed ones become antiquated before they can ossify. All that is solid melts into air, all that is holy is profaned, and man is at last compelled to face with sober senses, his real condition of life, and his relations with his kind.' The weapons of capitalist domination are the advanced 'instruments of production' and the 'immensely facilitated means of communication'. Capitalism is not satisfied merely by establishing domestic industry but by 'industries that no longer work up indigenous raw material, but raw material drawn from the remotest zones; industries whose products are consumed, not only at home, but in every quarter of the globe. In place of the old wants, satisfied by the productions of the country, we find new wants, requiring for their satisfaction the products of distant lands and climes.' Pasolini's charge of 'anthropological genocide' emerges from these lines: 'It [Capitalism] compels all nations, on pain of extinction, to adopt the bourgeois mode of production; it compels them to introduce what it calls civilisation into their midst, i.e., to become bourgeois themselves. In one word, it creates a world after its own image.' Even the beneficiaries of capitalism will admit the justice of this portrayal.

To re-make the world in its own image: herein is the key to the capitalist alchemy of mutation. Pasolini fixes on a particular example of mutation familiar to him in Rome's circle of plebeian districts:

> Between 1961 and 1975 something essential changed: a genocide took place. A whole population was culturally destroyed. And it is a question precisely of one of those cultural genocides which preceded the physical genocides of Hitler. If I had taken a long journey and had returned after several years, walking through the 'grandiose plebeian metropolis' I would have had the impression that all its inhabitants had been deported and exterminated, replaced in the streets and blocks of houses by washed-out, ferocious, unhappy ghosts. Hitler's SS, in fact. The young boys, deprived of their values and their models as if of their blood, have become ghostly copies of a different way and concept of life – that of the middle class.

Pasolini is looking back on his 1961 film *Accattone* and is non-professional cast of so-called 'plebeians', the sub-proletarians of Rome's crowded slum peripheries, with its 'exclusive culture' which gave them 'not only original psychological "traits" but completely original physical traits as well. It created a feral "race".' He is not sentimentalising the harsh oppressive life of petty criminals and impoverished marginals – or worse, 'aestheticising' them, an accusation of 'artistic nostalgia' often raised against him – but speaking for a vanished species of cultural vitality that has not gone for the better. He prosecutes in vain a crime that went unperceived, negligible, in the next levelling stages of Cold War industrial neo-capitalism in its hell-bent progress towards mass consumption and mass communications. A change occurring like this in the mode of production will also govern the production of human beings: superfluous commodities produce superfluous human beings.

> 'The new mode of production' has therefore produced a new kind of human being, that is to say, a 'new culture', which changes man anthropologically: in this case the Italian. This 'new culture' has cynically destroyed (genocide) preceding cultures, from the traditional middle-class one down to the various restricted and pluralistic popular cultures. For the models and values destroyed it substitutes models and values of its own – not yet defined or named – which are those of a new bourgeoisie.

Pasolini denounces 'perhaps the gravest sin in the whole of human history', in his view 'truly totalitarian', because for the first time in human history 'a unification of the bourgeoisie and the proletariat has taken place under the sign and by the will of the civilisation of consumer goods – "of progress".' Pasolini also names it 'the sin of the fathers', including himself among the old guard generation of the anti-Fascists, the Communists, the conservative post-war liberals – all proceeding on the guiding principle common to them:

> that is the idea that the greatest ill in the world is poverty and that therefore the culture of the poorer classes must be replaced by the culture of the ruling class. In other words, our guilt as fathers could be said to consist in this: *that we believe that history is not and cannot be other than bourgeois history.* (My italics)

I could add this 'sin of the fathers' to contemporary postculture, if not that the analytic vocabulary of 'bourgeois history' sounds antiquated to us today; as does the Marxian 'Historical Materialism' from which it derives. Evidently something *no longer of our time* has been removed from our recognition of history. What sort of history, in whose name, would be suitable to our contemporary next stage in the capitalist mode of production – the digital post-industrial hyperreality perching on the fault lines of recessionary crises, global competitive savagery and ecological meltdown? What sort of history is this which clings to the hemline of techno-science for its shreds of optimism? Can it be that a new mode of commodity production is developing, a new history of consumership, in which for the first time amnesiac mutation does not occur? No cultural genocide? Unlikely. The iron rule remains the same. Superfluous commodities produce superfluous human beings. Its success will depend on a further process of conformism which entails species mutation. Another 'anthropological genocide' is being staged – a way of being, lost; a varietal species of culture, disappearing. Pasolini's outcry had singled out only one small sector of vanished proletarian culture. The part can serve sufficiently as synecdoche for identifying the whole of our own.

Very well. I am mistaken. There is no threat of darkness on the horizon. I confessed my unwillingness to venture into this minotaur underworld of history. Pasolini went there, incautiously, and his footsteps can be seen ending at the scene of his murder on a dismal waste ground of the Lido di Ostia. He was himself proof of the genocide he sought to expose. But was it proof, really? His killing in 1975 – beaten to death in 'mysterious circumstances' – was the silencing of a way of being, a style of cultural expression, but did not finally make clear what had been lost. Only his mourning for a disposable, outmoded 'sub-culture', only the scandalous excess of his life as a 'gay Commie', in effect, the merely questionable is left to speak for his hallucinatory vision of a crime against humanity. An illustrious corpse is not evidence enough. Nothing *specifiable* appears lost, no one to blame. A waste ground…

1975 in Italy should give us pause, however. Pasolini's murder does not fall on that date by coincidence, at the very moment that the Red Brigades' subversion and the neofascist *everzione nera* were engaging in mutual acts of terrorism and sabotage, at a period when murky alliances of corruption had enmeshed politics within tentacles of complicity in high finance, the Vatican, the secret service, and at sediment bottom, the Mafia. It was a dangerous time to be dangerously outspoken. He was always so.

Pasolini published a remarkably foresighted anticipation of the migrant Syrian, Iraqi and other refugees braving the perils of the Mediterranean in frail craft to reach Europe's coast.

> Blue-eyed Ali
> one of many sons of sons
> will go down from Algiers
> on sailboats and rowboats.
> Thousands of men

will be with him
with little bodies and the eyes
of wretched dogs of the fathers
on boats launched in the Realms of Hunger

These verses from '*Profezie*' in the collection, *Ali dagli ocche azzurri*, 1965, had been preceded in 1964 by *Poems in the Form of a Rose*, in which Pasolini prophesied that the 'blue-eyed Alis', the youths of the Third World, would invade Europe and destroy its history.

They will destroy Rome
and on its ruins
lay the seed
of Ancient History...

His prediction became a triumphalist vow, half-a-century later, chillingly assured in an e-book published online by a British jihadi, Siddhartha Dhar, an Indian convert to Islam who joined Islamic State in Syria. 'When we descend on the streets of London, Paris and Washington...not only will we spill your blood, but we will also demolish your statues, erase your history and most painfully, convert your children who will then go on to champion our name and curse their forefathers.' I note, however, that Pasolini came to disown his Third World prophecy after the events of 1968. Why? It was

right at the time but only insofar as it was mistaken. It was a vital and fruitful caprice of political passion, a conscious and desired reversal of future common sense. [...] How then to account for the fact that this hope that was placed in the revolutionary potential of the peasants of the Third World is now mistaken? Because it is no longer seen in revolutionary perspective. The students in fact are bourgeois. They would like to exorcise the poor and preindustrial world, evoke it as a meta-historical entity, and put themselves in front of it like an apocalyptic guide. To make the Revolution? No, to make Civil War.

A dangling sense of unfinished business remains to comprehend Pasolini's withdrawal of hope in Third World revolution after the 'last bourgeois civil war' of 1968. The reason he gives, which I have cited above, censures by name only the 'bourgeois students', without specifying their segmented transformation into a militant elite, those who would next proceed 'to exorcise the poor and preindustrial world... [by putting] themselves in front of it like an apocalyptic guide', in the other words, the Red Brigades and neofascist terrorists. Why did he not name them as such? To answer that question would misconstrue Pasolini's revulsion with prophecy, because it was clear, all too clear, even in 1975, that the terrorist executioners did not and could not represent the revolution but only its suicidal stillbirth. So also, I can emphatically affirm here, Islamist terrorism in either its militarised or freelance enterprise versions is not and can never be the vanguard of Islam's *necessarily* revolutionary renovation. I say necessarily, but, alas, in agreed diagnosis with Pasolini, I fear that the moment of its revolution has passed. It has been overtaken by populism.

Pasolini risked himself in the intuition of a process at its unfolding stage of cultural levelling of a 'genocidal' type, as he identified it, advancing inexorably towards a mutation which eliminates any alternative to itself. Alain Badiou has since given the process a complementary name subsequent to millennial terrorism. 9/11 and America's war on terror compose a paired 'equivalence of nihilism' in Badiou's judgement. On the one side, the traits of 9/11 'indicate its nihilistic character: the sacralisation of death; the absolute indifference to the victims; the transformation of oneself and others into instruments'. On the other, there is America's colossal capitalism, 'nihilist in its extensive [worldwide market] form', nihilist in 'the absence of any project other than its perpetuation'. The prevailing capitalist hegemony is named 'the nihilism of virtual equality', by which Badiou means 'an egalitarian dogmatism', 'that of an equality in [the people's] placement in front of commodities. The same product is offered everywhere. Armed with this universal commercial offer, contemporary "democracy" can forge a subject from such abstract equality: the consumer; the one who, in his or her virtuality opposite the commodity, is ostensibly identical to any other in his or her abstract humanity as buying power... The principle is that anyone who is able to buy – as a matter of right – anything being sold is the equal of anyone else.'

I can imagine Pasolini and Badiou in dialogue across the intervening thirty-year gap of death, the subject of their discourse, terrorism. Badiou respects Pasolini's fidelity to the primary Communist truth of emancipation, a St Paul-like figure, fierce in protecting it from corruption alike by Communist Party or democracy's 'pragmatic realism'. Why then does he step back from the prospect of revolution – however disappointing, however ill-performed, however failed – that 1968 enshrines in form, if not in substance, a 'Communist formulation' as Badiou terms it, a merit which the subsequent Red terrorists acknowledged by willingness to perish for it. I recall what the Communist Ulrike Meinhof wrote in 1974 on the formation of the Red Army Faction: 'The comrades who joined the movement saw it as the only real way of doing their revolutionary duty… Not because they so misjudged the situation as to think the masses would simply rise at [their] signal. It was a matter of salvaging, historically, the whole state of understanding attained by the movement of 1967/1968; it was a case of not letting the struggle fall apart.'

Ulrike Meinhof, icon of the Red Army Faction, hanged herself on 8 May 1976. Pasolini had died a year before. Abjectly, one might say of these by-the-wayside dyings. And in the aftermath of Ground Zero, 2001, which Pasolini did not live to see, Badiou, in face of the 'disjunctive synthesis of two nihilisms', terrorism and globally diffusive capitalism, 'announces a formidable disaster.' Their dialogue resumes, the gap of years bridged, meeting in agreement.

Capitalist nihilism has arrived at a stage of the non-existence of any world, Alain Badiou says.

And the ghost of Pasolini replies, *I went ahead into the unforeseen to glimpse the world denuded…*

Alain Badiou: *There is no world simply because the majority of the planet's inhabitants today do not even receive the gift of a name, of a simple name. When there was class society, proletarian parties (or those presumed to be such), the USSR, the national wars of liberation, etc., no matter which peasant in no matter what region – just as no matter which worker in no matter what town – could receive a political name. That is not to say that their material situation was better, certainly not, nor that that world was excellent. But the symbolic positions existed, and that world was a world.*

Pasolini: *What has intervened is precisely the end of a world. Millions and millions of peasants and also workers – in the South and the North – who remained true to themselves over an epoch, certainly much longer than the two thousand years of Catholicism, have now been destroyed. Their 'quality of life' has been radically changed.*

Badiou: *Today, outside the grand and petty bourgeoisie of the imperial cities, who proclaim themselves to be 'civilisation', you have nothing apart from the anonymous and excluded. 'Excluded' is the sole name for those who have no name, just as 'market' is the name of a world which is not a world.*

Pasolini: *Excluded. Loss of world. I remember saying: One needs a great deal of vitality to love culture. Because culture, in the specific, or rather the class sense, is a possession; and nothing demands a fiercer or madder energy than the desire for possession.*

Pasolini repeatedly asserted that his denunciation addressed only the Italian context of his time. I believe that his vision extends beyond the singly admissible immediate of time and place. I can see it translated to the conditions of our mode of production. The forty years since his death at the midpoint declension of the Cold War have intensified those conditions to such a high-pressure degree that now confronts us with the urgent question: has the power acquired by the new globalised possibilities of production resulted in producing *social relations incapable of modification*? This is the essence of Pasolini's outrage: 'a final *identification* between exploited and exploiter' rather than a 'fight for civil rights in the name of a different order of things. Alterity – not simply an alternative – which by its very nature excludes any possible assimilation of the exploited and the exploiters.'

Our political systems are corrupt, not only because they nakedly, unashamedly and criminally protect the international interests of the high finance and super-rich kleptocracy, the minority against the increasingly pauperised majority; no, not only, but because they dare to say, 'we are all in this together', embarked on the ark of enterprising salvation. To which our implacable terrorists respond, 'Yes, and therefore within easy reach!'

Our terrorists. Ours indeed. But how so? Perhaps I have made clear the reasons for my reluctance to acknowledge them historically ours, and not posed simply as a 'generational threat', superficially understood to describe a replenishment of fresh recruits to Islamist terrorism. We have something worse to fear than a reservoir of alienated youths in our intimate midst from which in the twentieth century's Thirty Years' War of Red and Neofascist terror could draw and now Islamism does in its turn. I have called them 'body donors' to a cause — a cause, be it said, that has apparently different cultural and historical specifics, such as would befit a Red Brigades Italian, a Tupamaros Uruguayan, or Al-Qaeda Egyptian. I name only some representatives from Europe, Latin America, the Arab world in the spectrum of those ready to sacrifice their lives. Is there a moment of analysis that would refocus the multiple rays of this spectrum to one? Is there an imaginable situation in common which would override differences between those who choose the route of militant martyrdom? Alienation, social grievance, a sense of being purposeless in a society demanding economic success — all those ills that social theorists used to package in the categorical pathology of anomie — will not explain the 'generational threat' encountered in close-up domestic instances of the British-born jihadist of Pakistani ancestry, who is said somehow 'radicalised', who absconds to join the Islamic State Caliphate in Syria, of the Belgian citizen of Moroccan origin who returns from training in Syria to participate in the killing of 130 people in Paris, and so on, in Europe, in America, and elsewhere across the world, each different, all the same, converts to the doctrine of mayhem.

I have suggested an existential condition applicable to them, put to examination in psychiatric, anthropological and literary critical perspectives, but not in any sense to offer a 'cure'. There is none. It is too late for recovery. Nor could there possibly be one historically. I say historically, in the sense of an existential situation already befallen, which does not permit even to speak of 'symptom' or 'diagnosis' of terrorism. I say historically, because an immense anthropological genocide has occurred — on a scale unimaginable to Pasolini — in which entire differences of being in the world, entire variable species of culture have been annihilated. I do not single out the culture of Islam alone in this date of expiry but a multitude of diversity that in its particularities made up a life-world layer of resistance to assimilation. Assimilation to what? To the usual suspect, globalisation? Neocapitalism? Accelerated consumerism? And whatever else promises other lurking perils of Malthusian catastrophe? *Identification* is the symptom, not terrorism; vagueness, not of the uncertain diagnosis of terrorism but of assimilation, the after-effect of mutation which leaves the survivors of anthropological genocide unsure of what they have lost; homogeneity, like as sort of lobotomy that does not bring social tranquillity but restless anxieties. 'Our terrorists' — now we know them. They are Pasolini's 'washed-out, ferocious, unhappy ghosts' from the unquiet grave of postculture's genocidal assimilation. They are the last glimmer to reach us of extinction. This is the lesson of populism's loss of world.

THREE PROPOSITIONS

Sindre Bangstad

With the resurgence of the far right across wide swathes of the European continent, Brexit and the US Elections of November 2016, populism has become a publishing cottage industry. A number of academics from various disciplines are being asked to pronounce upon the phenomenon from their different angles. I am afraid I am no exception. I am a Norwegian social anthropologist who has to date not undertaken any ethnographic research on right-wing populists. Since Norwegian right-wing populists know perfectly well by now through my work as a public anthropologist who I am and what I stand for in relation to their life-worlds and worldviews, undertaking such research would present any number of difficulties in terms of access for me. I am not alone in this either. True to my academic discipline's long-rooted and often unthinking orientation towards exoticism, Norwegian social anthropologists have virtually flooded Norwegian mosques in search of proverbial Muslims to 'understand' and 'explore'. But hardly a single Norwegian MA or PhD has been written on the lived worlds and experiences of one's average Norwegian right-wing populist voter or sympathiser. It is not that these people are strangers to us: given that opinion poll support for the Norwegian far right Progress Party has varied between the 30 per cent recorded at the time of the so-called 'cartoon crisis' in 2005/6, to the 22.9 per cent recorded in the parliamentary elections of 2009 to the 13 to 15 per cent it currently records in opinion polls, it would be fair to assert that practically every white Norwegian citizen – educated or not – has some Progress Party supporters in their family ranks, close or distant, cousins or uncles or even the odd aunt. I certainly have.

In my youth, which I spent as an odd child born to middle-class parents in a then relatively bleak post-industrial working-class community which had turned into a commuter suburb to Norway's second largest city of Bergen on the West Coast of Norway, the Progress Party voters and sympathisers were relatively readily discernible. In the working-class community in which I grew up, there were actually some real immigrants to be found, due to the fact that the community has long hosted an asylum reception centre. We kept our distance, though one of my female peers at school at a rather precocious age fell for a man at this reception centre, and ended up having children with him. Though I vividly recall a fellow school pupil showing up at the school grounds one morning sporting a Nazi swastika on his leather jacket sleeve and promptly being escorted to the councillor, who no doubt told him that he would be facing expulsion if he failed to remove it by the next morning, the working-class community in which I grew up was not necessarily hostile to immigrants. There were to the best of my recollection few, if any, serious violent incidents to speak of. This community still remains a community in which the social democratic Labour Party is dominant; and in which the Progress Party, which increasingly touted itself from 1990s onwards as representing the interests of the 'ordinary' white working-class which had once been the core electoral constituency of the Labour Party, made limited headway.

But there were certainly Progress Party voters and sympathisers around even in this community. They were the male (for they were more often than not male) uncles and cousins who unfailingly felt that they 'had to' speak their minds about their dislike and contempt for those swarthy immigrants, a dislike and contempt which usually kept close company with their views on feminism, gays and lesbians. And they had by then already started their 'slow march through the institutions', a slow march which would culminate in the Progress Party entering a Norwegian government for the first time ever in the party's history as a coalition partner with the Norwegian Conservative Party after the parliamentary elections of September 2013. And they were increasingly vocal and vociferous about their views, a vociferousness which would by the 2000s once more make expressions of racism and Islamophobia quite commonplace and mainstream in Norwegian society. But this was a time before populist right-wing discourse in combination with an increasingly assertive Muslim identity politics had once and for all turned erstwhile immigrants referenced by virtue of their national origins into 'Muslims.' Which brings us to an important point which in the Norwegian and Scandinavian context regretfully cannot be stressed enough. Namely that the political influence and political power of right-wing populists and their discourses do not depend on right-wing populists alone, but the wider societal matrix in which they operate. For right-wing populists, much like fascists in the 1920s and 1930s Europe, rarely if ever come to political power on their own account, and their political influence over the wider field of politics is by and large determined by how more established and mainstream political actors respond to their messaging and popularity. In Norway, this has become very clear over recent years. Since 1987, the Progress Party has for all practical purposes established discursive hegemony over immigration and integration rhetoric and policies – and so much so that mainstream political parties, whether they be social democrats or conservatives, have virtually bent over backwards to accommodate their policies, if not their rhetoric on immigration and integration.

In the Norwegian context, one should also bear in mind that it was the Conservative Party, knowing fully well that it would not be able to return to political power without making the choice of going to bed with the Progress Party as an electoral partner, which brought the Progress Party into government. The decision to do so was made in 2009, after the Progress Party's most successful electoral campaign to date, which mobilised its electoral constituencies on a platform of far-right ideas and tropes about an impending 'stealth Islamisation of Norway'. A widespread notion among Conservative Party apparatchiks was that embedding populist right-wingers in government would make them more 'moderate.' It would be fair to say that this has not transpired: the Progress Party has since October 2013 been firmly in control of immigration and integration policies in Norway, and the rhetoric about Islam and Muslims in Progress Party circles has by no means softened.

To the extent that I can be said to have 'studied' populism, I have done so in the form of studies of right-wing populist discourses in Norway, and how these interact and converge with right-wing extremist discourses and Islamophobia. Let me note that there are very real methodological limitations in such an approach. Paraphrasing a comment made by the anthropologist Lila Abu-Lughod in a different context, one should not confuse 'theories of what it is to be a populist with populist experience'.

Even though the core anthropological methodology of ethnographic fieldwork makes anthropology seem more suited than most other scholarly disciplines to exploring and trying to understand the life-worlds, passions and motivations of right-wing populists, my own searches for anthropologists who have actually undertaken ethnographic research on and among these groups have yielded surprisingly few results. Instead, the scholarly literature and debates on right-wing populism continue to be heavily dominated by political science scholars. The dominant voices here belong to the likes of Jan-Werner Müller and Cas Mudde. The closest one gets to ethnographic accounts of right-wing populism at the time of writing, are the accounts of sociologists who happen to apply ethnographic methods to their sociological work. Here, I have in mind the work of Arlie Russel Hochschild and Justin Gest. It is not that I have anything against political science per se, but a political science framework and methodology, focused as it is on macro-level data relating to electoral and/or opinion poll patterns and behaviours and abstract theorising seem to me particularly ill-suited to exploring and understanding the micro-level processes at work in the rise of right-wing populism. Leaving aside these limitations, it has also become increasingly clear to me how political science scholars aligned with a liberal and centrist framework simply seem unable to adopt a critical stance towards the very interpretations of liberalism that have during the past thirty years or so prepared the ground for the current rise of right-wing populism. I have in mind here those same policies of neo-liberalism which have generated our recurrent political, economic and social 'crisis of inequality', which has resulted in a vast expansion of socio-economic inequalities across Western liberal democracies, the devaluation of manual labour and working-class solidarities and the disenfranchisement by means of a de facto political exclusion of people who are not of educated and middle-class backgrounds from our politics, the liberal common-sense about the importance of 'austerity' measures, the rise of a liberal and cosmopolitan elite of global 'frequent travellers' detached from the lives and circumstances of ordinary Europeans and Americans, and the albeit partial liberal accommodation of a right-wing nationalism and a xenophobia liberalism alone is deemed capable of 'controlling.' For in order to understand how we got into the 'dark times' that we currently inhabit, with Salafi-jihadist extremists feeding the uneven, but readily discernible rise of the far-right across Western liberal democracies, we need to be able to practise both critical introspection and to look critically at wider structural, political and societal shifts since the era of Thatcherism and Reaganism in the 1980s. One scholar who was able to diagnose these monumental historical shifts at a very early stage and as an embodiment of an authoritarian right-wing populism was the late cultural theorist Stuart Hall in his work on 'the great moving right show' and the 'rise of authoritarian populism'. This is, of course, not the same as saying that what Hall has to say about this issue is all that there is to say about it. But it is necessary to take his work forward. So let me attempt to do just that by making three tentative propositions about right-wing populism.

Proposition 1:The 'people' in populism is neither any people nor your people

Much scholarly ink has in recent years been spilt on figuring out exactly who 'the people' to which right-wing populists every so often refer actually are. Jan Werner Müller is clearly correct in noting that 'it is a necessary but not sufficient condition to be critical of elites in order to count as a populist', that 'populists claim that they, and they alone, represent the people', and that their claim to exclusive representation of 'the people' 'is not an empirical one' but is 'always distinctively moral'. Müller goes on to assert that populism is a form of 'identity politics', but stops short of the very obvious conclusion that if it is indeed so, it is a very peculiar form of racialised identity politics, namely a white identity politics. This is obviously not to say that there cannot be right-wing populist supporters who are not white: in Norway, the Progress Party has in recent years understood how important it can be to have party spokespersons of minority background covering immigration and integration policies. Their point man on this has for quite some time been one Mazyar Keshvari, an Iranian-Norwegian of nominally Muslim background. For the obvious reasons, most Norwegian-Iranians are either refugees or descendants of refugees from the horrors of Islamist repression in Iran during the 1980s and 1990s. In quite a few cases, as is the case with Keshvari, this has translated into active support of far- and populist right-wing political formations in Norway: to the extent that there are activists of Muslim background in Norwegian far- and populist right-wing formations in Norway, many of these happen to have explicit Iranian background. What is often left unexamined in these cases is the central role that racialised anti-Muslim nationalisms have long played in secular right-wing Iranian diasporic politics. Following the work of Ernesto Laclau, the referent 'the people' in right-wing populism must be considered a proverbial 'floating signifier'. The forcefulness of right-wing populists' invocations of 'the people' stem from the very flexible way in which 'the people' are constructed: it is a rhetorical construction which in Cas Mudde and Cristóbal Rowira Kaltwasser's terms 'appeals to different constituencies'.But though a 'floating signifier', the content with which the invocations of 'the people' in right-wing populism are filled is never completely empty. Right-wing populist politics are premised on the rhetorical exclusion of certain categories of people from 'the people'. In this sense, it latches onto the long-standing dual-faced nature of nationalism as entailing both inclusion and exclusion. One would hardly have guessed it from the work of liberal political scientists like Müller, but those most often excluded from the moral category of 'the people' invoked by right-wing populists across Europe and the USA are in our times one particular minority: namely Muslims. For as Farid Hafez and others have long noted, Islamophobia is the 'great unifier' among far-right and populist right-wingers in Europe these days.

The rise of right-wing populism across Europe and the USA has, since Brexit and the election of Trump, often been ascribed to a proverbial 'white working-class resentment'. This, as anyone who has studied the relevant voting patterns in any detail will know, is a highly reductionist account, which true to liberal elite forms displaces responsibility from liberal and conservative political establishments onto what remains of the working-class in Europe and the USA. The fact of the matter is of course that Hillary Clinton received a greater percentage of votes from people in the lower income brackets than Donald Trump, and that Brexit was supported in far greater numbers by Conservative and UKIP supporters than Labour Party voters.

Having said that, it is obviously true in many cases the rise of right-wing populism in certain countries is also fed by white working and service-class resentments over alleged 'favouring of minorities'. The Progress Party in Norway, for example, has the highest level of poorly educated voters and voters living on social welfare benefits of any established political party in Norway. It also happens to be the party with supporters with the highest levels of intolerance towards various minorities of any established party in Norway according to available surveys. However, it is one of the great myths that right-wing populists tell about themselves that they represent the interests of ordinary people. In the USA, the populist right-wing media campaign which prepared the ground for Donald Trump's election victory was in large parts funded by the libertarian corporate billionaire tycoon Robert Mercer, and the White House administration appointed by Trump in early 2017 has a higher percentage of corporate billionaires than any previous US Administration. In Norway, the Progress Party has for quite some time received millions in campaign funding from the right-wing corporate billionaire supermarket tycoon Stein-Erik Hagen, a man who, in spite of his vast fortune, pays hardly any taxes in Norway. Holding the post of Finance Minister since October 2013, Progress Party chairperson Siv Jensen has overseen unprecedented cuts in inheritance taxes for the wealthiest five per cent of Norwegians, a dramatic slashing of social welfare support for Norwegians who are too ill or disabled to work, and a significant increase in socio-economic inequality in Norway, affecting racialised minorities and their children more than any other Norwegian citizens.

Proposition 2: *It's not (only) the economy*

The advance of right-wing populism across Europe has been strong, but quite uneven, in recent years. It would seem that a number of southern European countries in spite of having greater levels of mass youth unemployment, increased levels of popular and general disaffection with dysfunctional politicians and politics, and higher levels of socio-economic inequality, have been relatively immune to the lures of right-wing populism. Countries such as Spain, Portugal and Greece. One possible explanation for this state of affairs is that these are countries with relatively recent experiences of Fascism, and that the void left by popular and general discontent with dysfunctional politicians and politics has in these countries been filled by a resurgent popular left in the form of, for example, Podemos in Spain and Syriza in Greece.

The rise of right-wing populism in Europe throws up a number of conceptual and analytical challenges for anyone wedded to deterministic Marxist analyses of contemporary politics. It is one of the greatest paradoxes of contemporary articulations of right-wing populist ascendancy in Europe that some of the strongest populist right-wing parties are to be found in Scandinavia (Norway, Denmark, Sweden and Finland). For, despite their differences, what Scandinavian countries have in common are societies characterised by comparatively low levels of socio-economic inequality, high levels of trust in public institutions and among citizens themselves, and comparatively low levels of mass youth unemployment. In other words, an account of the rise of right-wing populism in these countries which focuses only on socio-economic factors would be highly reductionist. Which is not to say that socio-economics does not matter. The Scandinavian countries have, much like other liberal Western democracies in recent years, seen a rise in socio-economic inequality, a rise of precarious work, a political and social marginalisation and denigration of people in working-class and service-class professions. What populist right-wingers offer to these potential electoral constituencies is a narrative which in Wendy Brown's apt terms 'culturalises politics' and renders socio-economic problems in cultural terms: if welfare state protections are crumbling, and the rich get richer whilst the poor get poorer, it is because of immigrants and their alleged 'culture'.

Proposition 3: For all their talk of 'religion', the faith of populist right-wingers is largely faithless

If there are fault lines in contemporary European and US politics that populist right-wingers have learned to instrumentalise to great popular and electoral effect, it is the fault lines of what the sociologist Rogers Brubaker has referred to as 'Christianist secularism'. For populist right-wingers across Europe have increasingly taken to positioning themselves as courageous defenders of a 'Christian and secular Europe' vis-à-vis the supposedly 'barbarian' invading 'hordes' of Muslim immigrants and minorities in particular. In Norway, the Progress Party recently adopted resolutions at its national party congress in May 2017 calling for the introduction of compulsory Christian services in Norwegian public schools, a ban on the wearing of the hijab for children under the age of sixteen in Norwegian public schools, a ban on the circumcision of male children, and increased monitoring and surveillance of Norwegian mosques in the name of 'preventing terrorism.' Progress Party politicians and cabinet ministers are nowhere received with greater enthusiasm than when making their yearly pilgrimage to a conservative Christian-evangelical gathering known as the Oslo Symposium, where they are surrounded by Christian-evangelicals whose views on marriage, gender equality and LGBT rights would make them completely anathema for the Progress Party were they anything but self-professed 'Christians'. The paradox is unmistakable: for the Progress Party was in fact founded in 1973 by the libertarian maverick Anders Lange as the Anders Langes Parti (ALP), on an anti-taxation and anti-bureaucratic platform. Lange was widely known for his boozing, hardly known for being religious, and would in all likelihood not recognise his political successors as kindred spirits. UKIP's Nigel Farage, for all his bluster about immigrants threatening 'European civilisation' is anything but a man of God. Donald Trump, a thrice-married serial philanderer and misogynist, made the feat of getting conservative Christian-evangelical Republicans to vote for him. As Brubaker rightly notes, 'the shift to a secularist and ostensibly liberal yet Christianist stance by national populists in Northern and Western Europe is partial and fragmentary. It is also strikingly contradictory. Its liberalism is deeply illiberal, and its identitarian Christianism is devoid of religious content. The contradictions are not surprising: bound by no stable substantive ideological or programmatic commitments, populism is distinctively and chronically eclectic, given to instrumentalising whatever issues seem exploitable at the moment.'

We have learned – or should have learned by now – that history is not written in straight lines and does not necessarily move forward. We should consider it as more akin to the swing of a pendulum. Western liberal democracies find themselves in a process of demographic and societal transition with consequences which cannot easily be foretold. Right-wing populism is in all likelihood here to stay as a permanent fixture of the political landscape in a number of countries. But so is the inescapable fact of the permanent presence of minorities – including Muslims – in these societies. And so it is to this 'politics of presence' and its co-imbrication with the everyday politics of 'conviviality' that one must turn in hope as the best defence against the right-wing populist tide. In noting that 'politics does not reflect majorities, it constructs them', the late and great Stuart Hall also charted the way forward for the hard, diligent and committed work required of us all in order to create and sustain the necessarily broad-based political, intellectual and social alliances called for if the pendulum is to shift against the current populist right-wing tide threatening civil rights and rights to equal citizenship in our societies.

NOX POPULI

Gordon Blaine Steffey

'There is no … guarantee that the "people" as a historical actor will be
constituted around a progressive identity'

Ernesto Laclau, *On Populist Reason*

'What do you want your world to look like? What do you want it to be? Do
you know that a wall has two sides? And nobody is free?'

Pussy Riot, *Make America Great Again*

Decades ago the Prince of Wales exhorted Britons to converse in 'proper'
English, by which he meant 'English English', and to resist the viral creep
of American English, users of which are inclined 'to invent all sorts of
nouns and verbs, and make words that shouldn't be'. We Yanks are mostly
inured to charges of barbarising the mother tongue, your Queen's English,
whether by invention or plain abuse. As American lexicographer Noah
Webster observed, independence requires a 'system of our own, in
language as well as government'. We are not therefore insensible to
degrees of competence or consonance in employment of the tongue that
binds and separates us. We recognise not without a tint of pink that the
rolls of our legislative and executive branches of government are spotted
with verbal barbarians. These brutes huddle deceptively in the lee of our
national altar to the artless and industrious common man wrestling every
inch of America from the frontier wilds. By the nineteenth century this
potent shade of the agrarian myth promulgated by worthies like Thomas
Jefferson was an ecumenical creed. To lay claim to this sacred history

(whatever its deficits, and including a presupposition of white supremacy) was to steal a march on political rivals and to bathe oneself in the headwaters of our 'more perfect union'. Studied black-and-white stills of President Calvin Coolidge haying in Vermont (or colour footage of George W. Bush clearing brush in Texas) circulated in compliance with the Jeffersonian axiom that 'those who labour in the earth are the chosen people of God ... whose breasts he has made his peculiar deposit for substantial and genuine virtue'. In our national lore, the exigencies and purity of simple practice, haying and clearing brush, absolve the 'common man' of his inarticulacy in 'our own' English.

Our current head of state, whom the defunct *Spy* magazine christened a 'short-fingered vulgarian', is on pace to barbarise even more expansively than several accomplished predecessors, including the 'misunderestimated' President George W. Bush and Vice President J. Danforth Quayle, III. While W.'s sins against lady English have been reported ad nauseam, 'the Decider' made marginal gains in presidential comportment across eight years. Such margins cannot rescue him from ranking among our worst chief executives, but political realities in 2017 have lent a shine to the reactionary 2010 meme depicting a grinning W. soaring above the caption: 'Miss me yet?' In 2010, I did not. Vice President Dan Quayle was so assailed by our media for his mangled semiosis that spouse Marilyn stormed to his defence with the unconvincing riposte that Dan 'tries to read Plato's *Republic* every year'. Despite this, she assured us, 'he isn't an egghead intellectual, which I think is very refreshing'. Quayle was variably given to using English like a person staggering toward sense after being roughly agitated from a dead slumber. Media feasted until gorged on Quayle's weirdly incantatory diction. On a stopover in our 50th state, Quayle whiffled, 'Hawaii has always been a pivotal role in the Pacific. It is in the Pacific. It is part of the United States that is an island that is right here.' Elsewhere he rattled, 'The Holocaust was an obscene period in our nation's history ... No, not our nation's, but in World War II. I mean, we all lived in this century. I didn't live in this century, but in this century's history.' Anxiety about his capability was tempered by his submission to George Herbert Walker Bush and by his sufficient sense to girdle himself with canny politicos. Careful and critical coverage of his myriad gaffes meant that neighbouring concerns about his fitness never fully evaporated.

My rumination on our recent political tempest takes wing with Quayle's observations on the state of our cultural union at the head of the last decade of the twentieth century. His observations have too many precedents to credit here, but it is vital to remember that evangelical Christians had lately overcome their longstanding aversion to politics, which had been motored in part by their view that social change was a consequence of individual spiritual regeneration. Their overcoming and political realignment to the Republican party was provoked by the perception of a sea change in social mores, which culminated terribly for conservatives in the divisive 1973 Supreme Court decision *Roe v.Wade*. That decision played a momentous role in persuading evangelicals to 'get their hands dirty' and it became the centrepiece in our enduring 'culture wars'. In the late 1970s and across the 1980s, the political action group claiming a 'Moral Majority' and its founder Reverend Jerry Falwell undertook to 'lead the nation back to the moral stance that made America great'. Falwell understood that 'we need to wield influence on those who govern us', and so they did. A corollary of evangelicals getting their hands dirty was the tinting of social and political difference in terms of Christian apocalyptic and the dispensational premillennialist ideology promulgated with the widely used Scofield Reference Bible. This was to be a 'holy war' against intramural 'evils', including secularist creep, legal abortion, homosexuality, pornography, socialism, and the 'deterioration of home and family'.

Quayle's 'Address to the Commonwealth Club of California' in May 1992 followed hard on the heels of the April riots in south central Los Angeles. The catalyst for unrest was the incredible acquittal of four white police officers charged with and filmed assaulting black motorist Rodney King. As fury cooled to outrage, Quayle chalked up 'black poverty' to the 'Great Society' programmes of President Lyndon Johnson, including several programmes imperilled under our current administration, and above all to a 'poverty of values' and to 'decades of changes in social mores'. Some gibed that Quayle belonged to another century indeed. Unbowed by gibes and rebuttal alike, Quayle insisted that 'I wear their scorn as a badge of honour'. In exposition of his honour, Quayle diagnosed 'two cultures' in the land of the free, one characterised by permissiveness and derision, the other by conviction and righteous indignation. The former pooled in 'newsrooms', 'studios', and 'faculty lounges' where 'sophisticates' mocked the traditions and norms that precipitated 'good and honest' lives in 'the heart of America'. The latter was that very *heartland*, a mythicised metonym and 'small-town' where the 'rest of us' worship, work, and weary of the derision of 'cultural elites'. To the extent that the heartland drops roots in actual soil, it is scarcely the kind of place where folks make an annual run at Plato's *Republic* or vault into senior leadership at a private investment firm now managing $30 billion. On the face of it, absurdities, ironies, and articulacy matter less there than a cathartic focus for escalating discontent with the transit of past securities, the decay of yesterday's dreams, and the daybreak of an alien and unwelcome America.

The raw materials for Quayle's construct lie scattered across U.S. history. Its precedents include our forefathers' declaration against the grasping 'abuses' of a distant king and the several nineteenth century agrarian and labour movements that joined to form the People's Party (known as Populists), which called on government to rescue 'the plain people' from the unjust predations of elites and *laissez-faire* capitalists. The critical difference between the construct and its historical precedents was Quayle's substitution of a horizontal spectrum for a vertical ladder. Quayle adopted a strategy gestating since freshly-minted Republican Ronald Reagan (on a doomed stump for Barry Goldwater) proposed a choice between 'self-government' or submission to an aloof 'intellectual elite', and Alabama governor George Wallace urged voters to stand with the 'average citizen' (Wallace himself) against the 'pointy-headed intellectuals who can't park their bicycles straight'. That strategy was elaborated in the blistering fulminations declaimed by fallen Richard Nixon Vice President Spiro T. Agnew against the 'national masochism' of 'well-to-do blasé permissivists' and the 'effete corps of impudent snobs who characterise themselves as intellectuals'. In his 1969 peroration on 'The Dangers of Constant Carnival', Agnew tipped a hand that would be replayed across ensuing decades: 'It is time for a positive polarisation ... time to rip away the rhetoric [this is not irony] and to divide on authentic lines'. It is difficult even now to credit that the divisions in American society in 1969 were bogus. Still, Agnew explained that 'for too long we have accepted superficial categorisation – young versus old, white versus black, rich versus poor. Now it is time for an alignment based on principles and values shared by all citizens regardless of age, race, creed, or income'. Positive polarisation would divide the 'common man' from the 'snobs' who 'disdain to mingle with the masses'. Asked to identify the 'cultural elites' of his decidedly more prosaic jeremiad, Quayle replied cagily, 'They know who they are'. In fact, they only might have known whom was meant, but they could readily be forgiven ignorance or incredulity because by the 1990s the French loanword no longer signified what the newly immigrant 'élite' once had.

You will protest that positive polarisation is a brazenly euphemistic strategy and a country mile past credible. Quayle nevertheless presupposed (what Agnew termed) 'constructive realignment' in his 1992 campaign speech to the annual meeting of the Southern Baptist Convention: 'The cultural elite in Hollywood and elsewhere may have a lot of money, they may have a lot of influence [notice the elision], but we have the power of ideas [this *is* the idea], the power of our convictions, and the power of our beliefs'. Positive polarisation was an idea so improbably powerful that the American left has yet to impair it appreciably, much less to refute it decisively. It has surely been abetted by media fragmentation, by a strong preponderance of right and alt-right opinion brokers, and by incessant recitation in a 24-hour news cycle. It posits an America savagely riven by antagonism between the salt of the earth and a 'morally cynical' bloc drawn from the fourth estate, the academy, and the entertainment industry. This depraved bloc will hereafter be reckoned elites. Such (mis) use excludes the normative reference of elite to la haute société or to the nexus of corporate and political executives driving and/or staffing the principal bureaucracies of state and society. A revolution comparable to the communisation of the English word gentleman befalls the word elite here. Conservatives crippled its descriptive range by perversely broadening it to include groups wildly ineligible according to established meanings. Redirected from those people 'up there' to these folks here, its misapplication required a concerted scramble to promulgate how it ought now to be heard, which included repetitively parsing its implausible membership and initially deploying modifiers like 'liberal', 'intellectual', 'radical', and 'cultural' ahead of it. Nietzsche recognised that 'what things are called is incomparably more important than what they are'. From Agnew to Quayle and beyond, conservatives (and liberals) have been 'making up people', to borrow Ian Hacking's expression for the interactive looping between naming and named that 'creates kinds of people that in a certain sense did not exist before'. Conservatives christened this new kind with a term already in circulation, a soft but conventionally stable term carrying social and political meanings incongruent with conservative usage. Mystification was in the offing.

How do the new elite compare to l'élite of yesteryear? If the metric is fiscal wherewithal and the multiple points of access wealth opens to the political directorate, thus to observable influence on U.S. domestic and foreign policy legislation, and further to favourable legal and regulatory outcomes, the answer is wretchedly, perhaps comically. That picture improves only marginally should we reckon cooperation between the political directorate and the academy through corporately financed networks of foundations, research institutes, and policy discussion groups. Untethered from its longstanding semantic orbit, 'elite' presents a puzzle. What do the disparate groups herded into its ample fold share; what strange accommodation whelms the media, the academy, and 'Hollywood' (and ultimately establishment Republicans)? Historian Eric Alterman observes that 'the crime is apparently one of mind, akin to such offences as "bourgeois sentimentality" or "rootless cosmopolitanism" in the Stalinist Soviet Union', a view seconded by linguist Geoffrey Nunberg and historian Beverly Gage, among others. Nunberg argues that the last vestige of the 'original meanings' of l'élite survives in 'the implication of insufferable pretension and an unwarranted sense of entitlement'. Gage agrees and sounds in proof the daffy Sarah Palin's matte analysis of elites as folks who think 'that they're – I guess – better than anyone else'. This transvaluation of elite essentialises a conceit redolent of but not necessarily actuated by real terrestrial privilege, power, and wealth. In consequence of this transvaluation, Nunberg rightly observes that 'when Americans hear elite these days, they're less likely to think of the managers and politicians who inhabit the corridors of power than of the celebrities, academics, and journalists who lodge in its outer boroughs'.

To judge by conservative media traffic, this assessment sinks straight to the roots. In the stale but stark litany of conservative radio personality Laura Ingraham, 'They [American elites] think we're stupid. They think our patriotism is stupid. They think our churchgoing is stupid. They think our flag-flying is stupid. They think having big families is stupid. They think where we live – anywhere but near or in a few major cities – is stupid. They think our SUVs are stupid. They think owning a gun is stupid. They think our abiding belief in the goodness of America and its founding principles is stupid.' Ingraham confirms that 'elites are defined not so much by class or wealth or position as they are by a general outlook', which she distills to an irrational 'core belief' that 'they are superior to We the People' (full disclosure: I think the latter formulation is 'stupid'). Conservative pundit Michael Barone swells the refrain, 'How stupid and vicious do they think we are? That's a question that I think explains a lot of things about politics and society today … The "we" in that question are ordinary citizens and the "they" are political and media elites who hold them in contempt.' Of course, the obverse side of 'making up' elites is making up the 'rest of us'. If a lack of real terrestrial privilege, power, and wealth cannot disqualify you from elite status, then having real terrestrial privilege, power, and wealth cannot disqualify you from identifying with the 'common man', 'We the People', or 'the rest of us'. Such mystification or essentialisation of attitude permits Connecticut-reared Ivy Leaguer Laura Ingraham (worth tens of millions) to play at being salt of the earth. It permits our vulgarian-in-chief to say 'I have a tremendous income' and 'I've made billions and billions of dollars' without waking suddenly to elite status. It permits Fox News opinion broker Sean Hannity and erstwhile Hollywood producer turned White House chief strategist Steven Bannon, whose fortunes are severally reckoned in the tens of millions, to smuggle themselves into the 'we' voiced by Appalachian coal miners. It also permits Bannon (lately restored to alt-right media) to explain the November 2016 election that landed the 'Make America Great Again' team in the White House as a rejection of 'elites', who 'have taken all the upside for themselves and pushed the downside to the working- and middle-class' (is that a straight face?). The mind reels when Bannon prophesies a 'restoration of true American capitalism and a revolution against state-sponsored socialism'. The temptation is surely to bawl: 'Soylent Green is people!'

In fairness to starboard-listing Americans, the left continues to misunderstand and mistreat cultural difference as 'false consciousness', taking a bourgeois 'class first' approach that reduces non-economic issues of voter concern to the status of pseudo-problems. In the notorious

'Bittergate' scandal of 2008, then Senator Barack Obama ruminated before potential donors: 'You go into these small towns in Pennsylvania, and like a lot of small towns in the Midwest, the jobs have been gone now for twenty years and nothing's replaced them ... and each successive administration had said that somehow these communities are gonna regenerate and they have not. And it's not surprising then they get bitter, they cling to guns or religion or antipathy to people who aren't like them or anti-immigrant sentiment or anti-trade sentiment as a way to explain their frustrations.' This is a toxic stew of stereotype, inexperience, and reductionism, and subsequent efforts to redress what his campaign speciously termed a misspeaking were as shabby as then Senator Clinton's effort to play working-class hero to Obama's 'elitist'. In the hunt for the Democratic nomination, Senator Bernie Sanders was invited to expatiate on the crisis of structural racism in the U.S. and tottered through an instructive exchange with activists from Black Lives Matter. Moving too soon from the stormy issues of race to the safe harbour of economy, Sanders was pressed by his interlocutors to recognise that 'a class analysis does not take the place of a racial analysis' or more pointedly that 'jobs and college don't stop the police from killing me'. The labour-liberal legacy of economic reductionism and the habitual dismissal of racial justice to the periphery understandably disaffects some black progressives, which is never to say that black progressives neglect economic issues or fail to fathom the imbrication of class and race. It is rather to say that Sanders' insistence on the priority of economic issues was tantamount to insisting that white lives matter. The left struggles to think past the mantra credited to strategist James Carville and on the back of which the 1992 Clinton-Gore ticket soared to the White House (defeating Bush-Quayle): 'It's the economy, stupid'. The American left may have a vision for a just, secure, pluralist, and generative America, but it has yet to execute a sound strategy for persuading working-class Americans of its vision in a way that neither neglects their mundane cares nor transposes them into terms that they do not own.

Positive polarisation did not gain sufficient traction to launch the 1992 Bush-Quayle ticket into a second term, but after more than two decades of accelerating demographic, economic, and religious change, the terrain is not the same. Persons of colour will soon constitute a majority of

Americans under 18 years of age. The Christian share of the population recently dipped below 70 per cent (from nearly 80 per cent in 2007), and formerly sovereign Protestants sit well below 50 per cent of U.S. adults. Traditional employments and industries surrender to forces of globalisation and automation amid widening income inequality. Pervasive change to the warp and weft of American society sources much of the uncertainty and insecurity that opinion brokers (and populists) convert into a generalised nostalgia for a (fool's) golden age. Such nostalgia rallies to working-class industries whose rehabilitation would be symbolic, unrealistic, and possibly ill-advised. The American coal miner is the latest iteration of the beleaguered 'common man' requiring rescue for the health of the Republic. This is not to trivialise the real lives encumbered by the loss of coal jobs in Appalachia and elsewhere (a loss of more than 50 per cent nationwide since the 1970s) nor the collateral withering of towns and regions nourished by that industry (which by some accounts now employs fewer Americans than the ten-pin bowling industry). Founder and CEO of 'the largest coal mining company in America' interpreted November 2016 as a 'victory for the working people' (over against you-know-whom), and in March POTUS (President Of The United States) signed an executive order rolling back several environmental regulations from the prior administration with the promise that 'we will put our [coal]miners back to work'. The same big coal executive who declared November 2016 a victory for 'working people' replied simply: 'He can't bring them back.' Reasons include changing energy markets, competition from cheap shale natural gas and renewables, and above all an industry preference for automated technologies. How then can November 2016 constitute a 'victory for the working people'?

Our momentary political convulsion in the long throes of the old 'West' has triggered a swell of scholarly and journalistic expositions of the watchword populism, as has Brexit in the UK and the challenge mounted by Front National in France. The moments sketched above are ingredient to this administration's populist Americanism, an iteration of populist logic particular to an American right as we near the third decade of the twenty-first century. I follow the late Ernesto Laclau in thinking that populism is defined not by ideological contents but by a 'logic of articulation' or formulary for the promulgation of any contents whatsoever. It is a logic with no specific commitments or, if you prefer, is open to any specific commitments, left, right, and centre. This is why it has been possible to describe Le Pen, Thatcher, Chávez, and Perón as populists, and why too our sitting President now joins this merry band. What defines populist logic is its embrace of diverse ideological demands and its homogenisation of their diversity in a shared antagonism to power. This embrace gives birth to 'the people' by drawing an 'internal frontier' beyond which prowls the source of 'social negativity', namely, the institutional order, the dominant ideology, or simply 'power'. Laclau observes that 'there is no populism without discursive construction of an enemy: the Ancien Régime, the oligarchy, the Establishment or whatever'. In the case at hand, the enemy beyond the frontier we call the elite. The recent, peculiar, and largely uncontested American construction of elite permits right opinion broker Ann Coulter to argue that 'every single elite group in America is aligned against the public—the media, ethnic activists, big campaign donors, Wall Street, multimillionaire farmers and liberal "churches."' Coulter's appeal to a 'public' beset by the elite points up the ambiguity of populist subjectivity. The public is at once the plucky underdog and an antagonist presenting itself as the whole community (wherefore sovereignty must be returned to it). Coulter's formulation confirms Laclau's view that 'populist discourse does not simply express some kind of original popular identity; it actually constitutes the latter'. Again, the heterogeneous demands gathered in this identity are homogenised in shared antagonism to power and homogenised too through the production of empty or 'floating signifiers'. In their emptiness or poverty lies their efficacy, which is to say that 'what it [a floating signifier] wins in extension it loses in intension'. Think here of 'Make America Great Again', which brings through its poverty 'equivalential homogeneity' to (for example) protectionists, nativists, and evangelical culture warriors. It effaces the separation between the demands, not the demands themselves, which will persist in a complex dialectic with the equivalential 'Make America Great Again'.

The American head of state is a populist demagogue in the mould of the Athenian politico Cleon, remembered by Thucydides for his 'violent' manner and by Aristotle for his 'abusive language'. He suffers the barbs of playwright Aristophanes in the delightful comedy *The Knights*, wherein a sausage seller is cajoled by a disgruntled slave to beat Cleon at his own game, namely, the acquisition and misuse of power through calumny, innuendo, mendacity, corruption, theft, and general villainy. When the sausage seller protests that he is unqualified to 'wield power', the slave answers that 'a demagogue must be neither a learned nor an honest man, but rather ignorant and repulsive'. Our vulgarian-in-chief fits this bill. His style or brand of populist Americanism is low and repulsive. His diction would not soon overtake the cant of an insolent tween with a stunted vocabulary and withered imagination. His infecundity scarcely requires exposition for it reliably tells in unscripted moments and in graceless bids to assert his brand over any given script. Disturbing and ill-advised tweets (which he characterises as 'MODERN DAY PRESIDENTIAL') deplore critics as 'bad' or 'sad', 'failing' or 'low rated', and are littered with exclamations and all caps. His fallow lexis is rarely starker than when his brain lands on 'big league' as a post-verbal adjunct to indicate intensity and extensity, for example, 'I'm a believer, big league, in God and the Bible' and 'Mexico is ripping us off big league' and the emphatic 'We're going to cut taxes BIG LEAGUE for the middle class'. His solecisms embarrass less than the often inane and occasionally vile commentary wherein they recur. Fathoms beneath his neurotic, masculinist, and vindictive tweeting and his extraordinary abuse of the fourth estate is a man out of his depth, a sausage seller unqualified to wield power arrogated to him by not even a simple majority of the people.

The populist is a strange symbiont, an antagonist defined by an other without whom there is no populist. In Laclau's formulation, 'the political dynamic of populism depends on this internal frontier being constantly reproduced'. Our vulgarian-in-chief excels in nothing so much as in this lifeblood of the populist logic, the relentless dichotomisation of social space. His discourse generates wall after wall, from a literal wall on our southern border to the figural wall erected daily between 'America first' and the fourth estate. His unflagging molestation of the media may have practical ends in view (perhaps the intimidation of media into softer coverage of his administration), but practicality is incidental to the constant reproduction of the internal frontier without which he becomes what he opposed. To be sure, undermining public trust in media is a profound threat to a pillar of democratic government (which always risks populism), but such threat has been facilitated by a recent construction of elite that encompasses the fourth estate (a construct that must be detonated if democracy and justice are desirable). In the wake of the election, chief strategist Steve Bannon observed that 'the media here is the opposition party', later characterising their opposition as 'corporatist, globalist' rather than 'nationalist', and thus colouring them as elites in league with Mammon against dyed-in-the-wool patriots. Bannon is wise to the transvaluation that capacitates this populist Americanism. Of the President, Bannon says, 'He's the leader of a populist uprising. But he's also an enormously successful entrepreneur who succeeded in real estate, media, and branding'. The but is fundamental and voluble.

The sternest test of any populist is actual rule, which requires cooperation and compromise with 'the establishment' and its institutions beyond the oppositional, shallow solutions to complex problems that earned ovations on the stump ('Mexico will pay for the wall!'). The desperately difficult task of governing risks alienating voters whose identity was constituted in the No that 'Make America Great Again' represented. In the trim maxim of Richard Heinisch, 'success in opposition – failure in government'. The populist grows thin on policy and fat on foes, wherefore may we fathom the abiding preoccupation of our current President with Barack Obama and Hillary Clinton, whose defeat may terminate in his failure. Hope in America Made Great Again consists in just that failure and in reconstructions of our deranged political lexicon so that people in America may enact creative, compassionate, and fair ways to be a 'people', both one and plural, without losing critical attention to the dangers of making up a/the people. We need more than new alignments, more than new words (of which we Yanks are fond indeed), we need new horizons, an ecology of new knowledges and practices for better understanding the processes by which sameness and difference are produced in an America of accelerating change and informational surplus.

MY DEMAGOGUE HERO

Barnaby Rogerson

Before the Qur'an was revealed, there were many books deemed sacred by mankind. Treasured tomes that could be opened at random in order to extract some advice of the moment, recited over the dead and dying, or written down as charms to heal the ill and the deranged. One of the most beautiful in language, but with the oddest morality for any modern reader to embrace, is the *Iliad*. Attributed to Homer, like the Qur'an it first existed on this earth as an oral recitation before it was committed (many, many years after it was first composed) into a written form. The *Iliad* was cherished by the Greeks (and then the Romans) for a thousand years. It inspired hundreds of subsidiary works, commentaries, translations and grammatical glosses. Scholars are still at each other's throats about re-assembling and agreed first written textual version of it, whilst others duel with each other as to how far back into history its composition can be pushed. Does it portray the events of a raid by a mixed gang of pirates from the Greek coast on a civilised Bronze Age city of Anatolia with documentary accuracy, or does it depict some of the anarchy with which the Iron Age Aegean was consumed, or does it also contain some fragments of ancient cultural memory from the lost homeland of the horse-riding Aryans?

Three thousand years after its first composition it remains one of the cornerstones of western civilisation, though people are now unlikely to turn to it for divination, or to tell them how to best worship the gods. Though there is not a year when it does not inspire a new play, a film, a novel or a new poet. I have been fortunate enough to hear two British poets of my chance acquaintance recite their own very powerful adaptations of portions of the *Iliad*. One was sitting in a courtyard in Greece, right towards the end of his long life, with his mind already confused but yet he remained razor sharp about these words. He was not a scholar translator, but someone who delighted in the constant emerging forms of everyday English, perfectly caught in the title of his last collection of *Iliad* derived verse, *All Day Permanent Red*. The other recital was in an attic-lecture hall in Somerset House, London. I had first met the poet when we worked together decorating an underground grotto with flints and bleached bones, but that evening she avoided all eye contact with any member of the audience. Like some ageless Sybil she addressed a distant corner of the room, with her words seemingly coming to her in a trance. What bound both poets together was that they had excavated the text of this ancient, classical work and turned the antiquarian dust of centuries of scholarship into a highly visual, and alarmingly vivid word entertainment about the pleasure to be derived from violent killing.

A dichotomy was being exposed, for in practically every other way, Western civilisation inherits a long tradition of absolute reverence for the culture that emerged out of ancient Greece. It is the centre of everything we not only venerate but continue to aspire to, whether one looks to the origins of painting, sculpture, architecture, medicine, ceramics, philosophy, history, theatre or athletics. Last year I wandered around the ruins of Olympia at noon in mid-August. It could have been a discouraging tourist-ridden process, but the crowds of sightseers, drawn from every corner of Europe brought home an insistent truth. The history of Western Art is in many ways just the story of how we have endlessly tried to copy the achievements of ancient Greece, century after century after century, and have also always failed. Nothing we create either quite catches the verve, the delicacy, the nobility, the severity, inventiveness, colour and playfulness of this period.

But beyond all the many intellectual and cultural virtues of Ancient Greece it also reigns in primary importance in the Western imagination as the birthplace of democracy. It can therefore be something of a shock to be reminded that all this superlative, inventive excellence yet co-existed with a spiritual holy book that continuously glorifies violence.

This violence is not just reserved to the battlefield. Book Two of the *Iliad* begins with a depiction of the Greek army being called together by King

Agamemnon who is described as with 'Eyes and head like those of Zeus, slender his waist like Ares, his chest like that of Poseidon, just as a Bull is by far pre-eminent among all in the herd'. Agamemnon knows that a plague and the absence of Achilles from their ranks, has discouraged the army. This is not the only time that the Iliad provides us with evidence of a form of proto-democratic gathering. An assembly of all sword-bearing soldiers including their tribal chieftains, captains, commanders gathering together to mull over the problems of the hour. Odysseus, one of the trusted leaders of the ultra-war party, is sent into the assembled crowd of soldiers and entrusted with the royal sceptre. He picks his way through the crowds of soldiers, acting all charming, civil and attentive whenever he spots a chieftain but he alternates this behaviour with that of violent bully whenever he meets a man of the people. Silencing some with threats, and physically beating others with his staff whilst telling them to keep still and listen to their betters. In Pope's version: 'But if a clamourous vile plebeian rose, Him with reproof he checked or tamed with blows.' The sole spokesman of the soldiers left speaking is Thersites who is 'loquacious, loud and turbulent of tongue: awed by no shame, by no respect controlled, In scandal busy, in reproaches bold: With witty malice studious to defame, scorn all his joy and laughter all his aim: But chief he gloried with licentious style, to lash the great, and monarchs to revile.' In Pope's lively verse translation Thersites comes across as the very model of a free-speaking journalist.

Thersites also has the wisdom to point out to his comrades that most of their problems derive from their leader, King Agamemnon, who not content with his tents stuffed full of war booty has proceeded to rob Achilles of one of his captive slaves, which is why the great warrior champion of the army has withdrawn from the fight. Thersites asks his comrades if it is not time they left Agamemnon alone with his treasures, for surely Troy had been punished enough for sheltering that pair of lovers Paris and Helen, and it was high time the army sailed home? It was a good debating point and true, worthy of some sort of reply, but rather than answering these charges in a rational way, Homer decides to damn this man to his imagined audience by describing Thersites as evil-framed, bandy-legged, lame in one foot, with rounded shoulders coming together in a stooped chest with a wonky eye on a thin head that bears but a scant crop of stubble. Odysseus does confess that Thersites is a 'clear voiced talker though thou art' but then attacks him 'no viler mortal than thou' for daring to talk of the affairs of Kings, no matter that an assembly of soldiers has been called. He then has Thersites stripped of his cloak and beats him into a bloody pulp with the royal sceptre in front of his assembled comrades until his face streams with tears and a weal of flesh rises up from his back. He is then driven from the place of gathering down to the ships. It is a humiliating public disgrace, his only crime to have talked some sense to his fellow men when they were asked to assemble for just such a purpose.

I can remember being bemused by this episode when I was first taught the *Iliad* as a boy. We are effectively being asked to join in with the cheers that salute a gangster-boss as he first humiliates, then strips, then beats a man into a bloody mass on the ground because he is not a handsome nobleman and he dared talk some common sense. Then as he crawled away in shame we are asked to applaud the wisdom of old King Nestor who dismisses 'holding an assembly after the manner of silly boys who care no whit for the deeds of man' and reminds the soldiers 'let no man depart homewards until he has raped the wife of a Trojan, and caused Troy's proud matrons to render tears'.

It is as if we are suddenly being told to sympathise with the temple guards and Roman soldiers who beat, stripped and humiliated Christ before he was made to carry the instrument of his execution. No doubt, I will not be the first commentator who links the ugliness of Thersites with that other ugly man who dared speak the truth, and who would be punished for this sin with his death, Socrates.

So I learned as a boy that one may delight in the language and imagery of Homer, but only with the same caution that one might now admire the innovative angled camera shots of Leni Riefenstahl, who made propaganda films for the Nazi Party, but remain vigilantly opposed to her politics. But this early lesson about the aristocratic spin embedded within Homer has a potent legacy.

Nine times out of ten when I have bought up the subject of a Demagogue, I have found that people naturally link the word in their mind with Demigod. There is an obvious similarity in English pronunciation, but the chance examples of Demagogues that I have gathered up in these conversations (which repeatedly included Robespierre, Pol Pot, Hitler,

Stalin and Mussolini) explicitly make this deluded messianic connection. A Demagogue is instantly presumed to be a bewitchingly brilliant speaker-leader, who achieves absolute mastery over his people through his evil genius and then like some mad self-selected demi-god leads them off towards their ultimate destruction.

Although this is true of the five characters named, it is not what the word Demagogue means. A Demagogue was initially just a leader of the people drawn from the people. James Fenimore Cooper in his essay 'The American Democrat' might define a Demagogue as 'leader of the rabble' but that is to misread Athenian history where Democracy first evolved. The Demos was not an ancient code-name for the lumpenproletariat, the unemployed and unemployable rabble of a city, that restless fickle mob. The Demos, the people, directly derived from the word Deme, the smallest unit of the self-governing City-state, an urban ward or a rural village which when gathered together was small enough for everyone to be able to recognise and attest to the identity of every other member of the community. A man could only enter the Popular Assembly of Athens by first being registered in the official roll call of his own village community, his Deme. To do this he would have to be 18 and sufficiently proficient in arms to join the roll call of his Deme when it formally gathered together as a militia. This group of men could then solemnly attest that this new member of the community was the son of free-born Athenians and neither a foreigner, a slave or a freed slave. In short you could not vote or take part in the politics of the Democratic city of Athens if you were not prepared to actively defend this city, and had been registered in your village muster rolls as such. To my mind this rather changes that nature of being a Demagogue. A leader of the community of men prepared to die in defence of their city.

But the men who wrote about the earliest democratic leaders, especially Cleon of Athens, were all aristocrats whose careers had in some way been eclipsed by such men. I venerate the works of Thucydides and Aristophanes as much as any amateur reader of ancient history, but it would be foolish not to recognise an innate bias towards the Athenian aristocracy in their writings, if not a sneaking regard for the aristocratic constitution of Sparta. We also know that Cleon was a real member of the working class, for he came from one of the most socially despised of all manufacturing trades.

He was a tanner and all leather worker who always used urine and animal shit in the smelly process of tanning skins.

The aristocratic historians who wrote about him were too clever to delve into the personal insults with which Homer besmirches Thersites, but they nevertheless slowly build up a hostile character portrait of a Demagogue such as Cleon. He will be shown to lack the natural caution, manners and dignity of an aristocrat on numerous occasions. He will be portrayed as too excitable, he will jump too quickly to conclusions, he will be too pompously proud of his civic dignity, he will be too aggressive in debate and too fierce with his enemies. Although his greatest fault in their eyes was almost certainly his ability to speak openly and honestly to their own people. For a Demagogue knew the real concerns of their comrades, they spoke their language, their dialect, and they could make them both cry and laugh. While the very definition of an aristocrat (within the context of Athenian democracy) meant that he was one of the 10,000 men who owned sufficient land to render their household and families completely self-sufficient. An aristocrat owned his own plough, oxen and horses and could happily survive from the income from their broad acres, their orchards and vineyards. Such men could never truly empathise with the artisans, seamen, labourers and small farmers who made Athens great and distinctive.

Roman democracy was based on a similar tradition to that of Athens. The Roman People became politically relevant when they were marshalled in the tribes and clans with which they would serve as citizen-soldiers in the Legions. This Popular Assembly had its own spokesmen, but in practice its duty was to solemnly applaud the decisions of the aristocratic Senate and acclaim the new Consuls, who would later become the commanding general of the Legions. Even the most radical of Roman politicians, be they the Gracchi brothers who tried to reform the social and political structure of Rome to help the lower classes, the Bobby and Ted Kennedy of the ancient world, or their political heir Julius Caesar, were aristocrats following a popular policy, not men of the people. The People of Rome were free to applaud or oppose, but effectively they were always led by a faction from within the Senate. The same restraining hand of the educated, office-holding gentry can be seen in the English Revolution and the French Revolution. For even during the height of the Jacobin terror, power never passed out of the hands of the committee of Public Safety composed of university educated lawyers and intellectuals. I like to remember that Robespierre, the great sea green incorruptible, the master tactician and architect of the French Republic, continued to dress in satin breeches and a powdered wig.

One should not insult the memory of Thersites and Cleon by allowing Trump and Farage to be rated as fellow Demagogues. But like Odysseus it would be foolish to underestimate either their charisma or their determination. They spotted that a broad consensus had developed within the ruling meritocratic elite (defined by their university education, their liberal-outlook, their salaries, their index-linked pensions and urban identity) who had imagined that the old working class was dead as an electoral force. The working class had indeed been driven from the land a hundred years ago by agricultural mechanisation and has now been all but driven out of skilled work in factories by robots and computerisation. So politicians now studied the fifty shades of middle class aspiration to identify the issues that attracted a caucus of supporters. They concentrated their energy on focus group analysis of this ever growing middle class block, especially that which identified the concerns of the 7 per cent swing vote which decides every democratic election. If market research could analyse the very small difference between Pepsi Cola and Coca Cola, or who shops at Walmart or Marks and Spencer, it could do the same job to sort out the slight difference between compassionate Conservatives and New Labour, between Republican and Democrat.

By contrast Trump and Farage had the Odysseus like ability to talk on their feet, to be seen to inhabit their own skins, rather than constantly consult a press secretary for the right response to tie in with the latest market research. They also had the ability to get things wrong but carry on smiling. For they knew that they could pull together support by just using one tool – fear. Fear of the outsider coming in to steal the last of the working class jobs, be it Mexicans or Muslims in the USA, or East Europeans and illegal migrants in the UK. This could be combined with fear that indigenous working class culture was being swamped by the existing immigrants. It could also be combined by manipulating the visceral dislike of the urbane liberal elites by the old working class living simpler, less cultured lives in the provinces. To get a taste of this, look at any successful American film which habitually presents the simple country dwellers as good folk and as the perennial victims of the Big City elite. *The Hunger Games* trilogy, though a fantasy, follows this trope to perfection.

But the political Fear has been used before, most especially in America, and it will no doubt be used again. If you look back over recent American history, it is a recurring theme, brought alive every generation. The American Party rose like a meteor in 1850 as a backlash against German and Irish Catholic immigrants flooding the land, repeated in 1880 by President Arthur Chester's Chinese Exclusion Act. Woodrow Wilson's fantastically enlightened vision of the League of Nations would be destroyed by American isolationism, which returned after the Second World War in Joseph McCarthy (the Senator for Wisconsin's witch hunt against Communists in 1950, who were invariably found to be both foreign and intellectual).

We just have to make certain that we don't cheer too loudly as Odysseus wields the royal sceptre like a club, raining blows on Thersites back until his body is soaked with tears and blood. It also brings to mind one of my favourite stories about the Prophet, chided in a verse of the Qur'an, for once turning his back on the complaints of a poor man, in order to pay attention to an elegant delegation.

FRAU PETRY'S DREAM

Leyla Jagiella

The world that we talk about is always our world, it is always my world. That's the only world that we can perceive and that we know to at least some extent. We start with ourselves and from there we gain cognisance of what surrounds us, while never at any point being able to fully escape the prison of our own subjectivity.

I am all too conscious of that fact and it is for this reason alone that I often like to engage in an exercise that others may deem a little narcissistic. I always like to start with telling something about myself before I talk about a specific topic at hand. It is, after all, only this 'myself' that would make it intelligible to my listener or reader why I see things in a certain light and why my judgement of the world around me is the way it is.

Before I talk to you about politics in Germany, let me first tell you when, where and how I gained cognisance of politics in Germany.

I was born in 1980, in a small rural town in a part of the German federal state of North Rhine-Westphalia. This was where I grew up, partly of an immigrant background (largely Polish and miscellaneous), always somewhat troubled about my gender identity and sexuality (I turned out a trans woman later) and identifying with Islam from an early age on. I have written in detail about these matters in the 'Men in Islam' issue of *Critical Muslim*. Why do I bring it up now, you may ask? I mention these experiences not only because they tell the reader who I am and why I might see the politics of my country of birth in a certain light, but also because all of these constituents of my identity have an immediate relationship, and not a friendly one, with the politics that I am going to describe.

I grew up in a landscape that was scarred by the remains of historical German nationalism, both of the Nazi variant and the older imperial one.

Only a few kilometres from my hometown stood the Wewelsburg, which Himmler had once wished to eventually turn into a world capital of the SS. Further to the North stood the impressive Kaiserzeit monument for 'Herman the German', imagined (anachronistically, of course) as a defender of the German nation against foreign imperialism.

The inhabitants of my hometown were overwhelmingly voters of the Christian Conservative CDU party. Not surprisingly, many people in my home town had difficulty accepting social change and diversity with ease. It was that particular characteristic that, after all, made them so fond of the CDU. Even though I was a white kid who had grown up with German as her first language, I remember several instances from my childhood during which my 'foreign' name alone sufficed to mark me as 'other' and to make some people view me with suspicion. Not all, of course. But some. And again and again. I also struggled as a child who did not conform to normative gender expectations. Everything 'foreign' was as much seen with suspicion by a significant part of the population as everything 'queer'.

Anti-Semitism was common as well. 'The Jews are still pretty bad,' is what was muttered when the Israeli army bombed Gaza. The Jews! Still! This reality in the underbelly of German small town society contrasted starkly with the image that the country at the same time portrayed to the world and for which its more urban elites congratulated one another: citizens of a country that had 'learned from its past' and that had successfully healed old wounds and confronted its fascist heritage. There was a clear disconnect between how these urban elites perceived themselves and their country and what people felt and expressed in the world that I grew up in. 'Not again!' moaned many students at my school, when the schedule asked them to talk about the Nazi era. Well, why not again, if you still haven't really learned your lesson yet? Their 'not again' mirrored the words of their fathers, of course, who constantly repeated the mantra of 'enough is enough'. It was, they said, all already too long ago and had nothing to do with Germans nowadays at all. In general, people had little awareness of historical responsibility. Although it can be said at least people knew something about the Nazi period. But they knew almost nothing about German colonialism and its brutal impact on several regions in Africa, China and Oceania.

Jews were disliked, but they were few in actual number. There were none in my hometown back then. Muslims, on the other hand, hadn't stepped much into the limelight yet. They hadn't started building too many mosques and they hadn't yet sent too many children to university. They were still mostly identified as *Ausländer* (foreigners; even if already third generation in the country) and *Gastarbeiter* (guest workers). Many, including part of the political establishment, still hoped that they would all return to their 'actual home countries' soon, after having worked for decades to enable the flourishing of the German economy.

What I am describing here is a world filled with prejudices and poor of much wisdom of anything beyond its 'edge of the plate', as we say in German. It was a self-contained world. People had their ideas about things, they had their sentiments. But these didn't really matter in practice. There was no synagogue (anymore) to burn down and there also was no mosque (yet) to protest against. And life was good for most people in this small-town environment. Fathers earned well and mothers largely stayed at home and took care of the kids. The worst decades of the Cold War had already passed and as such there was not much that people had to fear. And when people do not have much to fear then they also usually stay within their limits. Whatever their sentiments and prejudices may be, they still keep at least a certain minimum of *adâb* or social etiquette.

Things changed slightly with reunification in 1990. It made people feel uneasy about the future. Newcomers from East Germany arrived and were viewed with suspicion. Their habits, their fashion ... everything about them was strange, after all. But on the other hand, wasn't reunification what people had yearned for, for decades, both in the East and West? So, one put up with the reality of these newcomers in town, and the newcomers quickly adapted to the habits and fashions of the West. A bit more troublesome for the established population of our area were the great numbers of Russians of German descent who settled in our town with the advent of Perestroika. Chancellor Kohl had made immigration easy for them via a law that privileged people with 'German blood'. They were not German enough in the eyes of many in our town, though. They were always called 'the Russians', and stories circulated on their (supposed) dishonesty and unclean habits. The truth was, however, that most of them were actually extremely honest and clean because they belonged to a fundamentalist Christian sect that very much required them to be so. But their strange religion only set them further apart from the largely Catholic established population.

The 1990s was a strange time in Germany. On the one hand, it was a decade marked by optimism, thanks to the end of the Cold War and due to a dynamic social climate that dared to discuss many topics more openly that had hitherto not been referenced at all. I remember very vividly seeing for the first time people on afternoon television talk-shows speaking openly about their homosexuality or (what was back then called) transsexuality. It was also when I saw the first Muslims speak publicly about their faith. I became encouraged to entangle my own identities and consider how public I wanted to be about them. At the same time, however, there also was a discernible rise of nationalist sentiment in the public sphere. Germany had become bigger again. Could it also become a 'Greater Germany' once more? A number of bloody pogroms against *Ausländer* shook both West and East Germany at the beginning of that decade. Arson attacks on an apartment block mostly inhabited by Vietnamese immigrants in Rostock-Lichtenhagen in 1992, and on the home of a Turkish family in Solingen in 1993 – resulting in the murder of five family members, most of them children – are embedded in my memory. I remember the long lines of candle-carrying demonstrators marching in solidarity with the victims of these attacks. The haunting images were broadcast endlessly. But I also remember hearing local people bemoaning that the media was giving 'too much attention to these isolated cases of violence' and had blemished Germany's global reputation unduly. The reaction of parts of the political establishment also seemed bizarre at times: Angela Merkel, back then still a minister in the Kohl government, met with young East German neo-Nazis to understand their woes and worries. Yet I do not remember her visiting any of the victims or families of victims of neo-Nazi attacks. Throughout the 1990s, her party, the CDU, relentlessly stated the presence of 'too many immigrants' was responsible for growing racist sentiments amongst Germans and engaged in xenophobic debates incessantly. From the late 1990s onwards, their particular brand of centre right-wing populism repeatedly engaged the public in a tiring debate on *Leitkultur*, a dominant national culture that everybody living in Germany should agree on and that immigrants should assimilate into.

The 9/11 atrocity, which roughly coincided with the time at which I finally left my small town environment and started my own life as a young woman elsewhere, gave a new rise to racist sentiments all over Germany. As was the case all over Europe and in many other countries of what has been called the West, from then on the 'dangerous Other' has been more clearly defined as 'Islam'. That time also coincided uncomfortably with the growing confidence of Muslim communities in Germany as they started to build their own proper mosques and the children of Muslim immigrants started to appear in university classrooms in growing numbers.

Let me pause my narrative at this point, shortly after 9/11, and express in rather more pointed form what I wish to convey: Germany has been no stranger to right-wing sentiments amongst its population, or political populism amongst at least parts of its political elites in the times from the end of the Nazi regime in 1947 throughout the days of reunification up until 9/11. Right-wing sentiment and populist politics have continued to exist in Germany, at least as long as I can remember. I seek to emphasise this point because as far as I can see, most analysts of the rise of right-wing populism in contemporary Europe give far too much weight to hypotheses that attempt to explain that rise solely as a result of recent economic or social developments. While I do agree that such developments do play a role – and that is why I hinted at the connection between fear and the loss of political *adâb* earlier – I think it is crucial to understand that the ideas upon which right-wing populism in Europe currently thrives are the very same ideas that I heard many people express in my home town as I was growing up. They are the same ideas that led to bloody pogroms in the early 1990s. The very same ideas that led to the *Leitkultur* debate in the late 1990s and early 2000s.

What was quite different all throughout the 1980s and 1990s, and in fact the first decade of the 2000s as well, was, however, that German mainstream politics did not include any party that organised itself specifically along right-wing populist principles. There were the neo-Nazi parties, of course. But their success has always been limited locally. I remember very well how just ten years ago many people in Germany would commonly declare that a right-wing populist party could never become a possibility in Germany. 'Again', was often added as a conscious reference to Nazi times. Yes, we did have right-wing extremism, we had neo-Nazis, we also had regular dives of the Christian Conservative CDU and especially its sister party CSU into right-wing populist terrain but successful organised right-wing populism was considered an absurdity in the German case. The Dutch could do it; yes. The French; yes. Even the Austrians; yes. But never the Germans. 'Never again.' But, again, here did manifest some of the disconnect between the official self-image of Germany's elites and opinion makers and what has long been brooding in the underbelly of the country.

Just ten years later and much has changed. We now have a fairly successful political party representing organised right-wing populism in our political landscape, the AfD, *Alternative für Deutschland* ('Alternative for Germany'). Recent German media reports still seem to make it clear that the party should not be taken seriously. Their inner dramas and strivings are often emphasised and their idiosyncrasies exploited by the press. The public image of the party is largely one of chaos and instability, an image that does indeed describe the party accurately, to an extent. But this kind of reporting doesn't take into account what a worryingly quick rise the party has actually experienced in its young history already. Founded in 2013, it had entered the representative assemblies of several federal states of Germany within three years. In 2016 alone it managed to enter the representative assemblies of five federal states. Three more were added in the course of 2017, including North Rhine-Westphalia, where I had grown up. The AfD are now considered to have a good chance of entering Germany's national parliament, the Bundestag, during elections in September. Of course, nowhere in Germany during any election did the AfD ever gain percentages comparable to recent percentages won by right-wing populist parties in neighbouring countries such as the Netherlands, France or Austria; not to even speak of Poland or Hungary.

In the overall political landscape of Germany, the AfD still remains a minority phenomenon. Nevertheless, its dramatic rise is alarming in a country that didn't deem such a party even possible a mere ten years previously. Should the AfD indeed manage to enter the Bundestag later this year, it would be the first time ever since Nazi times that a clearly right-wing populist party manages to gain significant influence in our national parliament. 'Again'. Albeit with a manifesto that is, indeed, a chaotic conglomerate. The AfD embraces representatives of a 'new right' (think people like the Dutch Geert Wilders – clearly against the EU and immigrants but not officially anti-Semitic, in fact very fond of the modern state of Israel, and not necessarily opposed to all gay rights) with members from classically conservative milieus, and those with a very clear neo-Nazi tradition. What unites them all is mostly Islamophobia and a strong disdain for Angela Merkel's refugee politics, as well as conservative positions on such things as gay marriage, abortion and sex education in school.

There is something strikingly odd about right-wing and fascist movements of all provenances. As far as I am concerned almost everything about them is odd anyway, but here I want to mention one particular odd characteristic of this political plague. They spend the vast majority of their time and energy agitating against 'the Other', but when the time for mutual benefits arises, 'the Other' can quickly become their intimate. We see that in the odd global networks of modern Creationism and 'Pro-Life-ism', consisting of Christian and Muslim fundamentalists (amongst others) who usually hate each other's guts but who are willing to work together when it comes to fighting the eternal evils of evolution and abortion. Doesn't this reveal something about the fickle ideals of religious fundamentalism? That their fundaments are actually quite negotiable and not as solid as they pronounce them to be? The same is also true for the group of people which we may call, for reasons of comparison, political fundamentalists, and is also true of the strand of right-wing populism that has been on the rise all over Europe in recent years.

Each of these right-wing populist movements and parties preach a strictly anti-European political ideology. Their desire is to preserve and strengthen national sovereignty. They are also quite willing to rant against their own European neighbours, always 'the Other' of old. But, nevertheless, Europe suddenly matters to them when it comes to define it against a new 'Other', Muslims and non-European immigrants in particular. 'European values' suddenly become of weight within their discourse and 'the Occident' needs to be saved and preserved. To the extent that even the old eternal 'Other' of Christian Europe, which the larger part of Europe (let's remember: with Nazi-Germany and Austria at the forefront, but also numerous local collaborators in France, the Netherlands, Poland, Czechoslovakia, Hungary, etc.) sought to exterminate completely just a little more than sixty years ago, suddenly becomes appropriated in that discourse: Talking of 'Judaeo-Christian values' vs. 'Islamic values' has become established practice in many of these right-wing movements now, notwithstanding their own still existent anti-Semitism.

It is not only on the ideological and rhetorical stage that European right-wing movements discard all their ill-will against the inner-European 'other' when faced with defeating common, imagined or real enemies. This is also the case on the practical stage. One example unfolded in front of our eyes in January 2017 in the German city of Koblenz. Under the title *Freiheit für Europa* (Freedom for Europe), right-wing populists from all over Europe came together to form common strategies and celebrate each other. Of leading agency here was the AfD, who were gathered under the aegis of their chairwoman Frauke Petry. The French Front National had joined them with Marine Le Pen, as did the Dutch *Partij voor der Vrijheid* (PVV) with Geert Wilders, and the Austrian FPÖ. The crème de la crème of Continental right-wing demagogism were in attendance. Representatives from Italy and the UK were also to be found.

The event points to a curious international dimension of otherwise nationalist and parochial right-wing populism. Numerous laudatory speeches were made in honour of the newly-elected US-president Trump. Frauke Petry, amongst others, voiced her conviction that Trump's victory was a sign of good times to come for the kind of politics that she cherished. Previously, other members of her party had voiced support for the policies of Russia's Putin. In many ways, the Koblenz gathering was a reminder for the need to view the rise of right-wing populism in Europe in its global context and not just simply as a local and nationally contained phenomenon, as is often done.

In fact, the rise of Frauke Petry's AfD is itself a sign of how European and global discourses help to form tangible political realities within specific local settings such as Germany. Without doubt, the AfD's sudden rise has much to do with the specific history of German politics in recent decades and also with a very specific German-ness of its agenda. But its rise would never have been possible without the previous rise of other right-wing populist parties in Germany's neighbouring countries. The Dutch PVV, The French Front National and the Austrian FPÖ have all been known for successful voting outcomes in their respective countries long before the AfD had even become thinkable in Germany.

As I said: right-wing sentiments and a penchant for populist tactics had already been present in Germany for quite a while, long before the founding of the AfD. But it was awareness of the international sphere that made thinkable in Germany what had already been thinkable elsewhere. This explains at least in part the sudden rise of a right-wing populist party in Germany. But it does not give us the full picture.

To gain a better view of the full picture, we need to shift our attention away from the AfD for a moment. For, whatever percentages the AfD will reach in the upcoming elections in September and whatever its future will be, its rise should be seen as symptomatic of a general shift of Germany's political discourse to the right. Established parties in Germany have, in fact, also become increasingly devoted to populist discourses around Islam, refugees and other classical topics of right-wing politics.

As already mentioned, Angela Merkel's CDU/CSU has always been known to use right-wing populist trope and tactics in their election campaigns every now and then when it suited them. The CDU/CSU has been ambivalent in its dealings with the AfD and their policies. On the one hand, Merkel and others in her party have made it very clear that they consider the AfD's political agenda to be socially divisive and its style of politics intolerable. On the other hand, other members of the same party have publicly voiced sympathy for AfD voters and their 'fears'. It seems obvious that the CDU/CSU feels uneasy with the very likely possibility that it could lose some of its voters on the right-wing fringes to the AfD. This has led to an invigoration of old right-wing rhetoric and tactics in some quarters of the established conservative party.

In April of 2017, Merkel's party colleague and Minister of Interior Thomas de Maizière tried to again engage the public in a new debate on *Leitkultur*. The idea behind a German *Leitkultur* was, of course, always meant to define 'the Other' of German culture in a way that would further marginalise the cultures of immigrant communities. Since 9/11 this 'Other' has increasingly been defined as Islamic. In de Maizière's most recent variation of the idea, 'the Other' was now without doubt the 'problematic Muslim'. In a *Leitkultur*-agenda that he shared with the German public via the *Bild* tabloid, he expressed, amongst other things, that people living in Germany are expected to shake hands (even across gender lines, of course) and that 'we are not burqa'.

The CDU/CSU does not really surprise with such descents into dirty territory. Far more worrying, however, is that right-wing positions and populist tactics have become more acceptable in other established parties of the German political landscape as well. In fact, there simply is no established German political party anymore in which one does not hear right-wing populist sentiments from time to time. Sahra Wagenknecht, deputy chairperson of the Left Party (*Die Linke*) and herself the daughter of an Iranian father, has in recent years and with rising frequency voiced opinions on immigration and asylum seeking that could easily be confused with AfD positions. Several prominent members of Germany's Green Party have recently shown similar tendencies too. Amongst them in particular Boris Palmer, the Green mayor of the Southern German city of Tübingen. Palmer has become infamous (and in some circles probably famous) for diatribes on the political stage, on social media and in other contexts that cater towards racism and Islamophobia. In July 2017 he voiced the opinion that DNA tests should be mandatory for asylum seekers in Germany in certain cases. A Gambian asylum seeker in Tübingen had been arrested on suspicion of rape shortly before Palmer's public remarks. Palmer claimed that a 'mandatory DNA test for all black asylum seekers' could have prevented the rape. A few weeks before that, he complained on his public Facebook page, about young, confident, Arab-speaking men making him feel unsafe on the train.

As such, right-wing populism in Germany is not limited to the explicitly right-wing and populist AfD. It has entered all major political parties of the nation and it has also infected public discourse to a disconcerting extent.

This development mirrors a steep rise of attacks on asylum seekers, arson attacks on asylum homes and other racist attacks within the last few years. In fact, the number of such attacks has been as high in 2017 and 2016 as never before since 1947 in Germany.

There is but one more aspect that, at least for me, is the real missing link in explaining how this phenomenon has become such a strong force in German politics even beyond party lines. Populism, by common understanding, is derived from the word populus. The people; not in the sense of the full number of human beings belonging to a certain region but more in the sense of the 'plebs', the 'hoi polloi'. To cater to populist sentiment is supposed to mean that someone is catering to unrefined, unsophisticated and uneducated sensibilities. It also is supposed to imply that either the person harbouring these sentiments is himself unrefined, unsophisticated and uneducated, or deliberately uses populism as a strategy to manipulate the minds of those he considers more foolish than him.

The people seem to matter when it comes to populism, this is evident. They did indeed matter in the rise of right-wing populism in Germany, as we have seen. But are parties such as the AfD and populist politicians in all other parties just reacting to sentiments that have always been there? What has changed in German public discourse that allowed for such reactions, even though just ten years ago much of it would have been considered unpalatable? Is it simply the rise of right-wing populism in neighbouring countries that has led to this development?

A major shift in official German attitudes towards right-wing populism had in fact already arrived three years before the founding of the AfD and was initiated by a member of the social-democratic SPD party. Thilo Sarrazin, former senator of finance for the State of Berlin, had published a book with the rather populist title *Deutschland schafft sich ab* (Germany abolishes itself). The main argument of the book was that Germany's immigration policy and leftist-green ideas of multiculturalism have led to a state of decay in German cultural life and will eventually lead to the decay of German economics. He mostly blamed Arab and Turkish migrants for refusing to integrate properly into German society. He voiced strident opinions against the building of mosques and against women wearing the hijab while at the same time mixing his culturalist ideas with racist speculation on the influence of human DNA on such factors as success within the educational system. Sarrazin's book quickly ended up at number one in the German bestseller charts, despite the author's constant claims of representing an unwelcome opinion and being censored by the public. Apparently, Sarrazin had voiced a few attitudes that people in Germany really enjoyed hearing. Positions overflowing with racism and Islamophobia. The surname of the author, a version of Saracen, seems ironic. Maybe a subtle but apt reminder of how fragile these identities actually are that right-wing populism seeks to defend.

For me it was scandalous enough to see such a book rise up the bestseller lists the way it did. But even more shocking was what followed: Sarrazin, after all a respectable politician of one of Germany's most important established political parties, was invited to one seemingly 'intellectual' evening talk show after another and his opinions were discussed as valid and notable by opinion makers all throughout the German media world. A managing editor of the newspaper *Die Zeit* spoke out in his favour, as did numerous other journalists of the German feuilleton. Of course, immigration had been discussed before in the German media world. Islam has increasingly been described as a problem in the German media world since at least 9/11. But nobody ever before had made racism and Islamophobia as socially acceptable in the German media world as Sarrazin.

The floodgates that were opened by him - and by all the media who normalised his rhetoric and all the journalists that spoke in his favour - have not closed since. German media has been obsessed with racist and populist tropes from that point onwards. It had always been to some extent, of course, because media thrives on populism. But the Sarrazin debate had given decency to rhetoric that had not been considered decent previously. And since that debate, German media has indulged in these topoi as never before.

It was, in fact, a party colleague of Sarrazin, SPD-delegate Marco Bülow, who revealed the catastrophic scope that this development had acquired. He analysed 204 broadcasts of five of the most popular political talk shows on German state-owned television channels. The overwhelming majority of these programmes repeatedly discussed refugees, immigration and Islam as problems endangering German society, while topics such as racism or right-wing terrorism were highly under-represented in the shows. Topics such as poverty, social justice and climate change are likewise rarely featured. Political talk shows on German state television thrive upon problematising migrants, asylum seekers and Muslims. The same can also be said of much of German print media.

What we see here is right-wing populism spread for its market value. And there is a direct line from here to the founding and rise of the AfD and the spread of right-wing populism all across the German political spectrum. Right-wing populism sells. It panders to, and perpetuates, people's fears and captures their imagination with an addictive quality.

Audiences are in thrall and their appetite for fear and loathing seems endless. Nothing has ever been able to bridge the disconnect between Germany's urban elites and opinion makers and the prejudiced populus of my childhood small town as much as this sad but simple fact.

AWAAM

Raza Ali

The July 2017 decision of Pakistan's Supreme Court to convict Nawaz Sharif for his part in the Panama Papers scandal should not come as a huge shock. Since the country's inception seventy years ago, every single ruler has been forced out of office prematurely. The reasons have been multitudinous: military intervention, assassination and so forth. The surprise lies in the fact that a nation so numbed to the rotting corpse of corruption at the core of its political institutions should decide to hold its head of state accountable.

Sharif's party, the Pakistan Muslim League, has long positioned itself as the voice of the centre-right. What is interesting is that one of the protagonists in his downfall could be about to step into the vacuum he leaves behind. Step forward the populist hero of the moment, Imran Khan, chairman of the Pakistan Tehreek-e-Insaf (PTI) party. Khan has consistently demonstrated he is free from the financial sleaze that permeates Pakistani politics. His financial dealings have been notably and uniquely transparent since his cricketing days. But is he really the answer to Pakistan's prayers?

That depends on whether the alternative to rule by right-wing elites is the ushering in of right-wing populism. In Pakistan, populism is usually associated with *Awaam*, the Urdu word for 'the people'. Pakistan also has a popular saying, 'consider the voice of people, voice of God.' Politicians, political commentators and religious leaders all routinely use the term *Awaam* to refer to an entity which harbours the same emotions, hopes and opinions as themselves. Could this relate to the concept of 'popular agency', with the people proving a positive mobilising force, instrumental in building a democratic society? Or are the *Awaam* an emancipatory body that will change the status quo only through conflict and by creating 'radical democracy'?

Perhaps a more accurate assessment of the development of *Awaam* sees it as being centred around a charismatic leader who speaks directly to the masses but leaves a void in his or her trail. It has also manifested in a 'folkloric' style where unscrupulous front runners use whatever means necessary to garner media attention and public support against the 'elite'. It is in this way that the populists consider it their right to speak for this entity and often use this vision in opposition to the ruling 'elite' or *Ashrafia*.

Unfortunately, I have never had the chance to meet this faction called *Awaam* and have long considered it to be a mythical group. Opinion of the *Awaam* in Pakistan is divided squarely across the entire spectrum of political and religious views. Any one person speaking for them would be absurd, yet it is normal for the word *Awaam* to be bandied about ineffectually in Pakistani media. Accordingly, populism would have to be defined in opposition to something, but my sympathies lie with a more 'pluralistic' approach.

At the turn of the new century we are coming full circle to another right-wing populist scenario. Unconsciously, Pakistan has followed the global trend in its own journey. At its inception after World War II, Pakistan-in-the-making gave rise to its own right-wing uprising in British India driven by a nationalist philosophy, called the *Two-Nation Theory*. This founding philosophy of Pakistan states that Hindus and Muslims are separate and distinct *nations*, with their own beliefs and behaviours that must not be intermixed. India was partitioned to preserve the irreconcilable distinction of these nations. This narrative is referred to as *Nazariya-e-Pakistan* or the Ideology of Pakistan.

By 1970 populism had changed direction and two simultaneous movements emerged: The Awami League in East Pakistan and The People's Party in West Pakistan. Both left-leaning movements were advocating for the rights of the Pakistani people, yet their struggles were so antithetical as to break Pakistan in two. Since this convulsion, Pakistan has been steadily sliding further to the right, a move hastened by the dictator Zia-ul-Haq with *Nazariya-e-Pakistan* proving a handy tool in this reversal.

There is no better example of right-wing populist ascendance in Pakistan than the infamous words uttered by the scholar and celebrity Mufti Muneeb in March 2016: '*Between us and you are the funerals*'. His statement was in support of Mumtaz Qadri, who was executed for murdering Salman

Taseer, the then governor of Punjab. Taseer was targeted for his opposition to the death penalty for Aasia Bibi, a Christian woman who was accused of blasphemy. Blasphemy is a visceral religious and political issue in Pakistan where even false accusations can result in death - mostly at the hands of mobs and vigilantes. The words '*Between us and you are the funerals*' are attributed to Ahmed Bin Hanbal, the ninth century jurist who is the founder of one of the four schools of jurisprudence in Sunni Islam. He was persecuted by the Abbasid Caliph of his time for rejecting the creed of Mutazila, the rationalist philosophy of early Islam, which the state had adopted. Whipped, tortured and imprisoned, he responded with this retort. When he died in 855, the reported number of mourners at his funeral ranged from eight hundred thousand to over a million.

Taseer was shot 28 times on 4 January 2011 by Qadri, his bodyguard, who immediately surrendered. In October of the same year, he was sentenced to death by an anti-terrorism court but the charge of *terrorism* was dropped; although his intention had clearly been to terrorise. It took a further five years before his sentence was enforced, due to appeal after appeal being brought to court and even a mercy petition sent by his supporters to the president of Pakistan imploring a pardon. Despite high-profile defenders including the former chief justice of the Lahore High Court, all of the appeals were rejected and Qadri was finally executed on 29 February 2016, in the middle of the night in an operation shrouded in secrecy.

Reaction spilled on to the street the very next day as it became apparent the execution had been enforced not by the political government but the military establishment. As protests started and public property was damaged, people began gathering in Rawalpindi's Liaquat Park. This was the same park in which Benazir Bhutto gave her last speech to a massive crowd before being killed in a suicide attack. Strict security was placed in Islamabad and Rawalpindi to ensure that events did not spiral into violence. The BBC estimated that thirty thousand people attended the funeral on 1 March, 2016, but according to Mufti Muneeb the 'heavens had not seen a bigger funeral procession on this land of Pakistan' and he put the figure at two and a half million. Reminiscent of Hanbal's funeral, the 'millions' were his supposed vindication.

As the funeral procession travelled to its destination, rose petals were thrown at the vehicle carrying the body and people desperately tried to place a hand on it as though it was a sacred religious relic and a single touch could transform their lives. Had this been any another occasion, Pakistan's media would have covered every minute, but there was absolutely no television coverage. The media had been ordered to enact a complete black-out of the event, as if the funeral did not exist at all, and in response, Qadri's supporters took en masse to social media to ensure the world knew. For Mufti Muneeb this was an epic clash between a tiny but powerful liberal elite that ruled the country and controlled the media, and the great believing masses – the *Awaam*.

A year later a Facebook post caught my eye. It was a picture with two scenes side by side. One was the funeral of a young man named Mashal Khan, a journalism student at the Abdul Wali Khan University in Mardan with left-leaning views and a predisposition to Sufism, and the other was Qadri. There were less than a dozen people carrying Mashal's body for burial and no crowd of mourners paying their last respects. The cleric of the local mosque had refused to perform Mashal's funeral prayers as he too was accused of blasphemy. A day earlier, on 13 April 2017, a mob of students dragged him out of his dorm room punching and kicking, accusing him of blasphemy. He kept denying it, declaring his love for the Prophet Muhammad. They continued accusing him. Whipped up into a vicious frenzy, the mob flung him on to the grounds of the university, stripped and beat him with sticks. One of them shot him in the chest. They were about to set his body on fire when police intervened. By that time videos of his lynching were already circulating on social media.

When local media picked up the images, the nation was already reeling with shock. Religious groups issued qualified and impotent statements regarding mob justice, arguing that if the government had punished blasphemers appropriately in the past, people would not have resorted to taking the law in their own hands. However, this time the arguments didn't wash as the rest of the country could plainly see this was the blatant and sickening murder of a young student. The liberal media launched a campaign of condemnation and demanded swift action to punish those involved. The right wing media tried to play down the atrocity and described it as a covert attempt to harm the Blasphemy Law. When police investigated, the blasphemy charges turned out to be false and the administration of the university, which Mashal had criticised for corruption, was found complicit in his lynching.

The reaction of Mashal's father, a poet, was dignified to say the least. He demanded justice for his son but refused to be vindictive. He defended his son's love of the Prophet and rubbished all accusations of blasphemy. He remained calm despite the unimaginable tragedy and called for the government to punish those involved so that such horror would never again be repeated. During a media interview he recited verses by the Pakistani poet Ahmed Faraz and dedicated them to his son's memory:

All that I said was my eyes could see,
And the blind of the city trounced on me.

The murders of Salman Taseer and Mashal Khan serve to illustrate the steady right-wing populist trajectory taking hold of Pakistani politics, media and society. The path was already being paved when, in 2004, the first drone strike took place in Pakistan, targeting Nek Muhammad, a key Taliban leader, who had recently signed a peace deal with the Pakistani Army. His death triggered an angry reaction from Imran Khan, who opposed not only Pakistan's role in the US-led War on Terror but was also in favour of the peace deal. Musharraf, a military dictator and the then president and army chief of Pakistan, had already firmly set the course of right-wing populism in Pakistan when he decided to side with the Americans in their invasion of Afghanistan in the wake of 9/11.

This move was widely resented in Pakistan. The Pakistani security establishment has significant interests in Afghanistan with a view to protecting their western borders. In the 1980s, Pakistan had assisted the Taliban in their fight against the Russians, with support from the US. Religious rhetoric was employed to rally support for this cooperation between Pakistan and Afghanistan, with the Russians regarded as atheist, godless invaders. The military dictator of the time, General Zia-ul-Haq, flagged up concerns that Russia was trying to access 'warm waters' through Pakistan. The war became an existential issue for Pakistan. Islam was deployed to radicalise Pakistani society in an effort to keep public opinion on side, a move bitterly opposed by liberals who predicted eventual doom. Right-wing populism and its bedfellow religious extremism flourished but it was in post 9/11 Pakistan that it exploded. As drone strikes continued, a

word was added to popular media vocabulary, *Ghairat* or Honour. The
concept of honour is deeply embedded in the Pakistani psyche and it was
this idea that was skilfully deployed by the likes of Imran Khan as well as
right-wing religious groups and media commentators, to stir up nationalist
sentiment and harness the religious right populist trend. The Pakistani
nation felt humiliated, *Beghairat* or Dishonourable for allowing the US to
stomp on its sovereign territory and kill 'our people'. The suspicion that
Pakistan's military establishment had given covert permission for the US to
strike 'high-value targets' with their own drones in exchange for financial
compensation was widespread. This even prompted Pakistan's military
generals to claim responsibility for some air strikes, even though they were
in fact carried out by American drones.

Increasingly, honour has been propelled to the forefront of Pakistan's
self-defining narrative, with politicians such as Khan simultaneously
manipulating and grappling with this volatile national obsession. When
Pakistan's intelligence agencies colluded with the FBI to pick up high-value
Al-Qaeda targets in different areas of Pakistan, both Khan and right-wing
agitators cashed in on the popular appeal of this idea of 'selling our
honour'. The case of Aafia Siddiqui perpetuated this perceived insult. She
had travelled to the US to study, eventually settling there, marrying and
raising a family. After 9/11 she escaped to Pakistan and it is thought her
name was revealed as an Al-Qaeda associate by Khalid Sheikh Muhmmad,
a member of Al-Qaeda captured by the CIA. Pakistan's intelligence
agencies tracked her down and handed her to the Americans. Contrary to
how the world sees honour in Pakistan used against women, it was honour
or *Ghairat* that mobilised populist support for Aafia Siddiqui. One photo,
in which she seems malnourished and brutalised, was put side by side with
a young, beaming Aafia dressed for her graduation. The public was
incensed, blind to the contradiction that women are both killed for *Ghairat*
and paradoxically their helplessness evokes *Ghairat* in Pakistan.

It is too simplistic to say that right-wing populism was caused by 9/11,
although it was certainly exacerbated by the attack. The blame cannot even
be placed at the feet of General Zia. Switch back a generation to the 1960s
and 1970s where the liberal economic policies of the then military dictator
and president, Ayub Khan had created what popular lingo referred to as
the 'twenty-two families'. Capitalist policies had created a rich industrialist

class that was increasingly perceived to be the enemy of the poor, something Zulfiqar Ali Bhutto, who was the founder of the People's Party of Pakistan, was keen to exploit. He was a larger than life character, capable of evoking emotions amongst the masses like no other. Ironically, he was by no means a member of the *Awaam*. Descended from a landed feudal family, he studied at Berkley and Oxford and was foreign minister of Pakistan before founding his own party. The man who formerly, as foreign minister, had been presenting the case of Kashmir in front of the United Nations dressed impeccably in a tailored suit, was now addressing large crowds dressed in the plain native *Shalwar Kameez*, chest bare and cuffs unbuttoned, railing against the elite.

Bhutto's oratory and demagoguery remains legendary in Pakistan's history. In a fiery speech that was both populist and prescient he promised:

> I will fight for the rights of Pakistan. I will fight for the right of the poor of Pakistan. I am prepared to give my life for the rights of the poor of Pakistan. I am willing to sacrifice my son and my daughter…I am the son of a poor man. I have worked hard. It's my conviction that even if have to face death, I will face death but I cannot forget the words of Tipu Sultan. This nation is going to become a great nation. This nation will become the steel of this world. Do you accept that we will make it steel? So, will you serve? Will you work hard? Will you fight? Will you die? Will you struggle? Faithfully, will you? By God, will you?

It was evocative speeches such as this that captured the imagination of the people. Whether it was the poor working class or the educated white-collar middle class, they were all under the Bhutto spell. He won a sweeping victory in 1970 in West Pakistan on the slogan '*roti, kapra, makaan*' (bread, clothing, shelter).

This demagoguery is often blamed for precipitating the break-up of Pakistan. While he spoke for 'the people', the majority who did not vote for him lived in East Pakistan, later to become Bangladesh. Excluded and sidelined by West Pakistan, it was not long before civil war broke out. The Pakistan Army were brutal in their attempts to crush that popular and nationalist uprising but were ultimately defeated due to Indian intervention. Now Bhutto, in what is the present-day Pakistan, was the sole leader. One of his first acts was to nationalise the industries, undermining the capitalist 'elite'. He was seen as an alcohol-drinking, impious man by the religious right, to whom he famously retorted, 'I drink wine, I don't drink blood of the people.' In retrospect, history would go on to tell a different story. He became a popularly elected dictator who could not endure dissent and used his power to suppress it, eventually being tried and executed for the assassination of a political opponent, although his guilt remains disputed by his supporters. Even after death, his stature was such that his daughter Benazir would fight in his name, succeeding twice to become prime minister before her own assassination. To this day people in Pakistan refer to him to arouse emotions associated with a socialist utopia.

Jump ahead to 1996 when cricket legend Imran Khan founded *Tehreek-e-Insaaf* (Movement for Justice). Gossip about the former cricketer's personal life hindered his political aspirations. Intense focus on his playboy past, Western lifestyle and marriage to a fabulously wealthy English heiress wife proved relentless. Khan reacted in a most classic mode. He distanced himself from his past and reinvented himself as a *pukka* Pakistani, a member of the *Awaam*. His views shifted discernibly to the conservative right and he even sought co-operation with Islamist elements. His re-brand started to take effect and before long he and his cohort became synonymous with the word *Ehtasaab* or accountability. The word accountability had immense public appeal. So much so that Junoon, the popular rock band in Pakistan, wrote a song called *Ehtesaab*. In his autobiography, Salman Ahmad, the lead guitarist of the band hints that Khan may very well have been the inspiration for that song. Fast forward to 2016 and Salman Ahmad, now a social activist, is zealously campaigning for Imran Khan, even being arrested while protesting with him. The demand is still *Ehtesaab*.

When Musharraf overthrew Nawaz Sharif in 1998 in a military coup, it was seen as a popular move. Khan, despite being a democrat, was among those who welcomed this change. He recognised someone who could come in and shake-up the Pakistani *status quo*. When Musharraf organised a referendum in early 2002 to gain legitimacy, Khan was there to vote for him. While he cast his vote in Musharraf's favour, a person in the background screamed '*God is great*' — clearly this was a moment of significance. As the drone strikes began, he turned firmly against

Musharraf. It was one of the many U-turns that would earn him the title 'U-Turn Khan'.

The liberal minority within Pakistan opposed an imperial power running amok in Afghanistan but when it came to fighting the Taliban, America had their support. Khan labelled the liberals 'scum' and 'fascists'. He was not ideologically aligned with the Taliban but his vehement anti-American and Taliban-sympathetic stance earned him his second title, 'Taliban Khan'. He proved his credentials when he requested the Taliban offices be opened in Pakistan. His view was that there should be a point of contact, as every time a bomb exploded in Pakistan or a terrorist incident occurred, there was no one to reach out to. The liberals just thought he had gone mad and was trying to legitimise terrorists.

According to the New America Foundation, the number of strikes that took place from 2004-2007 totalled seven. This was during the *Bush-Musharraf* era, with Khan's agitation quietly riling the whole nation. What followed was the *Obama-Kiyani* era of drone strikes – a sum of 356 drones hit targets between the years 2008-2013. Khan advocated peace deals and was against the use of military force. A peace deal was indeed signed in Swat with the Pakistani Taliban led by Sufi Muhammad in 2009, during which an army man was famously pictured exchanging garlands with the militants. As part of the deal they enforced their own 'Sharia rule' and ran a criminal state within a state. It was tolerated in the interests of peace but that much yearned for peace remained elusive. When the Taliban shot schoolgirl Malala Yousufzai, for speaking out against them, one might have expected that there would be sympathy for Malala but on the contrary, popular feeling was against her. You didn't have to be an uninformed village dweller or a tin-foil hat wearing conspiracy nut anymore to believe that the whole Malala incident was staged. A university-educated and well-informed colleague asked me, 'how could a girl living in that tribal area speak such fluent English?' I replied that her father is an English teacher but that evidence was not sufficient. Those who hated her played on her surname and came up with *[Malala] Dramazai* as a moniker. This isn't the result of ignorance – but of the politics of a populist, right-leaning society that identified Malala as part of the global war against Islam.

Imran Khan tapped into this populist, religious rhetoric and played an equivocal game to serve his political ambitions. After visiting Malala in hospital he sparked widespread disbelief and outrage when he quoted from the Qur'an and implied that the Taliban were waging a 'jihad' in Afghanistan that was justified by Islamic law. His path to political prominence was firmly chosen. Khan would extrapolate the populist position until it afforded him success. It would be a further decade of struggle before he would finally see the day he would be taken seriously. It was not until 2011 when almost a hundred thousand people gathered to hear him around Minar-e-Pakistan in Lahore and the word tsunami became part of Pakistani dinner table conversation. Friends who mildly supported Khan became zealous enthusiasts, and those who had no other viable party became overnight supporters. They shared pictures of this overflowing gathering, imagining that this was not one hundred thousand but one million or even the entire *Awaam*. These minds and eyes were similar to those that saw Hanbal's funeral. The size of the crowd was vindication again. Political commentators were declaring that finally Khan had become a contender. He began prophesising that he would sweep the next elections with his massive tsunami of supporters. The idea was preposterous but in the face of such massive public display, it was difficult to make rational arguments.

Was this the result of Khan's decade of grafting, during which no one bothered to vote for him, or were other factors involved? Namely, the palpable lurch towards populism. The three years between 2008 and 2011 were characterised by extreme corruption, power shortages, inflation, terrorism and drone strikes. The country was at the edge of chaos and anyone who had the means left the country. Those unable to migrate, the over-whelming majority, had no choice except to endure and suffer. In the absence of alternative leadership, it was no wonder that a despondent people turned to Khan and his party to save them from imminent collapse. It would be the first time that people believed that Khan could change something. Then came the election and suddenly the elation turned into anger. PTI did not 'sweep' the polls. Khan was not going to be the next prime minister. For his fans, it was a moment of disbelief and shock. They could not foresee any other outcome. The shock and disbelief turned into accusations of rigging, routinely called '*Dhandli*'.

Suddenly Khan appeared in Islamabad, just a short distance from parliament, commanding huge crowds standing on top of what would become an iconic massive container. After *Drone* and '*Dhandli*', there would

be another d-word, 'Dharna', or sit-in; a form of civil disobedience that has
long been integral to Pakistani politics. The intention of Khan's impromptu
action was to force the prime minister to resign and trigger a public coup.
Once again, it was the size of the crowd that was of crucial importance. I
will add another d-word, Drama, to this situation as there was a great deal
of said drama from its frantic beginning to its tragi-comic end. I witnessed
many Pakistani friends now living abroad becoming sucked into the
frenetic excitement and filled with anticipation that a miracle was about to
happen. One person living in Dubai wrote a blog: a letter from a father to
his children. It described the current events as a historic moment, when
the direction of Pakistan would be changed forever and their father was to
be part of it. He travelled to Islamabad to participate in this historic
Dharna, took selfies with the crowd and with Khan's container in the
background and posted them on Facebook.

It all seemed to be going well until Khan uttered three words that were
seized upon by his opponents and changed everything. Fond of cricket
analogies, Khan said that 'the umpire's finger' would be raised soon. The
gesture by the umpire means that the batsman is out. But who was the
Umpire? It was speculated that by 'umpire' he meant the military
establishment, which would make him a mere puppet in their covert
operations. The mood waned irrevocably, and notable members of PTI
made for the exit. First to leave was Javed Hashmi, a stubborn and
principled democrat who was formerly a member of Nawaz Sharif's party.
PTI had been thrilled when he joined their ranks, calling him 'one brave
man'. But he had survived punishment and torture at the hands of military
dictators and when he heard rumours that Khan was in bed with the
military establishment, he quit. Khan hastily clarified that by umpire he
meant God, and later suggested he had been referring to the 'Awaam' or
'the people', but the damage was already done. Populism had reared its
ugly head to bite the hand that was trying to feed it. Imran Khan was once
again consigned to the fringes.

Pakistan has never been governed by a member of the Awaam. The
chances of a middle or lower-middle class person who is not a member of
the elite, or corrupt, or supported by nepotism, to succeed in politics are
slim. Thus those in power have had to pretend to play the role of the
everyman. The three military dictators who ruled Pakistan had to ditch

their uniforms and clothe themselves in a *Sherwani,* a traditional long coat, to prove their Pakistani credentials to the masses. Zulfiqar Bhutto switched to plain clothes and so did Imran Khan, Benazir donned the traditional female head-covering *dupatta* and Nawaz Sharif, like most Pakistani politicians, dresses in a white *Shalwar Kameez* and a waistcoat. Pakistanis like to see their politician as one of their own. But they are a world apart: they are all members of the elite.

Imran Khan promises to build a New Pakistan but the charming slogans are hiding a dark turn towards nationalist and religious populism. Irrational, unprincipled and populist behaviour is masquerading as democracy confidently threatening to take power back from 'the elites'. What is not clear, however, is whether this is the ascendency of the 'common man' or the basic man, whose urges and prejudices are amplified by numbers and given legitimacy as the voice of truth by opportunistic politicians. Sharif may have been run out but if the incoming batsman turns out to be Imran Khan, Pakistan is destined for a tumultuous and painful innings.

DESI POPULISM

Bhavik Doshi

Populism is a word that has re-entered our vocabulary with a vengeance. It first entered my subconscious in Autumn 2014 while I was studying for my MSc, albeit in a historical context relating to Latin America. The concept struck me as basic and simple; defined as political support for the ordinary or common (wo)man. There was an indistinct righteousness at the core of it that I found unsettling. It wasn't long before I discovered the way in which it was deployed as an ideological weapon for garnering any majority support regardless of political affiliation.

For me, the concept came alive during Narendra Modi's inaugural visit to London as the Prime Minister of India. It was October 2015, the run-up to *Navratri* and *Diwali*, and people of Indian descent lost their minds. Feelings of ecstasy surged through these communities nationwide but London proved the beating heart of blistering euphoria. An added bonus was that Modi was a *Guji*, Gujarati. I myself am Gujarati, and the majority of my Indian network are too. He represented commonalities amongst all Gujis as he seemingly symbolised the hard-working, determined, trustworthy and entrepreneurial character, which the people from the North-Western state of Gujarat are synonymous with.

I was utterly amazed how one man could spark off this instantaneous reaction of pride and joy. Since the millennium Indian politics had been contained within its bubble rarely connecting with the wider Indian diaspora. Enter Modi, a charismatic character who had captivated the hearts and minds of Indians and those of Indian descent in the UK, US, Canada, Australia, Europe, Africa, Oceania, the Caribbean and South-East Asia.

The Indian diaspora, and for me specifically the Hindu and Jain communities as they form the realm of my personal experience, is much like an imagined community – an idea conceptualised by Benedict Anderson. They comprise a nation-state which is a social construct, imagined by those who perceive themselves to be part of that group. This is even more important in the context of the Indian diaspora/transnational community as it forms a crucial linkage to how they identify and understand themselves in their current contexts outside of their country of origin.

I recall my mother being caught up in the hysteria over Modi's appearance at Wembley Stadium. 'Why do you like him?' I asked, to which she responded '*Modi Gujarati che, apprah lokha che*': Modi is Gujarati, he is one of us. It was at that moment that I realised what Modi truly symbolised and what his impact on the psyche of the Indian diaspora was destined to be. Modi had used populism to gain a majority. He was nothing more than a Hindu nationalist.

Populism in India is hardly a new phenomenon. Mohandas Karamchand (Mahatma) Gandhi brought peasants and artisans together in an anti-colonial movement fighting for Indian independence in 1915. More critically, he widened his appeal to areas of the diaspora such as South Africa, Fiji, Mauritius and propagating anti-colonial sentiments to Indians overseas. Hindu missionaries from different sects such as the Arya Samaj and Sanatan Dharam took this anti-colonial populist message to Caribbean states including Trinidad, Suriname and Guyana. Once independence was achieved in India, it inspired a chain reaction for independence in other British colonies. Of course, this was populism manifested as an anti-colonial message which did a great amount of good in empowering Western colonies around the world. Populism during this period represented a form of political communication enabling the masses to resonate and interact with the anti-colonial movement. This was against the backdrop of the creation of a nation-state and so the complex myriad of religious and nationalistic pursuits were not yet existent in true form. In contrast, the populism we see today is a combination of right wing conservatism, nationalism, fascism, racism, sexism, homophobia, Islamophobia and xenophobia which makes for one volatile and destructive formula.

To the vast majority of the world, Modi is just a man who adores hugging people, mainly other politicians and dignitaries. This cuddly persona distracts us from the fact that he is leader of the Hindu nationalist Bharatiya

Janata Party (BJP). The BJP is inextricably linked to Shiv Sena and the Rashtriya Swayamsevak Sangh (RSS), the Volunteer Organisation or as they are better known the National Patriotic Organisation. These formalised organisations amongst others advocate advocate *Hindutva* or Hindu-ness as a 'legitimate' ideology – which was naturally adopted by the BJP in 1989. Modi was previously chief minister of Gujarat, and presided while the Gujarat riots of 2002 occurred, during which over a thousand Muslims were murdered and many were horrifically injured and raped. The state called this a 'communal riot', but it has been widely denounced as a pogrom. A pogrom, as Werner Bergmann notes, is 'the collective attribution of a threat, the pogrom differs from forms of violence such as lynching, which are directed against individual members of a minority, while the imbalance of power in favour of the rioters distinguishes pogrom from other forms of riot (food riots, race riots, or "communal riots" between evenly matched groups), and again low level of organisation separates them from vigilantism, terrorism, massacre and genocide.' This distinction warrants concern as it reveals how the push for *Hindutva* as a political discourse has infected the populist movement in India to such an extent that it incites violence.

Over 700 cases of communal violence occurred in 2016, injuring 2,361 and killing 86 people. Muslims have felt the full force of these crimes falling victim to mob lynching, forced conversions, attacks on mosques and constant bombardment of threats. Given the number of incidents that go unreported, the figures are undoubtedly higher, particularly in light of the recent ban on cattle slaughter and the witch-hunts surrounding the enforcement of these new regulations. Modi's regime has indicated in every way that it is using populism to dominate – they are the 'people' by their definition: simple, anti-plural, anti-elite and monolithic.

Modi's embrace of the Indian diaspora and its NRIs (non-resident Indians) was an opportunistic means of grasping political and economic power. In return the NRIs were seduced by a carefully constructed sense of identity and reconnection to a land which they had either left behind or formed part of their heritage. The 2014 general election permitted NRIs who had retained Indian citizenship (approximately 10 million people) to travel to India to cast their vote. For decades, transnational politics has played a role in disseminating ideas, but for the first time transnational diplomacy looms as a critical feature of Indian governance. Preparations are underway for the next general election to offer an e-voting ballot for NRIs in a calculated move to maximise Modi's core support. This will add renewed vigour to attempts to transmit this right-wing doctrine to Indian communities overseas, inevitably exacerbating social divisions and communal tension.

The right wing rhetoric that dominated Modi's election campaign utilised a combination of nationalism and populism in extreme and peculiarly Indian form. It is strange to say that we live in a world whereby the US and India are similar — after all they are both religiously and ethnically diverse, yet these two main players on the world's stage are headed by ego-obsessed leaders who have used the rhetoric of 'sovereignty' to gain popularity. Trump and Modi both identified the rising anti-establishment movement in their nations, and manipulated this sentiment to seize political power. Both share an almost identical stance on Islam and Muslims, although conveyed through two different modes of transmission — the former being overtly crude and the latter attempting to be subtle (and failing mightily). Similarly, both are reticent in their condemnation of threats and violence against Muslims, illustrated by the laws they seek to impose such as Trump's Muslim ban and Modi's crackdown on cow slaughter. Much has been made of Trump's surprising success with the Hispanic vote, but there has been less focus on the significant numbers of Indians who turned out to vote for him. Trump's message spoke volumes to many Indians desperate to differentiate themselves from Muslims, with whom they were constantly being lumped together. Hindus, Jains and Sikhs share a common culture with Muslims and all were seen as part of the same ethnic bloc lauded for having assimilated themselves successfully as a minority community. But the Muslim bit of this equation is problematic. Indians see themselves and are proud to enjoy the status of 'model ethnic minority' or the term I prefer is 'obedient ethnic minority'. Indians in the US had basked in an image of themselves as successfully absorbing American values and norms, and fully integrating themselves as acceptable, good immigrants playing a crucial role in developing the nation — its politics, its economy, its society, its culture. Whether this is a conscious or unconscious mindset is another matter, but within most areas of the diaspora, Indians have been able to assimilate using this model. As far as they are concerned, it is another story for Muslims.

Since the rise of anti-establishment and populist politics across the world, there has been a growing acknowledgement of the so-called 'rise of Hindu nationalism'. Hindu nationalism has become increasingly contagious and developed into a movement framed within the political sphere, yet we cannot forget that it has always been a latent part of India and its diaspora. Hindu cultural and religious groups have long been a tangible mechanism for the nationalistic agenda of *Bharat* – India. Chetan Bhatt has shown how this transnational network has proliferated into a number of affiliated groups and peoples in the UK such as the Labour Friends of India, NHSF (the National Hindu Students Forum), among others. In particular, the RSS has established 'cultural centres' where Indians have settled globally, calling themselves the HSS (Hindu Swayamsevak Sangh). It is a like-for-like organisation with the same structure and ideology as the RSS with the aim of creating *shakas* (ideology training camps) and *sangathan* (organise and strengthen Hindus). In 2015, they were exposed on UK television when one of their tutors claimed that there are very few 'good' Muslims. This provides only a brief insight into the indoctrination that takes place in these types of organisations; constant repetition of the superiority of Hindu culture and values, which they believe to represent India in all of its glory and riches. This method serves to brainwash those who no longer or have never lived in India despite their origin. It is purely down to a very simplistic idea of feeling a cultural and national attachment. These linkages reiterate the political power such networks carry in spewing out disturbing Hindu nationalist propaganda, which feeds Modi's tactic to keep the diaspora close to him as his weapon to reaffirm his place at the top of this monolithic structure.

The anti-Muslim sentiment found in India and its diaspora is not based on encompassing and overarching resentment for all Muslims, but is framed within the framework of politics of Pakistan and India. Islamic kingdoms historically dominated India in the Middle Ages but this was centuries ago and is unlikely to hold any validity for the rhetoric that exists today. Yet fierce Hindu fanatics are still willing to use this as their 'rationale' for holding anti-Muslim views. More likely it is the British colonial rule and postcolonial legacies such as the Partition of India that precipitated this visceral hatred within the Indian sub-continent. This is not to say this is the only type of Islamophobia, but the narrative connecting 'Islam' or 'Muslim' to Pakistan looms large. Such a distinction is critical in understanding how this rhetoric manifests itself, as it displays this entire reality that exists within a bubble of itself.

My relationship with India and its diaspora has allowed me to understand the similarities and differences between the 'Motherland' and its imagined communities overseas. I was born in the UK while my mother was born in Tanzania and my father in India. My frequent visits to India, as well as Tanzania, Zanzibar and Suriname, all of which are proponents of the Indian diaspora, have led me to the realisation that anti-Muslim rhetoric does not necessarily present itself in the form of violent and abrasive actions, but can be covert, subversive and nuanced. In India there is open prejudice against Muslims as it can be seen manifested in policies and violence. In the diaspora, however, I gradually picked up on the plethora of nuances which provided further evidence of anti-Muslim notions. I remember as an adolescent I purposefully did not grow my facial hair in order to distinguish the fact I am Indian not Pakistani, almost as if it was a subconscious decision ingrained in me. Gradually, as my awareness of these nuances developed, I managed to dismantle them. Yet, even now, family members suggest I might want to shave off my beard, teasing that it doesn't 'look good' or it doesn't 'suit you', whilst turning their face in a kind of sweet disgust. On some occasions, they can be more direct and complain that I look *Musulman,* Muslim (ironically a Gujarati/Hindi word derived from Persian). Even the manner in which they would speak the word betrays an underlying disdain, as if Muslims were anathema. This is a distinction in the stereotypes attributed to those of South Asian descent, as even within this group anyone who has a beard is judged to be a Muslim. Attempting to be rid of stereotypes is part of enacting cultural change, it is a long and arduous process without necessarily yielding results.

The other manifestation which is rather more obvious is packaged in the configuration of relationships. I am able to recall countless scenarios whereby people within my 'Indian network' would talk about so-and-so's quest for a husband or wife. An unwritten but perfectly understood 'policy' that informs the quest for a suitor within Indian communities is B.M.W: 'no Blacks, no Muslims, no Whites'. My experience may be specific to the UK context, but I have heard of similar notions indicated in the diaspora. Indians who move to the UK have assimilated into British society in some way, shape or form, and some have become relaxed regarding their views on interracial and inter-faith marriages. But (and this is a big but) there are few exceptions for Muslims, it is a boundary that can rarely be crossed. Those who do cross that line can expect a harsh and potentially severe reaction.

Being a second generation British Indian like many of my family and friends, I have been brought up according to Western ideals, while maintaining my heritage in some way, shape or form – be it through doing morning *puja*, wearing a *rakhi*, celebrating Diwali or even eating *roti dhal bhaat ne shakh*. There has always been this idea that second-generation kids are very liberal, open and forward-thinking, whereas our parents are cast as backward-thinking and stuck in a bygone period. But assumption has never been true. There are many of my own generation who are just as prejudiced as their parents, who emphasise the differences between us as Indians and them as Muslims. Despite sharing a culture in a completely different geographical environment, where we have been allowed an opportunity to understand theories and thoughts from across the world, there are some who are still stuck in the past, and use that as a reference for their sentiments in the present. The very accentuation of 'us' and 'them' is a clear articulation of the divide that exists, as well as the desire to differentiate themselves from the pariahs in a society that they have been brought up in and sought to assimilate into.

These nuances are not a part of the populist agenda, which have been transmitted through transnational networks, instead they are deeply ingrained cultural legacies. It is almost as if anti-Muslim rhetoric is part of the tradition of being an 'Indian'. It is passed down from generation to generation, and must be maintained. In this way, populism has worked to enliven anti-Muslim feeling through Modi and Trump, but it revives this sentiment from historical memories of India. It is the transmission of this rhetoric that can also act as a portal to perpetuate the linkages between the past and the present allowing for the persistence of this attitude. These historical memories can be anything from major events such as the Partition of India to personal attachments of families.

If a person is a Hindu nationalist then by definition that person must also be Islamophobic, the two are inextricably linked. Of course, I believe that when *Hindutva* was first conceptualised, it was India's ideological weapon against the British Empire and colonialism. However, the concept evolved, as the nation-state developed, into something more extreme and violent, which is what exists in the modern day. It is not to say that being an Indian nationalist is wrong – although I personally believe nationalism is a tool used to control the masses and distract from social injustice, I can see its benefits in uniting society and crafting a shared cultural identity and experience. However, Indian nationalism cannot truly exist while India is unable to separate itself from Hinduism and Hindus.

In India, populism has legitimised the anti-Muslim rhetoric into mainstream thought. Fervent Hindu nationalists or fanatics use the presumed subjugation of the people as an excuse to commit violent acts against them. From the Mughal Empire to the Partition of India, the saga allows for brutality, as it unfolds with a series of violent riots and pogroms. The state, or more the JP, is more than complicit in its maintenance by reducing and minimising the insidiousness of such thinking as 'reckless acts caused by a minority of society'. In reality, it is actually a majority which is feeding and funding anti-Muslim attitudes into practical actions on a national level through its expansive web of subsidiary groups ready, willing and primed to take the necessary steps. This is in tandem with the Indian government 'weakening the rule of law' to reduce Hindu nationalism to a minor altercation as Amnesty International reported. In the diaspora, it is a different story as Indians are a small part of a larger cultural society from the UK to the US. Violence enacted by Indians upon Muslims is thankfully rare, but this is why poisonous views are taking hold by stealth. There is an external, outward facing persona which is open, warm and accepting to all *masksa*. There is also a subversive internal personality that trembles with underlying bigotry. And this is purely driven by an obsessive desire for self-preservation of a constructed public perception that they hold in the highest regard.

At the outset, I mentioned the idea of righteousness being entangled in populism. Three years on from that moment, that unsettling feeling is still there, and in fact it has taken on the idea of fear. Fear, in that populism has spread like a contagious virus across the world to the diaspora. I do not know if this 'fear' will subside, but one thing I can note is that we are living within one of the most transformative epochs.

A BRIT IN THE BIBLE BELT

Sughra Ahmed

Posters depicting hordes of people queuing, snake-like – we would be forgiven for thinking that these were produced by deeply intolerant regimes of times gone by. Nazi propaganda, perhaps? Sadly, these images of men and boys who looked foreign and poor made their rounds in 2016, in the midst of the referendum on the UK's membership of the European Union. Did they successfully persuade some people that Britain was no longer able to welcome those in need, or those who had a right to come to the UK?

The message in these posters was clear – our country's doors were no longer open for the free movement of people across the EU. 'Foreign folk' could no longer turn to the UK as a place of safety or refuge. Phrases such as 'breaking point' and 'take back control of our borders' became commonplace in campaign literature. Right-leaning tabloids fed these sentiments with headlines like 'Who do you think the EU are?' and '1m migrants to rush in before EU exit', even referring to High Court judges as 'enemies of the people'.

In the EU referendum and, later, the presidential election in the US, many of us saw a sea change in the tone of public debate. Racism and xenophobia were used to push people into voting against a mythical monster that was supposedly coming over to take our jobs and swamp our lives. According to *The Independent*:

> ...the Leave vote on 23 June last year prompted a wave of hate crimes based on religion and ethnicity, and have led to calls for the Government to 'urgently' review its response to such reports. Gwent in Wales saw the highest increase, with the number of incidents rising by 77 per cent, from 367 to 649. Reports of racially and religiously aggravated hate crimes also rose considerably in Kent (66 per cent, from 874 to 1,452), Warwickshire (65 per cent, 286 to 471) and Nottinghamshire (57 per cent, 681 to 1,071).

The changing tone of the public debate in the UK – and in the US – made me want to find out how people were really feeling and what issues were on their minds when voting. I needed to push the papers and magazines aside and meet some of these people for myself. I wanted to listen and find out what they stood for. What mattered to them and their families? What were their values and how did these guide their big and small decisions in life? Did they really hate immigrants? Were they the racists and misogynists some sectors of the left-leaning media had made them out to be and what had persuaded them to vote in the way they did?

The opportunity to embark on such an adventure presented itself late last year. I became a Greenberg World Fellow at Yale University in August 2016. Life was insanely busy up to this point. I had a full-time job in faith and public education, headed a national Muslim charity, and was a trustee of various organisations specialising in interfaith relations and cultural diversity in Britain. I loved what I did. I worked constantly – weekdays, evenings, weekends and holidays.

Looking back now, I realise that something had to give. I needed to reclaim some work-life balance and some head-heart space to think about the future – my future and the future of a fast changing world. So many of us seemed to be desperately firefighting terror attacks, racism, and violence against religious and other minorities. We were trying to tell the world that there is more 'good' than 'bad' in what we read about on our screens. I was looking for the time and space to reflect on how I was feeling about where I fitted in all of this. What would my future look like if it weren't dictated by these circumstances? What did I want to do and, most importantly, why?

I decided I needed to revisit what I thought I knew. I stepped down from all my responsibilities in Britain before going to Yale. And this freedom is what allowed me, a British Muslim woman of Pakistani descent, to go on a trip which began in Connecticut, and took me through the mid-west, Massachusetts, Vermont, Washington, DC and New York. Between the US elections and the presidential inauguration, I also took a road trip across the Bible belt – including Utah, California, New Mexico, Texas, Louisiana, Mississippi and Georgia.

I arrived in New Haven to embark on my fellowship in the midst of the buildup to the election. I paid close to attention to discussions in the media and the presidential debates. Then I watched the election results unfold. I sensed the nation splitting into extremes. I watched the Obamas say goodbye, the inauguration of President Donald Trump, and then the millions of people taking part in protests in the US and abroad. At same time, my circle of friends became increasingly diverse over the months as I witnessed both heartbreak and jubilation as Trump become the forty-fifth President of the 'Free World'. Throughout these diverse encounters, though, two recurring themes stand out – the centrality of attitudes about salvation and abortion. Both issues were key in shaping voter attitudes during the Presidential election. In fact, most people I met were single-issue voters who seized the opportunity to ban a woman's right to abortion, an idea that they connected intimately with God and salvation.

Salvation

I landed at Austin–Bergstrom International Airport on a Tuesday evening in early January 2017. I grabbed my case from the carousel and, as instructed by the lady I was going to stay with for the next three nights – (we were to meet for the first time that night) – I downloaded the Lyft app and booked a car to take me to the first of my three Texan homes.

I was excited and nervous. I had no idea of what lay in store. Texas had a reputation in my mind – cattle ranches as far as the eye could see, rodeos, gun-crazed and meat-loving Americans who preferred women to stay at home doing the washing and the cooking whilst the men went out to work. A long conversation with an old friend, who hailed from Texas, did little to free me of the Hollywood stereotypes that filled my imagination.

It didn't help that most people I'd previously met in New Mexico encouraged me to skip Texas for my own safety. When I got to Texas and shared my wonderful experiences of Santa Fe and Abiquiú in New Mexico, the Texans I met were equally dismissive. I was puzzled by this rivalry, since both states clearly shared a lot by way of trade and travel. On my first night in New Mexico, driving from Albuquerque to downtown Santa Fe, our bus passed cars with mostly Texan license plates – I later learned that they were holidaymakers who were over for the skiing season. The whole thing reminded me of the War of the Roses – the rivalry between Lancashire and Yorkshire that had been in the background as I was growing up in the mill towns of Lancashire.

The Lyft driver and I got chatting pretty easily. He was around twenty-five years old and had been living in the US for around six years, working hard to save enough money before returning to Nigeria. Danny missed his family and friends – and life in Nigeria – terribly. One of the few joys of being in Austin, for him, was the devotion to his religion and Lord. He was a Pentecostal Christian belonging to an active church where he not only went to worship but was keen to bring others, too. He became more passionate about his faith in Austin, which encouraged me to ask lots of questions. He was patient, calm and generous with his answers – particularly given we had only just met.

He explained that this particular type of Christianity was the same kind most of his family belonged to 'back home', but he'd become more zealous since settling in the US. I asked him if there were any services that I could join. He got excited that I asked. It did feel like the old evangelical tradition of witness and conversion but I was willing to set my discomfort aside – he was young and passionate, it was no big deal.

'We have church on Sundays where you would be welcome,' he said. 'In fact, we have a minibus to make pick-ups. We take people who are interested in observing our worship to our church, but I'm sorry – we only have that on Sundays.' I was in town from Tuesday to Thursday. I still wanted to know if there was anything else I could attend.

'We have Bible Study on Wednesdays. It's not glamorous or anything, not formal, you see. But you'd be welcome. It's tomorrow night, if you can't get there I could try to give you a lift. Would you be okay to call Lyft again tomorrow? I don't know whether I will be in your area but I will be going to church myself.'

I had no idea about the local geography nor of my itinerary for the next few days. On the other hand, this was too good an opportunity to miss. As I weighed my options to myself, we talked about my road trip and the string of events that had led me to Texas.

The next morning, I bid my host – a kind and generous Egyptian woman studying for her PhD and teaching at Texas University – a good day and, armed with a bottle of water and a fully charged phone, headed out to the see the sites of Austin. As evening fell I found myself in the same part of town as the Bible class Danny had talked about. I decided to call him - he agreed immediately to pick me up on his way.

As a British desi (someone with ancestry from the Indian subcontinent), I realised soon enough that my Nigerian brother was running on desi time. We arrived at Amazing Grace, the Redeemed Christian Church of God, an hour later than expected but he didn't seem fazed. I, on the other hand, felt awkward and embarrassed. We walked into the room where everyone was informally sat on rows of chairs, all facing the 'front'. The study was well underway. Hardly anyone turned to look at us as we stepped in. I thought we'd be able to slip in quietly and take a seat at the back of the room – not in a Pentecostal church in the Deep South, you don't! The pastor welcomed us with a joke to relieve my awkwardness. Still, I could feel everyone looking at me wondering what I was doing there. He was a vibrant, middle-aged man with a twinkle in his eyes.

'Welcome, guest, welcome. Come to the front row! I was told you may be joining us tonight and I hope you got the message about your talk. We're looking forward to hearing from you in a couple of minutes.'

I replied without missing a beat, 'Absolutely, I'm looking forward to it.' He laughed warmly, in a way that made me think of Archbishop Desmond Tutu.

The pastor continued to preach the Bible for the next couple of hours and the congregation – all African-American women, men and children of Nigerian background – were responsive throughout. When he talked about stealing, fornication and excessive drinking, the congregation shared their stories of how they'd been affected when family members had engaged in these sins. Mothers talked about the absence of their husbands, which affected the whole family and community. It was clear this community was in pain and the Pastor acted as a healing agent. He confided that in his youth, he had also 'indulged' but had since seen the error of his ways. That's why he decided to help others by becoming a priest. His personal examples made him appear all the more real and human – he was showing his flock that he was just like them and could understand their pain. Watching and listening to him reminded me of the stories of Jesus meeting people in the public square, reaching out to them in a language they could understand and with empathy.

After the service, the Pastor invited me to join him. Whilst volunteers cleared up the space, we began a conversation. 'It's very nice that you came here tonight, I'm really happy that you joined us. Tell me, do you believe in God?'

'I do,' I said. 'I'm Muslim and follow Islam. I feel blessed to have spent this evening in your company – thank you for welcoming me.' Danny was hovering in the background – although we hadn't agreed to anything, he was clearly waiting to take me back to where I was staying. Feeling as though I had to be mindful of time, I decided to cut to the chase.

'Pastor,' I said, 'I've listened to you preaching for the last couple of hours and I have a serious question for you.' He encouraged me amicably. 'If, as you say, Heaven is the ultimate goal for those who believe, then it's the big prize that will make everything worthwhile, right?'

'Yes, that's right, exactly right. The Lord God will grant us Paradise.'

'So, in your vision of Paradise, do you think there is any room for someone like me?' The Pastor was quiet for a moment and then let out of one his laughs before trying to explain in a long-winded fashion that Paradise is for special people – God's people.

'But Pastor,' I said, 'Does that include me? It's not a trick question, I'm just curious as to whether, in your opinion, I'm also eligible for the big reward.'

'No,' he finally said. 'There is no place for anyone who doesn't believe the Holy Spirit moves through them. You don't believe in the Holy Spirit so, no – not for you.' I understood where he was coming from, but felt saddened nonetheless. I had truly enjoyed his wonderful preaching and forgot that, to him, he belonged to an exclusive club. I know only too well that this attitude is not confined to some Christians. Too many other religious ideologies would assert that 'our path is the only righteous path and everyone else is wrong'. I personally find this exclusivist approach arrogant. How can any of us truly know whether our specific flavour of 'truth' is God's only truth? But at the same time, I warmed to this Pastor – a lot. That's why I took a risk with what I said next.

'Pastor, let me mix a few theologies here,' I began. 'If on the Day of Judgment I'm at the front of the queue waiting at the pearly gates and I'm given my scroll in my right hand and welcomed into Heaven by St Peter himself, then I will come and find you in the queue, take you by the hand and beseech St Peter on your behalf. I will tell him that you're a good man and led a goodly life on earth, that surely a man who overcame challenges and changed his life to become a source of good in helping people deserves a place in Heaven. I believe in a Heaven that welcomes the goodly and the kind.'

The Pastor looked a little stunned and didn't quite know what to say. I put my hand on his arm and said, 'You don't need to answer, I understand. I wasn't planning on saying any of this but listening to you tonight has clearly triggered some thoughts in my own mind.' He replied by saying he had never heard such a thing from someone of a different faith tradition – he certainly hadn't expected it from this evening's visit. He asked that we keep in touch, so I left him my email address.

In the car, the driver gave me a copy of the Bible which came as a complete surprise. 'This book changed my life and I hope that when you open it, it will change yours forever too.' I tried to assure him that I was happy with my life. I added that although his gift was generous, I was way over my luggage allowance and already had to take a few kilos out of my case each time I checked in at the airport. Not to mention that I already have a Bible – not the New King James Version but a perfectly good one that had been gifted to me one Christmas. He wasn't convinced and insisted that the book was now mine and that I should be prepared for my life to be changed by it. It was a thoughtful gesture and it meant a lot. Still, I had to leave the bible on a bookshelf at an AirBnB in New Orleans some days later – but not before I took a picture of the message inscribed inside: 'Sughra, this is a gift with treasures to be discovered and I hope it transforms you as it did me. Nice to meet you. Danny.'

This encounter is something that continues to inspire and challenge me. On the one hand I was smitten by a group of warm, generous and loving Pentecostal Christians in the Deep South. They welcomed me with open arms. Yet they were hoping that I'd change in some way, that I'd find the real truth at last. And until I found that truth, they couldn't imagine me entering Heaven. The combination of intense love and sadness this evoked in me was a defining feature of my road trip across the rest of the Bible belt.

Underpinning salvation were a host of issues that remained at the forefront of people's minds. During his campaign, President Trump had promised to abolish abortion across the country. This was an opportunity these believing folk (of different ethnicities, I must stress – Black, White, Asian and Hispanic) couldn't afford to miss. In other words, the single, overriding issue for the vast majority of people I met was abortion. They were going to vote for the person who was doing God's work.

Abortion

I was totally unprepared for the kindness, generosity and good nature that I found in people all the way from Utah to Mississippi and beyond. Additionally, the long conversations I had in people's homes and airports, on trains and buses, in diners and whilst sharing car journeys, often included religion whether we were reflecting on politics, public personalities or our own private pledges. The people I met were really open about sharing their religious traditions and beliefs, often unprompted, which told me something about the place of religion in their decision-making – personal, professional and political.

Many of them would confide that they could be more open in discussing issues like politics, religion, sexuality, gender and human rights with me compared with their own families and neighbours. The risks of creating discord and arguments with their nearest and dearest made them refrain from talking about where they stood on important issues which were being wildly debated in political and media circles. Casey, a fellow passenger on a bus journey said, 'You're real easy to talk to and you ask lots of questions, which makes it easy to share.'

He continued, 'These things, you know – banning abortion in my country and pushing people to go get a job – are important for us all.' Casey had taken the final empty seat next to me. Our little bus was carrying seventeen of us from Salt Lake City to St George, Utah. The winds were pretty strong and we swayed side to side down the I15, passing mountains with huge letters carved into them – local school children visit these mountains to carve the letters of local universities. As you pass Provo, for example, on the left is a mountain with the letter Y on it in white, standing for the famous local Mormon college – Brigham Young University.

For the first twenty minutes, Casey had earphones plugged in and leant his head on the seat in front of him. Glancing through the corner of my eye and trying not to be obvious, I figured he wasn't in the mood for conversation. He was probably listening to something important and hoping – even in the most uncomfortable of seats – to get some sleep. Eventually, however, he pulled his earphones out and broke the ice, and I realised he was feeling nervous about the weather and our safety. Living in St George with his family – a wife and two grown-up daughters – and working in Salt Lake, he travelled this bus every week but had rarely experienced such severe winds. He explained this just as the driver, once again, swerved from right to left and back again, punctuating this with, 'Whoa, that was close! These storms sure will keep us awake folks.' When someone suggested we pull over for a little while, the driver explained his company wouldn't like that and that we, in fact, had to speed ahead to make up for a delayed start.

Casey and I started talking, both trying to distract ourselves from the weather conditions. Before we stopped for a quick break in Fillmore, we managed to learn about each other's families, professions, road trips and travels, and had shared interesting stories about the people in our lives. Three hours had passed by in a flash and I was grateful. A five-minute break in Fillmore meant everyone had to visit the restrooms and get something to eat at breakneck speed – the driver was determined not to be late and nobody was prepared to upset him lest he started driving even more erratically.

Casey pointed to a diner and said, 'You don't want to eat from there.' I thanked him for his advice and headed to the shops before joining the queue for the only other eatery at this pit stop – a Mexican diner. We bumped into each other again – the place wasn't very big – and Casey insisted on paying for my meal. 'I think what you're doing is amazing,' he said. 'You're getting to know my country and my people, you'll soon know more about the South than I do. Let me have a small part in your journey and buy you this meal.' I was struck by his thoughtfulness and how much he valued what I was trying to do. I understood his logic and accepted his kindness.

But back on the bus, we soon discovered we didn't agree on everything. In fact, we vehemently disagreed on one subject especially – abortion. Casey was anti-abortion and proud of it. He was clear and firm about his views – in the eyes of God, abortion is illegal and should therefore be made illegal throughout the USA. 'For the first time in my life we have a President who has promised to ban abortion in every state. He understands it's wrong and is doing God's work.'

I tried to reason with him and talked about women I knew who had had abortions in the most awful of circumstances, that there wasn't even one of them who wishes she could have made a different decision. Context and circumstance should count for something when women – and it's always a woman's choice – find themselves in a situation where abortion must be considered. Casey wasn't accepting any of this. For him, Mormonism came first.

'God has souls waiting to come to earth and nobody has the right to decide that a soul won't make it. It's a woman's job to understand that this is a life she is taking and it's not her right to decide what God has already decreed. If we continue to allow women to have abortions then we are challenging God instead of following His plan. Trump is a Christian – he understands this. He understands that God comes first and will do as he's promised. I'm sure of it.'

I didn't know what to say. Our previous silences were few but never awkward – this one was absolutely awkward. I felt deep sadness that once again I was hearing that God was to blame for our prejudices and intolerance. 'God says we must....' I've heard this used so many times to rationalise people's feelings, misunderstandings and control. I personally cannot believe that anyone's God would risk the life of a woman so that a child could be born into this world.

Casey broke the silence and tried his best to share his own perceptions about women who sought abortion. He explained that women slept around and had abortions as an emergency measure, like contraception. In his mind, women were irresponsible and should take ownership of their decisions to sleep around. I replied that most women would not be in this position and many would have health, socio-economic, and other reasons to consider – painful choices often made without the support of the person also responsible for the pregnancy. 'Do men bear no responsibility for their actions? Are they not around when you're thinking this through? Why are they allowed to remain invisible in this despite being irresponsible, too?'

Casey felt this was a problem too but still couldn't justify abortion. 'Why should I have to pay for someone's abortion when my faith tells me it's wrong?' he replied. 'If they want to sleep around and then get abortions, they either have to pay for it themselves or go underground. The only option remaining is to have the baby which means that a life will be saved.'

Women were meant to have children and that was that. I asked what made him believe that women were using abortion as an equivalent of contraception. 'You hear about it all the time, especially on the east and west coasts – it happens all the time.' We talked for a while about whether he knew of women who had done this. He didn't. I said that I knew women who had felt abortion was the only option for them. But I was talking to a family man, proud of his religion and of his wife and two daughters, who felt very strongly about being able to support them all financially. He'd worked hard, was still working hard and felt that every other American should work hard, too. He was not paying forty per cent tax to support those who were too lazy to work or wanted an abortion.

Casey got off one stop before St George and asked his daughter to pick him up on her way home from work; he couldn't tolerate the 'drivesmanship' anymore. Halfway out of his seat he quickly said, 'Can we stay in touch? I'd love to hear from you.' He passed me his card. 'If you ever travel to Utah again, you must come and stay with us in our home. My family will love you and we can tell you all about Mormonism,' he continued.

'Would that be in an effort to convert me?' I asked with a big smile. He smiled back and said, 'No, I don't think we could but it would be a pleasure to host you.' With that, we parted company.

Southern hospitality wasn't just reserved for bus rides. Many of my encounters took place over dinner or coffee where families, religious leaders and groups of friends were open about their traditional values on how women and men should live their lives. I heard repeatedly that a woman's role is to look after the home, to have and raise children whilst her husband takes care of the finances and is the head of the household. This included leading prayers – male leadership was not confined to just the secular realm but was an active religious role too.

As generous as the people I met were, they seemed to have little or no room for trying to understand how other Americans might experience entirely different circumstances or a lack of opportunity. Where you live, the colour of your skin, the accents you speak with or even being a victim of crime are serious issues that affect people's lives. Therefore, it follows that people must have the right to make choices for themselves, whether they are Mormon, Southern Baptist, Evangelical or Pentecostal Christian – these are just some of the faith communities I had the privilege of being with. And so, a woman's decision about what happens to her body should ultimately be her right alone. This was a view that very few of the people could appreciate.

After the New Year, I made my way to Texas, to a small town called New Braunfells. I stayed with a fabulously kind and glamorous young woman, Juliet. She was around twenty-eight years old and rented her extension out as an AirBnB. She was a professional hairdresser living in a small town, right by a village where America's oldest dance hall was still hosting bands. Gruene Hall is an old wooden building that looks like a barn with high wooden ceilings and cracked floorboards. Round the back of the hall was a bigger barn – the dance hall. It was rustic and laid back with long wooden tables and benches for seats. Locals were the primary customers in this village, from grandparents to grandchildren, and all generations in between were gathered listening to Bret Graham, from Oklahoma, who'd been playing country music here for twenty years. Some of his songs were covers like 'Rock Me Mama', others he'd written himself, including religious songs like 'He Found Me'. Although it was a cold night, the atmosphere was charged with patriotism, spiritual joy, and there was a real sense of togetherness. A dozen or so elderly couples took to dancing at the back of the hall, which raised a cheer from everyone.

Juliet, in her good nature, had offered to drive me around a little whilst I was staying with her for a couple of nights. By now, I had learnt the hard way that walking rarely gets you anywhere, especially in these parts. Also, in small towns, everyone knows everyone and word soon got out that I was in town to get to know people. By now I'd realised that this wasn't unusual. It's easier getting to know strangers from foreign lands. People were curious, and I too wanted to make the most of my time with these folks.

One night, after some reluctance on my part, I went to dinner with Juliet's family where I met her brother's wife. At a family restaurant in Gruene village, we were getting on reasonably well, especially as her three-year-old was keeping us all entertained whilst we waited for our table. The little girl and I had a walk and dance around whilst the others chatted. Juliet's sister-in-law was expecting her second child in a matter of weeks, which is why when someone around the dinner table raised the topic of abortion, I found it extremely hard to have an open conversation – I certainly didn't want to offend my host's family. Juliet's sister-in-law, however, was very open about her anti-abortion views. She was a Southern Baptist and said, 'God's word is decree and should therefore be upheld no matter the situation. He's the master of all and knows what's best for us and so we should pray and trust in Him.'

Juliet was clearly uncomfortable with this view and countered, 'Well what about when someone is really sick and they need to have an abortion otherwise they will die from the pregnancy or labour?' Her sister-in-law wasn't interested, and said a true believer would trust in God's plan for them and not pretend they know better. 'What about a woman's right to choose though? Should she at least have the responsibility for deciding on what's best for her and the baby? Could we not give women at least that much?' I said.

Juliet's sister-in-law was having none of it and became slightly agitated and frustrated that I was unable to accept her position as my own. 'A woman has her own authority. She cares for her husband, looks after the home and brings up the children. That's a lot of responsibility right there. This is not about that. Abortion is against God's law and therefore must be against man's law too. I'm confident that by voting for Trump we voted for God too.'

Lessons

One evening a Southern Baptist who voted Republican invited me over for Thanksgiving. As we were chatting about something and nothing, she asked me to pray for Trump so that he would succeed during his term in office. 'After all,' Denise reasoned, 'we've been praying for Obama for the past eight years so that he was able to be a good President.' It didn't connect with her that praying for Trump's success meant building a wall to keep the Mexicans out, practically endorsing a witch-hunt on minorities, especially Muslims, and supporting the mass uprooting of undocumented people, many of whom have worked and paid their taxes in the US for generations. It was too painful for me to think about. But I could see her pain too as she talked about trying to make things work these past eight years whilst fervently disagreeing with Obama's policies and decisions. Our conversation ended in silence. I could understand where she was coming from but couldn't bring myself to oblige her request to pray for Trump's success.

I didn't only meet people who were fervently religious. I also had deep conversations with people who were born into particular religious denominations and had fallen out of love with them as they grew into adulthood. They had encountered a hatred of others through their religious communities which they felt was profoundly unjust – prejudicial attitudes to sexual minorities, single parents and gender equality were at odds with their sense of justice and fairness. After struggling with these, and other ideas, they took the grave decision to leave their religious traditions and communities. This had a profound impact on their whole lives. Many were excommunicated and had to leave all they had known behind. These women and men were in a good place today, but they had struggled and fought against ingrained intolerance in the name of God. I was in awe of their courage and strength.

At other times, I found myself taking comfort, oddly, in encountering extreme religious intolerance from other groups. It reassured me that the extremists are not confined to Islam and Muslims but are living amongst all of our traditions no matter the god, ideology or geography.

I associate values such as justice, fairness and equality with God and creation. For me, these are intertwined and cannot be separated. It follows for me that whether we are Catholic, Southern Baptist, Pentecostal, Jewish, Muslim or of no faith, that we must have a sense of justice, compassion, love and mercy for all. This is especially essential for those who are different to us, whether they are within our religious, cultural or social group, or on the outside.

A leading American historian, Timothy Snyder, was the final speaker at our Good Society Seminar at Yale University. He shared his now famous '20 Lessons from the 20th Century', of which number sixteen particularly resonates with me:

> Learn from others in other countries. Keep up your friendships abroad, or make new friends abroad. The present difficulties here are an element of a general trend. And no country is going to find a solution by itself…

Stepping outside of my comfort zone and taking a walk on the wild side at a volatile time proved to be an exciting learning curve both for me and those I met. My time in the US, as a fellow at Yale and throughout my trip, brought me into close contact with different people. It expanded my world in a way that could never have happened if I'd continued to do what I was doing. In order to understand seismic changes, I had to create a seismic shift in my own life. The power to deal with crises, negotiate our differences and think beyond ourselves lies with us, not only within political circles. The idea of listening to the Other and creating space for what they have to say in us cannot be underestimated in understanding the two great shocks of 2016 for me – Brexit and Trump.

CAIRO

Eric Walberg

I stumbled into Cairo determined to learn Arabic, read the Quran, experience Muslim culture first-hand and test my enthusiasm for Islam. I found the Fajr Centre for the Arabic Language, founded in Cairo in 1995, online. The new session was beginning in January 2007. Fajr (dawn) is for new enthusiasts and prospective imams, affiliated to the Egyptian Ministry of Education and al-Azhar, and located in Medina Nasser (Nasser City), which I was to discover is a sprawling suburban near the airport. Transportation in Cairo is a nightmare, be it by taxi or public transit. Virtually all Fajr students share digs near the 'institute', which is modest to say the least, but I immediately liked it, despite the anonymous suburban clutter. The administrators and my teacher were clearly devout Muslims, and warm, friendly people. This was not for rich secular westerners, who studied at the AUC or one of many private institutes down town, at three times the cost.

I heard of a Canadian-Egyptian artist who lived in Manial, the southern-most large island of Cairo, perched just upstream from more upscale Zamalek. Anna responded to my query, offering the vacant apartment next door. The 'apartment' was one of two shacks atop a 9-storey genteel 1930s apartment building on the east shore of the island of Manial, with a channel of the Nile and the Corniche directly underneath, in the heart of Cairo. Straight out of *The Yacoubian Building* (2002), the best-seller by Egyptian author (and dentist) Alaa el-Aswany, made into a film as I was packing my bags for Egypt in 2006, and into a TV series in 2007. A good omen, I thought, and it became a kind of Bible for me, where I learned my Arabic watching the daily episodes, along with other *musalsal* (tv soap operas) over the few years, like a textbook, as I struggled with Arabic. It is set in a real-life, dowdy, but still elegant Art Deco-style 1930s apartment building in downtown Cairo, much like the one I was to call home for the next six years, populated by a bizarre cross-section of Egypt.

My rooftop eyrie with its ghosts of past rooftop dwellers, was a scaled-down version. The real thing was a whole village, crammed onto the roof. The book-movie is a biting condemnation of a nation that has squandered its promise and which has been forced to compromise its own principles, resulting in a corrupt and undemocratic political system dominated by a single party (the fictitious 'Patriotic Party', a thinly veiled version of Egypt's National Democratic Party under Mubarak), a society whose most talented members abandon the country for promising careers abroad, and an increasingly disenchanted and restive populace that has no loyalty to the government and which sees extremist Islam as one of the few viable options to counter growing poverty, economic stagnation, moral degradation and social alienation. Despite its unremittingly devastating dissection of Cairo, its colourful characters make it a compelling, heart-warming read. I visited the real Yacoubian Building on Talaat Harb Street (still referred to by its old name, Suleiman Pasha, Muhammad Ali's French-born general). It hasn't changed much over the years, but its entrance gate is more securely locked than mine in Manial against gawkers like me.

One look at the panorama of the Nile below my eyrie and I was determined to rough it out. It sounds great in retrospect, but over time, proved less and less a place to actually live. My eccentric rooftop neighbour Anna Boughiguian, the Armenian Egyptian author of *Anna's Egypt: an artist's journey* (2003), spent months at a time visiting artist friends in Germany and following the trail of the Dalai Lama. Her flat was more a studio/ storage shack. The lock on the iron gate at the entrance was mostly broken or left unlocked, which made it convenient for visitors, both expected and unwanted. She was a militant secularist, representing the large and frightened class of westernised bourgeois who thrived under Sadat and Mubarak. She had no use for either Nasser's national socialism or the Muslim Brotherhood, both of which I cherished. Over time, I came across many such Egyptians.

Manial's claim to fame on its north end is the Manial Palace, built by Prince Mohammed Ali Tewfik (1875–1955), the uncle of King Farouk, between 1899 and 1929, in a style integrating Art Nouveau, Rococo and Islamic architecture. It was endlessly under repair when I lived there, now mostly just a nice bit of greenery without a sidewalk accessible by pedestrians, hence, a rare stretch of the Corniche without garbage thoughtlessly tossed down the embankment. Much of the palace land was requisitioned to build a Meridian hotel. On the south end of Manial there is the Nilometer, original dating from 861 AD, but the modern structure is just an anachronism, after the completion of the Aswan Dam in 1970, as the water level of the Nile is now regulated. The dams on the Nile, the first built by the British in 1902 and the monumental Aswan Dam in 1970, built by the Soviet Union, dominate Egypt-Cairo's life, having tamed the Nile, with all the advantages and problems that dams entail.

The students I met at the Fajr Institute mostly ended up just conversing in English, French, Russian, Bengali, etc., while diligently parsing difficult classical Arabic grammar and memorising passages. Most could read Arabic script fluently, as they were mostly Muslim by birth and had attended classes to learn to read the script, but without any understanding. That was not what I had in mind. I wanted not only to understand what I read, but to gain enough fluency to function socially. The six-week course at Fajr taught very little grammar, and no conversational skills, but it was a start. The textbooks were Saudi – big and shiny. My class was level one, a wonderful group of nine, mostly from the former Soviet Union, which meant we spoke more Russian than Arabic after class.

'Welcome to Egypt!' I heard this many times during my four hours of crowded, stuffy buses each day. People from all walks of life, most of whom don't know another word in English: the policeman calmly flashing a toothy leer at a chaotic intersection between Medina el-Gadida (New City) and Medina Nasser, who stopped traffic to scrawl instructions; the helpful bus traveller flashing his toothy, yellow smile as I haltingly asked which buses go there for future reference; the long-suffering, bored bus driver who promised to tell me when to get off and promptly forgot, graciously allowing me to ride back free and stopping till I did.

My thirst for Muslim experiences led me to an American Sufi, a American University in Cairo sociology prof, Abu Hai Naq, who related the numeric significance of the Semitic scripts on our hour-long car ride to a Thursday evening *zikr*. An eleventh century mosque in Aleppo was built according to the the the architect's wife's name. The builder was a Sufi and the dimensions derived from her name. I was sceptical of this magic totemism but Naq argued that just speaking the ancient sounds brings one closer to God. Idris Shah counters this in *Learning How to Learn: Psychology and Spirituality in the Sufi Way* (1996) by saying prayers by rote, without understanding, is useless. I wanted to side with Idris Shah, but my own fascination and obsession with learning Arabic suggests the sounds have a special quality. I want to articulate (even by rote) the sounds the prophet used to transmit the message from beyond. But just as important, to understand them. My enthusiasm for real understanding of Islam just by learning Arabic flirts with misplaced concreteness, but is a blessing as well. The blessing being the challenge of the arcane text, forcing me to be creative in deconstructing the text, fashioning the meaning based on reason and study, a kind of *ijtihad*. There is no excuse for intellectual laziness in Islam, but true understanding requires going beyond mere words, whether in Arabic or English.

The *zikr* was at a spooky Ottoman mosque/graveyard buried among modern blocks of flats. Sufism is generally frowned upon in mainstream Egyptian society, and there are only a few mosques which allow *zikrs* 'after hours', so it was an adventure. The Shia-like chanting, reaching an ecstatic state with clapping and singing, was followed by a tasty repast. The Sufism of Cairo is the Naqshibandi *tariqa* (path), which dominated religious life during the middle of the nineteenth century in Egypt. This colourful mysticism was frowned on by the British occupiers, Nasser and, since the 1970s, the secular establishment and Salafi. The Turkish Cypriot Sufi Muslim Sheikh Nazim is the spiritual leader of the Naqshbandi *tariqa*, and on my ride home, French-speaking Fazil urged me to '*venez avec mois a un festival cet ete avec Sheikh Nazim en Chypre.*' We were listening to Cairo radio's Chopin hour (syrupy nocturnes), driving on the spaghetti expressways weaving through Cairo in his Lexus, and I thought: nice and cultured as Fazil was (we went to a bridge club a few times), I was not here to listen to hackneyed Chopin, play bridge, or to flit off to Cyprus to follow the guru of westernised Muslims. This is not the Cairo I'm looking for.

Omar, a Surinamese, born in Holland, befriended me on the bus near Fajr one day, and invited me to iftar in his digs (with five other students) and prayers at the nearby mosque. 'We must love each other as Muslims. We must share equally.' Much like my teacher Fuad says, 'I teach you because I love you as one Muslim loves another.' A fascinating variation on the Christian 'fundies' I have experienced in Canada. I use this diminutive not as a slight, but rather to suggest the refreshing naivete of the best of both Christian and Muslim fundamentalists. My US cousins in Minneapolis are evangelicals, never missing a Sunday service, and attending a Bible study group every week. They volunteer for charity work (mostly with the elderly rather than the poor). But they are literalists, reading the Bible like Omar reads the Quran and sunnah. There is no sense that one must wrestle with the scriptures to make sense out of them in today's world. They mean well, but this bad epistemology is sterile, if not downright dangerous.

What a contrast with the very westernised Sufis I've encountered here, though the Sufis strike me as naive in a different way, following a guru, justifying their bourgeois lifestyle with ecstatic *zikrs*, but also disconnected from the social, political and economic challenges of the world around them.

And then there are the westernised lumpen Egyptians, more cynical than naive. Waiting for the creaking rusty trolley in a car-infested suburbia across from a stately mosque, I spotted a teenage girl in an orange headscarf with a tight, black t-shirt barely containing her hanging breasts with 'Love Boat Have the Girls' emblazoned in complementary orange caps, chewing her bubblegum. An act of defiant protest, though the angry girl doesn't know against what.

My touristy activity in Cairo was attending jummah at different mosques, the most imposing ones luckily within walking distance or a short 'marcheroute' (van-bus) ride from Manial. My favourite was the Salah al-Din mosque, a nineteenth century tribute to 'Saladin', on the west side of Manial at the bridge to Giza. The al-Rifai Mosque (1869–1912) is across the Nile, visible from my eerie, named after the medieval era Islamic saint (1118–1182), founder of the Rifai Sufi order, born in present-day Iraq. With a touch of twentieth century irony, it contains the tomb of the

Shah of Iran, who Sadat invited as the Shah was wandering the world, abandoned by his patron the US, dying of cancer in 1979. This homage is a conflicted one, only a modest posy of flowers at its base when I visited, attracting a few westerners and stray Iranian emigres, the Shah's legacy as an abandoned US puppet having no more than curiosity value today.

Also within walking distance was the Mosque of Amr ibn al-As, originally built in 642 AD as the centre of the newly founded capital of Egypt, Fustat. The original structure was the first mosque built in Egypt, the site of the tent of the commander of the Muslim army, general, a companion of the Prophet and credited with the conquest of Egypt in 640. One corner of the mosque contains the tomb of his son, Abd Allah ibn Amr ibn al-As, but the rest is the result of reconstruction over the centuries. A visit during Ramadan in 2009 to pray was awesome, feeling the weight of history, the mosque bright, spacious and packed. Unfortunately, there is little greenery around any of these places of worship, only clogged roads and crowded sidewalks. I also prayed at the more modest prayer halls dotting the streets, small narrow rooms wedged between stores and residences. It was delightful to just slip in to one when the muezzin called to prayer, like a social instinct, kept in tune by the thousands of centres scattered everywhere.

I found I was not really welcome beyond superficial polite hellos in my building. My shack's previous tenant (French) was a bit of a scandal, using it as a bachelor's flop house, as Anna explained later during one of our few interludes of truce. I never came to know many of the building tenants. Occasionally on the lift, I would greet a Saudi in full regalia, and learned that several of the flats were used by vacationing Saudis. But they are even more aloof with foreigners than Egyptians. Thousands of Saudis spend months in Egypt, mostly in the summer, Egypt's furnace being a refreshing relief from the Saudi furnace. It is a chance to unwind, drink booze, and wallow in decadent quasi-Muslim culture. Cairenes have a love-hate relation with Saudis, envious of their wealth, but secretly contemptuous of their boorishness, lack of culture, seeing Saudi Arabia as a kind of rich purgatory, best reserved for the hajj. Egypt is tied to Saudi's purse strings, and Egyptians bridle at the Saudis flaunting of wealth, their love of prostitutes and the purchase of young Egyptian brides. The protests over Egyptian President Sisi's 'gift' of the Tiran island to the Saudis in 2017 highlights the widespread resentment – and Egypt's dilemma – a rare example of public protest in today's Egypt.

Internet cafes dot Manial, and being without a computer, I made daily excursions to one or another of them, still looking for a silver bullet for learning Arabic and deciphering Cairo. The Fajr programme was oblivious to the use of Arabic as a *lingua franca*. An American woman I met later at *al-Ahram*, Julie, told me, 'I studied four years of classical Arabic at university in the US, came to Cairo, and asked where I could buy a fishing rod, and was greeted by shock and laughter.' (It struck me they may have found her request just as bizarre as her *Fus-ha*.) I already sensed that, and found a lead to the University of Cairo, which I discovered just across the Nile in Giza.

My Arab Godson

This time my stumbling landed me at the Centre for Eastern Studies in Cairo University, offering Arabic and Hebrew, though only Arabic seemed to be taught, located in a small, dilapidated palace of a princess near the Cairo Zoo (one of my few concessions to tourism was taking visitors to the zoo as you would to the CN Tower in Toronto or the London Eye). I registered for a month, joining the last half of a class of Korean students. It used the same wooden, tedious methodology of Fajr, guaranteed *not* to result in any ability to speak Arabic. But with advantages: 1/ it was nearby, a must in Cairo, where a normal commute takes one and a half hours, 2/ with a friendly young office clerk, a new father, Mahmoud, who I quickly befriended and convince to teach me colloquial Arabic at home. This was strictly forbidden–no private coaching–but we made a secret pact, and a blind eye was turned (if it saw anything), as Mahmoud's salary skyrocketed from $8 a month, most of which went to pay for three 'marcheroutes' from his village Nikla, twenty miles north in the delta.

I felt like my real voyage of discovery of Cairo and Islam had finally begun. Mahmoud Shaaban more or less adopted me (his father had died of Nile liver disease at the age of forty). He spoke little English, though he had studied it all through school and college, which helped us without him constantly breaking the spell of my thinking in Arabic. For the next five years, Mahmoud would slip away twice a week after work (as a school, the Centre ended its workday at 3pm) with a cardboard container of *foul* (beans) and *chipsty* (freshly made potato chips) from a street kiosk. When in season, he would bring artichokes, which he tore into and ate raw, with relish.

For a Muslim, to 'sign up' a convert puts you on the fast track to *janna*, so Mahmoud insisted on taking me to al-Azhar one day to the department for registering new Muslims in the Office of the Grand Imam, where I recited the *Shahada* and *Fatihah* and signed on the dotted line. It was almost worth becoming a Muslim just to feel the joy in Mahmoud, his family and the Azhar sheikh.

Cairo has the world's second-oldest university, al-Azhar University, founded in 970 by Sunni Egypt's Fatimids, a now forgotten historical footnote. You might think it makes Egypt the perfect intermediary in Sunni-Shia understanding, and indeed, al-Azhar recognizes not only the four Sunni schools of jurisprudence, but the Shia Jafari school. However, virtually all Egyptians are disdainful of Shia, both the devout – suspicious that they are trying to convert Sunnis with their veneration of Ali and Hussain – and the secularists, fearing Iran as a dangerous example for Egypt's Islamists, intent, so they assume, on creating a 'Islamic state'.

Mahmoud and I also went to the theatre, which I didn't really understand, but knew was 'good for me', and Mahmoud enjoyed himself immensely and would explain the plot. He had never been to the theatre, and his life with me was a new life, challenging his beliefs, as he imparted his own deep faith and gave me insight into his life as a poor young Egyptian villager, struggling with the temptations of cosmopolitan Cairo. Our attempts to travel beyond Cairo and his own village were not much success. Neither of us were tourists and Egypt is not tourist-friendly for simple people or free spirit middle-aged *hawagas*. The 2-3-hour trips to his village Nikla were exhausting (what isn't exhausting in Cairo, in the chilly, unheated winters, and blistering, merciless summers?), though the last bumpy, crowded hour out of Cairo was at least dotted with brilliant green fields of sugar cane or vegetables, a view of the Great Pyramid, and *felaheen* toiling away. But also passing through cluttered, unkempt villages, where garbage was piled randomly and stagnant canals were full of slime.

Always a tasty meal, served modestly by Mahmoud's lovely wife Nagla, with his daughter Miriam and son Abdul-Rahman crawling over us. Usually just Mahmoud and me, but sometimes his closest friend and nephew, Muhammad, and others. I met one of his six brothers once, another Muhammad, who was a bit of a rake and offered me a toke, much to Mahmoud's dismay. Mahmoud later confessed he smoked dope on occasion, but considered it *haram* and refused to help me obtain any. 'I can't be a corrupter of you. That would mean I'm doing Satan's bidding.' I suspect Mahmoud didn't really want to share me with anyone else, or maybe his brothers were suspicious of this *hawaga* friend.

My life with Mahmoud encapsulated much of Cairo with all its contradictions for me. Sincerity of belief, abiding friendship, politeness with foreigners, but hunger for the promise that western media held out and that I symbolised, suspicion, resentment, disdain ... It's hard to put my finger on it. I suspect it's the traveller-writer's bane: you never really integrate, you are grateful to find and cultivate a friend or two.

One evening after our lesson, met Mohammad, the fruit drink seller, shuttering his shop.

'Ali, where have you been? Come to prayers... Have you prayed today?'

As it happened, I had. *Fajr* (three hours late), *Zuhr*, *Asr* (with Mahmoud). Mohammad smiled to hear that. We were joined by his two young cousins and an older brother and wound our way through the twisting back allies to the eighteenth century Ottoman mosque, open in the middle with the sky glowing above, with solid stone walls and ornamental painting on the lofty ceiling. It was angled, almost triangular in shape, making it seem even more unworldly than usual, with *jallaba*-clad men lined up with blue-jeaned youth in t-shirts. We first made our ablutions in the clean but very wet washing room. Then I went with a young cousin to pray and ended up beside a handsome, modest teen, who was not embarrassed by physical contact of feet and shoulders with this odd visitor, as Muslims are instructed to do during prayer, though on my other side, the fellow did not touch, and seemed resentful of my invasion of his world.

These thousands of men of all walks of life all touching as we prayed tonight in the majestic cathedral mosque in the dirt poor neighbourhood aren't just having the second-hand brief spark of experience that, say, we achieved at a suburban United Church in Ontario. They do this five times a day and really believe it. They have conserved their spirit, inculcated since childhood and maintained through the years by the constant prayer, gruelling fast and intense celebrations that characterise Islam. Hence the naiveté of Muslims masses. That's why they can't seem to make the real world work to their advantage. It's just not important enough. Their real life is on another plane, and their crass political leaders are the real chumps (fat cats though they be).

The subtlety of determining how intimate your fellow supplicants want to be is perhaps a secret chance to share a moment of spiritual connection, with only Allah observing. I marvelled as I wandered out of this magical journey into another dimension, and put my sandals back on with Mohammad, that Muslim men have a wonderful channel for intimacy, alien to western secular behaviour, which dehumanises, reduces everything to sex and money, creating slots for humanity, be they race, class, sexuality. I often think of Malcolm X's epiphany at Mecca in 1964. In letters from his trip, he described scenes of unimagined interracial harmony among 'tens of thousands of pilgrims, from all over the world. They were of all colors, from blue-eyed blondes to black-skinned Africans.' His greatest struggle was to bow down and touch his forehead to the ground in humility. He got up and shed his hatred of whites, embracing Islam and equality of all peoples.

Another high, talking about Sufism, Islam, Handel's *Messiah*, and glimpses of heaven, as medical student Haitham and I leisurely crossed the Nile on the Gamaa bridge from Giza to Manial, watching lovers leaning over the rail, the ferries floating past, the cool, clean night wind blowing in our faces, the wedding cortege (clap-trap b/w taxis) with young Egyptians hanging out the windows by their knees, hooting and waving. There is no end to the wildness and chaos, the *joie-de-vivre* here, all sans alcohol. Such a sense of grubby, but real civilisation, without the sexy ads celebrating the drunkenness that is so ingrained in partying in Canada.

Recovering from the usual *hawaga* digestion problems, I decided to risk a lunch of *qushari* (lentils and macaroni). I wanted the nice half-litre plastic container for my kitchen set, and the meal costs only 2LE (Egyptian pounds). The server stood at the raised counter like a high priest surrounded by huge vats of lentils, chickpeas, macaroni and crispy fried onions, like the percussionist in an orchestra surrounded by his shiny timpani and kettle drums. Before I could catch my breath, he had scooped up the macaroni, flourished a dollop of lentils and threw a large spoonful of chickpeas and onions in the air, catching them expertly in the container, dropping in pouches (plastic of course) of hot sauce and vinegar as he smiled at me. A magic trick, an offering to the gods (just joking). Speaking of which (another day's topic) you don't joke about religion here. From starving street persons to fabulously rich businessmen, this is indeed sacred (even secularists are careful), though I'm constantly flummoxed by the unbelievable disparity in incomes. Only the Muslim Brotherhood addresses the economic disparities, and of course is harshly persecuted as a result.

Al-Ahram

My life was up for grabs after Fajr. I was still 'full time' enough at the University of Cairo to extend my visa for a year, thanks to Mubarak-era lax visa requirements. Could I aspire to study Islam at al-Azhar University? No. Prospective students from abroad spent at least two years intensively studying classical Arabic, as I had witnessed at Fajr. After two years, they still couldn't converse easily on the street, and that was my priority. My love of writing (and adventure) trumped my desire for a scholarly background in Islam. With no income, my only hope of staying was to work. In the past, I had worked as a freelance journalist in Moscow and Tashkent, and as a translator of books, and English stylist at newspapers, but that was from Russian to English. My Arabic would never be good enough for translations, but there were at least three English-language newspapers, and I made the rounds over the next month, stumbling—again—across a copy of *al-Ahram Weekly*, which I found buried among the Arabic newspapers of a street hawker in Giza, near the university. You never see foreign language newspapers as a rule, so my sojourn at the university was a lucky stroke. Ahram means ruins, as in pyramids, which is the newspaper's emblem, fitting in more ways than one as the leading newspaper in Egypt, home of the pyramids and a country in ruins. *Al-Ahram* was founded in 1875 and is the most widely circulating Egyptian daily newspaper since Nasser, state-owned.

There was an email address on the editorial page, and without any expectations, I fired off a letter touting my credentials and availability. The next day at the internet cafe, I was pleasantly surprised to see an answer, asking me to come immediately for an interview. Chapter two of my life in Cairo was beginning, as I took the metro to Urabi station and queried my way to the imposing twelve-storey Ahram buildings (I & II) on Galaa St. The English edition (founded in 1991) was on the ninth floor of the old building, and I entered its mini-labyrinth, had several interviews, and was given a trial, along with the other prospect, who had already been interviewed. I had sent my application just in time to give editor-in-chief Assam el-Kirsh and managing editor Galal Nasser a choice. My competition was Mel Frykberg, a tough-as-nails South African/Australian journalist (like me, of Swedish descent), who had already lived and worked for eight years as a correspondent in Israel. Sounded like a walk-over for Mel, but I *had* to have this plum job. Did I have a chance? We were asked to work in tandem, writing something for the paper, and editing some copy of the local journalists, who all wrote in passable English. Despite her many years' experience, Mel knew less Arabic than I did, and my Cambridge degree (and gender, as 80 per cent of the staff were women) tipped the balance with these secular Anglophiles.

The *Weekly* staff was in two camps: militant secularists and a smaller contingent of quiet, devout Muslims, who lived peaceably, respecting the differences, with a surprising lack of censorship, though the limits of the state-owned paper were more or less clear. Most of the women were sans hijab, pampered children of the old secular elite, though a couple would flirt with hijab from time to time, more as a fashion statement. I moved between the two groups, my disputes being with the secularists, who viewed my praying in the hallway with the believers with curiosity and even amusement. I sometimes missed the adhan, hard at work with a deadline. The praying staff were a minority, mostly the errand boys/men and other service staff, but with some journalists. There was a prayer cubby hole in the waiting room for women and others who disdained the mostly plebeians praying by the elevator.

The secularists accepted that I was still a plus, despite my eccentricity, there being only one other *hawaga* on staff, the pompous Brit Nigel, who was even more eccentric, my secular nemesis, now a recluse, refusing to come to work, sending in his copy from home. I reluctantly entered a Paul Bowles world of the decadent expat, who relies on his passport and foreign chicness, his violation of the status quo tolerated more for his entertainment value than his productivity. There was more in common between myself and the secularists in tastes and life style, though that changed over time. The chain-smoking atheist culture editor, Yousef Rakha, gave me free rein on book reviews, my articles on culture clash, reading the Qur'an, and western converts to Islam, and my obit for Osama Bin Laden. As long as it was readable and intelligent, he was happy. We even squared off on Judaism vs Islam.

Nigel was the culture hawaga, a cynical secularist, so he was not happy with me horning in on his territory, but perhaps my Islamic bent was seen as providing the balance that was sorely lacking at the *Weekly*. Instead of feeling threatened, he made use of me as a stop-gap, disappearing into Sinai to write a novel, where he lived in a cabin on a mountain side during my last two years at the *Weekly*. He would have been out the door in a western paper, but this was Egypt, where socialism survives, if only in terms of job security, though Assam never seemed to get around to giving me a contract, leaving me at the whim of management. I sensed that I was not indispensable if someone else showed up, but who knows? However, relations remained friendly, and in the end, it was my choice to leave.

The *Weekly* was a godsend for me, as I was soon promoted to the 'American correspondent', writing about Canada, the US and Palestinian-Israeli issues, which are inevitably American issues. My patron was Gamal Nkrumah, son of Kwame Nkrumah, Ghana's first president, ally and soulmate of Gamal Abdel-Nasser, heir to the heady secular socialist project of African and Arab unity and socialism. Gamal, like his father, is a larger than life persona, living in the family mansion on the Nile in Helwan, built by Nasser on the southern outskirts of Cairo for Kwame Nkrumah's family after he was toppled in the 1966 coup. Gamal liked my anti-imperialist credentials, my love of socialism, the Soviet Union and third world liberation – my earlier incarnation. He was a reluctant Muslim, divorced with two young sons. He never saw his father after the coup, spirited out of Ghana on a military plane which Nasser sent for the Nkrumahs. Kwame chose to go into his own exile, first to Guinea and then on to Romania, where he died in 1972. Gamal was the foreign news editor and was happy to unload much of the foreign news onto me, more interested in doing restaurant reviewing, interviews with visiting media stars, and culture pieces.

The Soviet Union was Egypt-Cairo's third motherland, replacing France and Britain, as Egypt's sponsor under Nasser, but very much the unloved stepmother. The engineers who came to build the Aswan dam were watched by their KGB minders, and Nasser was a reluctant Soviet ally, wanting the financial and economic support, but also wanting his own version of a socialist Arab nationalism – Nasserism, and control of Middle East politics. It's hard to say what would have happened if Nasser had been more obedient as a Soviet ally. He was caught between the Muslim Brotherhood, whom he ruthlessly repressed, and the nationalist westernisers, who were mostly cynical about his socialism, but happy to promote Egypt as the head of the Arab world, abiding his dictatorial regime, as it kept the Islamists in check. When the shock of the 1967 defeat by Israel receded, Egyptians felt betrayed by their socialist stepmother, and when Nasser died in 1970, his successor Anwar el-Sadat maintained the Soviet alliance only long enough to get the arms necessary to launch a replay against Israel in 1973 to regain Sinai.

Over the next five years, I wrote mostly about politics, mobilised by Gamal to write weekly on whatever crisis was brewing or breaking. But that veered into Islamic politics and during Ramadan, articles celebrating Islamic history and culture, including Iran, in defiance of the overwhelmingly negative view or just absence of Iran in Egyptian news and thinking. To me, despite its ostracism as the only Shia country, Iran is at the heart of modern day Islamic affairs.

Much like the other secularists on staff, Gamal found my bumbling efforts to be a Muslim amusing, recounting his own earlier attempts. 'The only time I was able to fast, was in London in the 1970s, when the day was only six hours long.' Like me, he had Christian parents, his mother, a Coptic Egyptian beauty, a lowly bank clerk in 1950s who caught the eye of his father, a secularist with both native and Catholic religious background, who Kwame had met on a visit to Egypt shortly after Ghana achieved independence in 1957. It was a political marriage but a successful one. Gamal had accepted Islam only as a matter of protocol when he married. Being a lapsed Christian (Coptic) was not a plus on his resume and passport, and he had lost any Muslim fervour as his marriage disintegrated, enjoying his drink and occasional pork.

I was in awe of his legendary father, and was delighted to make a second home at his villa on the Nile in Helwan, where he grew up, attending the elite English-language Victoria College. Gamal is a tantalising mix of Ghanaian high forehead and afro hair, the flashing eyes, jolly humour, wild laugh, resonant voice, regal paunch, and the Copt oval face, large round eyes, romantic character. His own biography is populated by larger-than-life events – studies in London and Zimbabwe, before settling into his position at *al-Ahram*.

My debut as an anti-imperialism correspondent was an account of the sixth (and last) international Cairo Conference against Imperialism and Zionism in 2008. Egypt was in the dying days of dictator Hosni Mubarak's regime, caught between the anti-imperialism and socialism of Nasser and his pro-American successor Anwar el-Sadat. Sadat, to his credit, was trying to move forward when he made peace with the enemy in 1979. But his embrace of Israel and US neoliberalism won him no supporters, and his assassination in 1981 resulted in no outpouring of grief, unlike the death of his beloved predecessor in 1970. His plodding successor, Hosni Mubarak continued Sadat's policies, Egypt regaining membership and headquarters of the Arab League in 1987, and maintaining a pseudo-democracy under US tutelage, where real opposition (the Muslim Brotherhood) was repressed.

Gamal took me to the conference at the Journalists' Union building near *al-Ahram* and introduced me to some of his Egyptian colleagues, but slipped out to do a restaurant review (i.e., gorge himself), commissioning me to write up the conference. I was overwhelmed with the cacophony of the cross-section of the Egyptian opposition. (No officials from the government were there.) The conference featured children of jailed Muslim Brothers, bravely pleading for public awareness about their fathers being tortured and robbed. Egyptians are uniformly hostile to Israel, the cause of unending tragedy, not only for Palestinians, but for Egyptians, so holding the conference was good politics for the unpopular Mubarak, despite its strong anti-US tone, the presence of major Egyptian opposition representatives, and the lack of any Mubarak supporters.

Fourteen members of the Canadian Peace Alliance and from student organisations represented Canada. Delegates to this and the previous Cairo conference were attacked in the *National Post* and *Ottawa Citizen* for consorting with 'terrorists', and 'shouldn't be surprised if they come under scrutiny of the Canadian security services', simply for their willingness to dialogue with Muslims fighting the various wars now being inflicted on them. My article 'Zionism in Canada: Political poison' prompted a reference to me in the Canadian *National Post* as a 'terrorist', and derided my comparison of the struggle of Canada's natives and Palestinians. My reply to the *Post* was not printed, nor did I get an acknowledgment, but my first thrust into Middle East and the world of Islam had had some ripples, which was encouraging. It convinced no one that I was a danger, but gave me a platform and an incentive to continue the battle for Palestine. These were the fraught days before the whirlwind of 2011, after which open defiance of imperialism and popular support for the Muslim Brotherhood and Palestine blossomed. Halcyon days before an even more brutal dictatorship emerged, when no public expressions of anti-imperialist and pro-Palestinian sentiment were possible anymore. It turned out Mubarak got the last laugh.

Mubarak days are remembered now with nostalgia by the intellectual elite. Life was boring but safe. Mubarak was a wonderfully unifying force, making unlikely allies of secularists and devout Muslims on the staff, while not torturing as much as Nasser or Sisi.

Once the Arab Spring exploded, militant secularists had a field day, shouting their promises and demands loudly. The Muslims were quietly using the vacuum in society to rebuild their forces, jails were now emptied of members of the Brotherhood, even while daily crises grew, to which only the Muslim Brotherhood had a tradition of grassroots help, from doctors, to school books, to meals for the destitute. I witnessed this frequently outside my apartment building in Manial, where tables were set up, and school books and notepads were distributed. In 2012, the Brotherhood mobilised its cadres to clean up the worst trash in the streets, for which they were derided by the secularists. There were many such local activities across Egypt in villages, unheralded or at best ridiculed in the negative press. Any such altruistic efforts to follow the teachings of Islam were greeted with scornful taunts of 'Down with the rule of the Supreme Guide!', conjuring the spectre of Iran.

Bringing down the Brotherhood

The Egyptian revolution was brought down by an unholy alliance of '*fuloul*' (beans, remnants, referring to the old guard), the army, and so-called liberals. The latter loathed the Muslim Brotherhood in the first place, the old guard second, the army a bit less, and despised the people, thinking they could use them, despite the clear evidence in repeated elections since 2011 that they would elect an Islamic government. Given the collapse of authority in 2011, this was a recipe for disaster. The Muslim Brotherhood was elected, but its government was sabotaged by the bureaucracy, army, police and liberals, most of whom were eager to abandon the fragile democracy. 'Better dead than Islamic.'

The fanatical Islamophobe at *al-Ahram* turned out to be Khaled Dawoud, whose (second, and short-lived) wedding I attended at the ritzy Shepheard Hotel in 2008. A former CNN stringer, he became spokesman of the Constitution Party of Egypt in 2011, and later for the National Salvation Front (NSF), hastily thrown together in November 2012 to overthrow the Muslim Brotherhood government. He resigned from his political life in August 2013 in protest at the police violence against Morsi supporters, and was stabbed by a Morsi supporter on 4 October 2013, but survived and still works at the *Weekly*.

The liberal star of the coup was a stand-up comic, a young doctor, Bassem Youssef, who used YouTube to launch *El-Bernameg*. ('You are watching the program *The Program*!' opened each show.) It ran from 2011 to 2013, uncensored despite its increasingly *ad hominem* attacks on Egypt's first democratically elected president, promoting the opposition's distorted exaggerations of actual events, claiming that Morsi was becoming a dictator. As the campaign of subversion intensified on all fronts, Youssef (dubbed the Jon Stewart of the Arab world) let his program, fresh from witnessing the overthrow of a real dictator (Mubarak), set the stage for a new, more vicious dictator, what the army had intended all along, from the opening shots of January 2011.

The army hated Mubarak as much as anyone, and let the revolution of 2011 proceed under their control, though they had no use for either the liberals or the Brotherhood. The plan was to give the Brotherhood some rope and then take charge and hang them (metaphorically and literally), responding to the vengefulness of the old guard and the naive, screaming liberals. The liberals were weak, and could be conned into supporting a coup, and then easily brought to heel with a few arrests and massacres.

Youssef, nominally a Muslim, was sponsored by Egypt's top billionaire, the secular Copt Naguib Sawiris, mobile phone magnate and owner of ONTV. Youssef's parodies originally targeted genuine buffoons like TV show host Tawfik Okasha, minor figures like Salafist presidential candidate Hazem Salah Abu Ismail, and even respected liberals such as Mohamed ElBaradei, former head of the International Atomic Energy Agency and onetime presidential candidate. In June 2012, Jon Stewart invited Youssef to *The Daily Show* in New York. Youssef recorded one of the highest viewership ratings in the world on both TV and internet, with 40 million viewers on TV and more than 184 million combined views for his show on YouTube alone. He was a political power by social media.

But Youssef also alienated his new TV sponsor CBC with insults to the management and they cancelled one program, a warning of what was to come. Caught up in his ego trip and adulation of the US, he emulated Stewart, his hero, through increasingly outrageous skits ridiculing Morsi and the vision of an Islamic government. Instead of using his immense popularity to help calm waters and to support the fledgling democracy, he used these few precious months of disorganised 'freedom' to discredit and bring down the democratically elected Brotherhood and Egypt's first legitimate president. Brotherhood criticism of Youssef was muted. He was never arrested. The Brotherhood did not control the media, and his program continued unhindered, to whip up ever great anger and protests.

As the coup loomed on the horizon in June 2013, Youssef appeared again on *The Daily Show* in New York, and Stewart came to Cairo as a supposed terrorist on *The Program*. As the coup took place, Youssef, like my *Ahram* collegue Khaled, watched, first ecstatic, then as if in surprise, in shock, as thousands of devout Muslims were mowed down and the Brotherhood leaders arrested and condemned to death. His *Program* was closed after two post-coup episodes. He managed a few more *Programs* on satellite

MBCMasr before a suit by CBC (claiming his contract was broken for not providing acceptable content) was decided in CBC's favour, and Youssef was ordered to pay US$1 million.

As thousands were killed, tortured, left in prison limbo, Youssef fled Cairo, and in the venerable tradition for pro-US dissidents, was given an appointment at Harvard's Institute for Politics. In an adulatory documentary *Tickling Giants* (2017), he is clearly shaken but insists (feebly) that 'If I could it do to again, I would do the same.' In 2013, Youssef was named one of the '100 most influential people in the world' by *Time* magazine and one of *Foreign Policy* magazine's 100 Leading Global Thinkers. In November 2013, he was awarded the International Press Freedom Award by the Committee to Protect Journalists.

I watched Youssef on TV before I myself fled the growing nightmare of Cairo in 2012, but he didn't really register with me. Humour in another language is always difficult, and petulant stand-up comedy mocking politics never appealed to me, attacking personal foibles, actually diverting the listener from serious political issues. The writing was on the wall as Egypt descended into chaos and experienced a collective mental breakdown, laughed at by satirist Youssef et al, and I left in bitter disillusion. As much as I had come to love Egypt, it was not my breakdown. *Hawagas* were more and more seen as at best irrelevant and nosy parasites, at worst, traitors and spies.

Sisi – Muhammad Ali redux

From my rooftop, I often sat watching the dusk transform the Mohamed Ali Citadel, the 12th century citadel build by Salah al-Din, containing the Mosque of Muhammad Ali, built between 1828 and 1848, perched on the summit of the citadel. As a new Muslim, I watched the phases of the moon, like a slow-moving backwards clock, from my perch in Manial, unhindered by clouds. It's hard to imagine anything more magical than the full moon rising behind the minarets of the sprawling mosque on the Muqatam hills. Even more magical was a crescent moon at midnight, feeling the power of the lunar calendar in action, the spiritual timepiece of Muslim worship.

The Citadel was fortified by the Ayyubid ruler Salah al-Din (Saladin) between 1176 and 1183, to protect it from the Crusaders, and was the seat of government until Khedive Ismail moved to his newly built Abdin Palace in the 1860s. The Ottoman mosque was built in memory of Tusun Pasha, Muhammad Ali's second son who died in 1816. However, it also represents Muhammad Ali's efforts to erase symbols of the Mamluk dynasty that he 'replaced', and to keep Egypt's image firmly Muslim, even as the British and French were taking control, and as the Ottoman Caliphate was giving way to the new imperial high-tech world. The Citadel is the most popular tourist site in Cairo after the pyramids, with Japanese cameras casually documenting worshippers at prayer. There is a small museum of Muhammad Ali's collection of paintings and artefacts, and a very large museum of Egyptian military history, which—until 2011— featured a massive mural with Mubarak as father of the people.

When friends visited, we would make the excursion to the Citadel, and nearby al-Azhar Park, another hilltop fort lavishly restored with funds of Aga Khan IV, a descendant of the Fatimid Imam-Caliphs who ruled from Cairo in the eleventh to twelfth centuries. But I was a very poor tourist, never actually standing at the foot of the Giza pyramids or in line at the Egyptian Museum in Tahrir Square, though I passed it hundreds of times. I did visit Saqqara, thanks to my USAID friend Robert, who came to Cairo to see how I was faring. Robert reserved a taxi for the day and invited me along. The tourist shtick of Giza was too much when we stopped there, a gaggle of sloppily dressed Russians haranguing a camel driver. Saqqara was much better, if only because it is far from downtown Cairo, with no metro stop, so gets fewer and more serious visitors. To my shame, I never did the Luxor pilgrimage to the Valley of the Kings, not even the tourist's *de rigueur* camp-out on an oasis. When you live somewhere, suddenly you're not a tourist, and touristy things are for 'them'. None of my friends had any interest in them. I avoided falling into the expat rut of English-language NGO and diplomatic parties and excursions. I was in Cairo to learn Arabic, experience Muslim life in the flesh, to see and feel the real Egypt-Cairo, to take the local pulse. Each day spent with an expat was a day wasted. When Egypt collapsed/rose up in 2011, that put touristy things even lower on the totem pole. My balconies were my daily dose of Egyptian history (the opposite balcony faced the Giza pyramid, though it was rarely visible in the smog).

Sisi is beginning to take on traits associated with this nineteenth dictator-pasha Muhammad Ali, beloved of *Ahram* Raya. She no doubt saw the parallel between Sisi's slaughter of thousands of Muslims, and Muhammad Ali's clever invitation of all his Mamluk rivals to his citadel, where he proceeded to slaughter a thousand of them to consolidate his rule.

A legend of the pasha was that he had 300,000 street children rounded up and shipped to Aswan where they were taught skills and became assets to his construction of a new Egypt. Sisi launched just such a program 'Homeless Children' in May 2017, planning to gather up street waifs and whisk them to an army camp for training. This nostalgia for the secular past is perhaps a stab at taking the wind out of the ISIS types, yearning for the caliphate, but is just as misguided as ISIS itself. That was what the Muslim Brotherhood could have tackled, but not a secular dictator persecuting devout Muslims. On the contrary, terrorism has increased dramatically since 2013.

Another bright idea to model a compliant youth is the Ministry of Education's decision to airbrush the whole revolution-coup experience out of Egyptian history. They decreed that the revolutions of January 25, 2011 and June 30, 2013 will no longer be mentioned in high school history textbooks. This followed protests over an exam question: 'How would things be if Abdel Fattah al-Sisi had never given the June 30 speech?' Countering incredulous protests, Mamdouh Qadri, history adviser for the Ministry of Education, said the answer to the question is clearly defined in the curriculum, and that students were only asked to stick to the textbook without giving any political reasoning or personal analysis. Only the most hardened Sisiphiles could swallow that. Better 'out of sight, out of mind'. The Egyptian revolution and 2013 coup no longer exist. 'Welcome to Egypt!'

I look back on those years fondly, especially the Mubarak years (yes!), as do all Egyptians, even the Muslim Brotherhood, who bore the brunt of the *fulul* and the army. The dying years of Mubarak's dictatorship look rosy now - the straitjacket was loosening, if only because of the internet, which acted like a solvent, dissolving the rusty veneer and allowing the now notorious social networking, the bain of cruel dictators and a breeding ground for world terrorism. Camelot had its fleeting moment, the iron fist came down, and the oppression of Muslims increased far beyond

Mubarak's tired efforts. The Brotherhood (and all devout Egyptians and even *hawagas*) had a brief window of light for two and a half years. I'm not in a rush to go back to Cairo, but my memories are robust, and my thoughts are there, if only as I read the Quran, and recall when and where Arabic words and phrases were hammered out courtesy of my long-suffering Mahmoud.

ARTS AND LETTERS

MONUMENTS TO HUBRIS

Marjorie Allthorpe-Guyton

From being the Olympics of the art world, the Venice Biennale has now become a *'Game of Thrones'*, where powerful countries, institutions, backers, curators and artists are seriously challenged by hitherto marginalised others whose strategies, activism and events grow in influence and relevance. But the struggle is hard, even the established art critics have to compete for entry to the three opening 'professional days' with 'VIPS' who can buy their way in. It is a symptom of that misalignment of art, money and value which was addressed in the 2015 Biennale by Okwui Enwezor, the first African born Curator of the Biennale. While Enwezor acknowledged that 'art has no obligation, it can choose to stay silent' in the face of growing inequality across the globe, he saw that the 'exhibition has limited leeway for withdrawal': it is a public space for creating meaning. His Biennale exhibition *All the World's Futures* was a full-on engagement with the political moment and was criticised for it. In terms of reflecting what the Biennale President, Paolo Baratta, calls 'the Age of Anxiety', the exhibition was an unqualified success.

In 2017 anxiety has deepened for many to fear and loathing which in the US and Europe has found expression in political upheaval and the resurgence of populism with disquieting impacts. Even in the privileged and protected space of the Venice Biennale, which in 2015 had half a million visitors, we might expect an unequivocal critical reflection on this psychological trauma. But for the 2017 Biennale, the Biennale Curator, The Pompidou's Chief Curator, Christine Macel sought cheerfully to return art to art with the clarion call *Viva Arte Viva*: a humanistic celebration of the power of art as 'an act of resistance, liberation and generosity'. This noble universalist ambition is reflected in the global and generational reach of the hundred and twenty artists selected, of which a hundred and three are first time exhibitors in the Biennale. That this ambition failed is a result of the disconnect between Macel's presentation and that of the urgency of much of the art in the National Pavilions and collateral events across the city of Venice. While Enwezor could be accused of joyless, opportunistic heavy-handed didacticism, Macel is curiously ingenuous to claim a discrete space for art: 'a realm for dreams and utopias' at a time when artists are more socially engaged than ever. At the opening night of this year's Biennale, the New York art and activist agency, Creative Time held a conversation 'Art in Precarious Times', which aimed to reflect on the implications of 'the global shift right for creative practices and collective futures'. The panel included Ann Marie Peña, curator and founder of Hands Off Our Revolution, the global art coalition founded in November 2016 to resist the rise of populism and its negative impacts, especially in

Diaspora Pavilion, International Curators' Forum Exhibition,
Palazzo Pisani, S. Marina, Venice

Europe and the US. The coalition's project to 'bring into public view statements, questions and reflections on the state we are in' runs counter to Macel's unapologetic turn inwards, to the spiritual and material needs and state of the artist. While none would doubt the centrality of the artist to the Biennale, it may not be the moment at a time of instability for the lives of millions, to dwell on the privileged creative 'space of productive idleness', as she writes in her introduction to the Biennale short guide. Or to showcase, for example, the conceit of the sleeping artist in the work of the Zagreb conceptualist artist Mladen Stilinović (1947-2016). However relevant the existential non-gesture is to an art of resistance, it rings hollow in current conditions with the growing displacement and poverty of peoples, even in the rich urban centres of the west.

Dwelling: in this space we breathe is a series of small self portraits by British Gambian artist Khadija Saye. These are works by a young artist at the very beginning of her career. Their quiet darkening power resonates besides

Khadija Saye 1992-2017, *Dwelling in the space we breathe 2017*
Wetplate Collodian Tintype, Diaspora Pavilion

more declamatory works at the Palazzo Pisani S Marina, the venue for *Diaspora* one of the must-see collateral exhibitions of the Venice Biennale. The exhibition, described as 'tactical interventions' by the curators David A. Bailey and Jessica Taylor, has nineteen artists, both young and established, such as Isaac Julien and Yinka Shonibare, linked by their varied diasporic experiences. It stands as a beacon of clarity for the impact of migration on cross cultural exchange, exposing the confusion and contradictions in Venice, the mother of all Biennales, still wedded to the permanent National Pavilion.

Collaborating with the artist Almudena Romero, Saye used wet plate collodion tintype, a traditional photographic process imbued with nineteenth century western narratives and forged a contemporary transnational feminist and emancipatory art. She wrote 'the work explores Gambian spirituality that transcends specific religion and locale through the nineteenth century process.' It became her medium through which a black woman's life of Gambian ritual and belief, of purifying baptism, is re-enacted through the physical process of submerging the plate into silver nitrates, with no final control of the outcome. It is a scandalous national outrage that *Dwelling* became the artist's memorial. Khadija Saye died, with her mother Mary Mendy, in the Grenfell Tower fire, London 15 June 2017. She lived on the twentieth floor of the unfit social housing block with the many other immigrant families and unknown numbers of friends and relatives who lost their lives. She was born in 1992 in London and came from a multifaith and multicultural background; she attended a Catholic school in London and was awarded a scholarship to Rugby, a top UK private boarding school. After a degree in photography and work with PEER, one of London's successful small independent galleries, Saye achieved a social mobility which eludes many young Britons. This has profound implications for the cohesion of British society. It is one of the widespread factors for the rise and success of the populist surge which has weakened left and centre political parties in the West and shaken the arts world.

The contemporary visual arts, in particular, has long proclaimed its concern with issues of equality, identity, race and gender, but often fails to acknowledge that this is from a privileged and conflicted position, that of an educated elite whose universalist values are at odds with nationalist and, importantly, the communitarian narratives of family, religion, place and tradition which the right has harnessed with such devastating success. The internationalism and liberal values of contemporary art cannot comfortably confront populism when the art world is not only awash with laundered money, but it is dominated by internationalist, rootless people who flock to Venice and countless other Biennials worldwide, those who David Goodhart has defined as 'the 5 per cent belonging to the more extreme sub-group that I call Global Villagers'. Even the relatively poor and nomadic artist is compromised; dependent less on the public purse, than on patronage from these globetrotting collectors, private institutional grandees and their favoured curators. The art world overall has always been particularly self-satisfied about its left leaning empathies, but the shock of the seismic swing to the right in the US and Europe has been a wake-up call. How deep is our knowledge of and empathy for the real causes of the populist revolt? Viewing the Biennale through the lens of current political conditions not only stiffens the heart and mind against art's more self-regarding tendencies, but throws into question the paradoxes and confusions of the Biennale project. How far does the Venice Biennale 2017 reflect on an urgent and troubling political reality, or have artists and curators retreated to an Art which Christine Macel describes as 'the last bastion, a garden to cultivate above and beyond trends and personal interests'? The works and shows that do stand out as relevant and compelling are those that are not circumscribed by the Biennale thematic.

This year there are, in effect, two Biennales; that of Macels' Biennale Exhibition spread over nine 'Trans-Pavilions' in the Giardini and the vast colonnaded Arsenale and that of the independent eighty six National Pavilions and the twenty three collateral events staged throughout the city of Venice. The processional route of the Giardini gardens is headed by the French, British and German Pavilions and crowned by the elevated neo classical portico of the British Pavilion. Macel's vision seems to float free, in a bubble of undaunted optimism, curiously detached from the National Pavilions' more sober presentations. These are most brutally epitomised by the performance piece in the fascist architecture of the German Pavilion. *Faust* is a dystopic nightmare; outside chained and caged snarling Doberman Pinscher dogs, inside, gaunt and pale faced goths, youths of indeterminate gender, howl, crouch and make violent, vaguely drug induced movements between and under dangerous glass screens, thrilling and threatening the audience like beasts in a zoo. The artist, Anne Imhof won the Biennale Golden Lion.

Paolo Baratta describes Macel's exhibition as an epic poem in nine chapters beginning with a prologue, *The Pavilion of Artists and Books* which sets the scene of over reaching ambition with the 'dialectic that involves the whole of contemporary society, beyond the artist himself, and addresses the organization of society and its values', and then proceeds to take the viewer into the internal worlds of the artist's studio. This philosophical dwelling on the enquiries, roles and values of the artist feels over determined when the art speaks for itself, or not. The room devoted to the *Skoobs* of the British artist John Latham (1921-2006), plaster objects embedded with books from Latham's universal metaphysical cosmology, is for most viewers bewilderingly elusive. In contrast, the exquisite diairies of Abdullah Al Saadi, born 1967 in Khorfakkan (United Arab Emirates) where he lives and works, immediately captivate, even though they are written in Arabic which will be read by few visitors. These small notebooks and rolls kept in sardine and tobacco tins are influenced by the artist's study of the meticulous nihonga painting tradition in Japan, redolent of nature, ancient place, tradition and memory. Al Saadi is no outsider artist and he is internationally exhibited and celebrated, but his work is exceptional; it is rooted in his culture and identity, speaking to the values of place, home and community. Another artist who embraces and lives her heritage, wearing her identity, is Taus Makhacheva, born in Russia in 1983 and living in Dagestan. Makhacheva's family roots are in the Avar ethnic group of the Caucasus. *Tightrope 2015*, is based on the collection of the Dageston Museum of Fine Arts and is an enthralling, if nail biting video of a famous local tightrope walker as he carries sixty-one large paintings, one by one, from one mountain top to another. As the artist writes, it is 'a half-seen, levitating, weird regional art history', with all the poetry of forgotten narratives that enshrines.

After the integrity of these works, what are we to make of the project of Olafur Eliasson? Born 1967, Eliasson lives and works in Berlin and Copenhagen and has brought his internationally feted collective studio practice to the heart of the Biennale Exhibition with *Green light- An artistic workshop*. Viewers can look down at a hive of activity where tables are set up for invited refugees, migrants and asylum seekers to make clunky polyhedral lamps from recycled materials. The lamps are on sale at €250 for charity. In January an African refugee drowned in the Grand Canal and was filmed by tourists who did nothing to save him. Eliasson's project of welcome and support is undoubtedly an act of recompense, as Venice's history as city of sanctuary becomes threatened, but it comes at a cost. An exhibition is always a site of spectatorship and it is questionable whether refugees are appropriate subjects. More persuasive and challenging for the spectator as a response to the rise of populist nationalism and its Kafkaesque impacts, are two independent projects which tackle the issue head on. NSK (*Neue Slowenische Kunst*, or New Slovenian Art), was created by artists in 1984 when Slovenia was part of Yugoslavia. After the break-up of Yugoslavia, NSK State was set up in 1992 as a fictional state without borders. There are over 15,000 NSK passport holders throughout the world. NSK State even issues postage stamps. For the 2017 Biennale, the NSK collective IRWIN commissioned curators and the Turkish émigré artist Ahmet Ögut who worked with refugees who take the role of 'officers' to set up a National Pavilion, an 'Apology for Modernity'. Showing in a room of 'global disorder' are responses to questions on Europe such as 'what do you want to take with you from the heritage of your own country (as you understand it) to help build a new and better world?' Applicants for the NSK passport are subjected to a bureaucratic trauma of endless absurd physical obstacles, including bouncing off a small trampoline to reach the desk. The project, a 'State-in-Time', is 'a tool to rethink citizenship, common heritage and the purpose of the state. It raises issues that most trouble the political state today – migration, history and identity'. At an NSK Citizens Congress in Lyon 2011, Alexei Monroe said the aim was to make people aware 'that totalitarianism isn't a discrete historical phenomenon which went on from 1933 to 1989 and then it's over so let's have a nice triumph of liberal democracy'. Unfortunately the NSK project has since been hijacked by scammers in Nigeria and Egypt who have issued desperate people with NSK passports, which of course have no official validity. The NSK pavilion, as 'a parallel project in the context of the Biennale', opened in the Palazzo Ca'Tron, Iuav University of Venice with a packed public lecture by NSK citizen Slavoj Žižek. There is no reference to the NSK pavilion in the Biennale *Short Guide*.

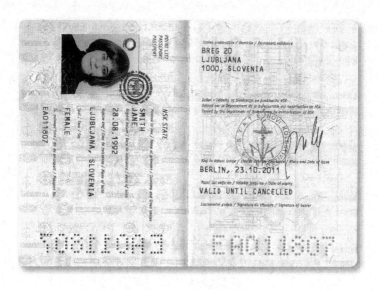

NSK Passport, NSK State Pavilion, Ca'Tron,
IUAV University of Venice, 11 May–15 July 2017

The Tunisian pavilion, Tunisia's first since 1958, is less a long lived conceptual project than a temporary timely intervention, *The Absence of Paths* has three small military style kiosks, one in the Sale d'Armi, the Arsenale, which issue the *Freesa*, a 'universal travel document', a mock passport bearing the inky finger print of each holder. The four anonymous young migrants who man the kiosk, and hand out the cleansing tissues for the fingers of fastidious applicants, were granted visas for one month only by the Italian authorities. The project is a collaboration with MOAS, the Migrant Offshore Aid Station which has helped over 35,000 migrants since it was founded after the Lampedusa tragedy in 2013.

These projects stand against the softly, softly approach of Macel's Biennale Exhibition which claims to take the visitor on 'an experiential journey from interiority to infinity'- like an overpriced course for the late twentieth century self-creating-self. In the *Pavilion of the Shaman* the viewer is introduced to the well-worn idea of the artist as shaman, but with little irony. Participants link hands in *Um Sagrado Lugar,* a large tent installed by Brazilian artist Ernesto Neto, born 1964, where he adopts the 'Cupixawa', a ceremonial place of the Amazonian Huni Kuin Indians complete with shaman. Sadly, it is hard to resist the thought of dressed down hedge fund managers chilling out in Ibiza to the drumbeat as the sun sets on Benirrás beach. The strongest works in the 'Pavilions' have no need of being corralled in these groupings of *Joys and Fears, the Common, the Earth, Traditions, Dionysian, Colors, Time and Infinity*, when their meanings are typically ambiguous and multivalent, eluding such categorisation. This is the dead hand of curatorial sorting out for the viewer which erodes difference and distinction and diminishes the art. The haunted and harrowing large canvases of the late German-Syrian émigré Marwan (1934-2016) loom before the visitor, powerful traditional portraits, testaments of exile, loss – and freedom. They hang in the *Pavilion of Joys and Fears* along with the lush futuristic film animation by the New York artist Rachel Rose, born 1986. In Rose's *Lake Valley 2016*, a little creature, a cross between rabbit and dog wanders, curious and unafraid into a strange fairy garden where even the stones alter shape and substance. This is a cartoon world for real. One which is inhabited by the artist himself in *Laws of Motion in a Cartoon Landscape* by Andy Holden. Holden, born 1982, is showing in the collateral exhibition of the Pinchuk Future Generation Art Prize 2017. Rose and Holden represent a younger, fearless generation who embrace, even relish hybridity and change.

Generations and cultures cross in Macel's *Pavilion of the Common*. The coloured abstract modular structures *Zero into Infinity 1968-2017* by the British artist Rasheed Araeen, born in 1935, have little *in common,* other than Aareen means his sculptures to be interactive and participatory, with *Atrato 2014,* a film of water drumming with expelled Columbian communities by Marcos Ávila Forero, born in 1983. Forero joins the struggle of peoples displaced by armed conflict, while Aareen is making a riposte to the high minded purist aesthetic of American minimalism. In art historical and cultural respects these two works are poles apart. The curatorial project here is a simplistic attempt to harness art to show detraditionalisation, the losses of identity, culture and community to individual self-interest, market forces and capitalist globalisation. Art is not so easily co-opted. Much international art presented in global Biennales is postmodern and is itself post traditional. It has no sense of place because it could be produced anywhere, and often is, as artists live by taking up paid residencies abroad. A more direct challenge to an international art language and to the impact of what Susan George calls 'casino capitalism' on lives worldwide is the Korean Pavilion exhibition *Counterbalance: The Stone and the Mountain* with works by Cody Choi and Lee Wan. A silent room of six hundred clocks, each engraved with the names, nationalities and occupations of an individual, the hands moving at different rates to set the time it takes for each person to earn enough for a meal: *Proper Time* by Lee Wan, born 1979, is a potent revelation of the inequalities of production and consumption. Cody Choi's work rejects sentimental nostalgia for home and country and confronts the reality of being in the schizoid gap between cultures where identity becomes provisional and conflicted. His *Venetian Rhapsody, The Power of Bluff* mocks the art world's complicity with the commercial circus which is now Venice and calls the lie to the delusions of Asian emulation of the West. A riotous rooftop forest of neon signs and

Lee Wan b. 1979, Seoul, *Proper Time* 2017
Installation, Korean Pavilion, Giardini, Venice

hoardings, the images from two cities, west and east, Las Vegas and Macao, stand as paradigms of fantasies about western culture and Americanisation. Choi, born in 1961, a Korean immigrant to the US who returned to live in Korea, writes that his work 'suggests that casino capitalism signals the death of art, but also presages a new kind of hope for its resurrection in the era of speculation and excess.'

That hope takes a battering from an alternative attraction which is stealing visitors from the Biennale shows. Damien Hirst's audacious two site *Treasures from The Wreck of the Unbelievable* is presented in The Palazzo Grassi and the Punta Della Dogana. It is a Disneyesque immersion, a story of exotic wealth accumulated by an ancient potentate, a freed slave whose ship sunk with all its treasures in the Indian Ocean and which were dredged up from the seabed, encrusted with corals in 2008. Hirst's vast and costly show parodies the desire for gold (the Collector), authority (the Museum) and the semblance of authenticity (the Market). This 'post truth' extravaganza, a confection of false history, fake materials and objects, overproduced to maximise sales, is a remarkable achievement, the culmination of ten years work with teams of technicians and artisans. It has divided critical opinion. Perhaps the most perceptive comment is made by a British artist born in 1974 showing in the Grenada Pavilion. Jason deCaires Taylor first began making sculptures underwater in the Caribbean island where I met him in 2004. His aim was to draw attention to the fragility of the marine environment. He says of Hirst: 'his marine facsimiles are very different in context from my living installations...nature does not lie'.

In the year of the centenary of the October Revolution in Russia, perhaps the most relevant exhibition showing in Venice is the exhibition of the Moscow based V-A-C Foundation which launches in Venice its first permanent public venue in the Palazzo delle Zattere. Presenting early twentieth century Russian art, *Space Force Construction*, is a lesson in history, art and ideology and, through the lens of contemporary artists, a warning. The opening had a performance by the Biennale artist Taus Makhacheva evoking the starvation of millions through Soviet policies in the 1930s. Uniformed girls serve toffee lollipops in the shape of Lenin's head. The US artist Barbara Kruger responds to a multimedia construction conceived by the propaganda artist Gustav Klutsis in 1922 with texts, which she notes, 'loiter around ideas of power, control and the grotesqueries of dominance'. Wolfgand Tillmans, the German photographer, who is a significant voice for European transnational inclusion, shows an image of a vast agitated ocean, *The State We're In, A* 2015.

While Macel's 2017 Biennale Exhibition has some arresting works, it is overall a lost opportunity. I have two enduring images of the Biennale. Phyllida Barlow's British Pavilion, transformed by her raucous colour and fearless use of stuff of poor materials - cardboard, wood, concrete, scrim, plastic bin bags; the vast sculptures' huge and jagged ledges and ash grey towers now take on a more sinister cast. She talks of hoardings, evisceration: 'Something that is foolhardy, or stupid, something that is a pretence...' She called the work *Folly. The Golden Tower* 1990, by the legendary US artist James Lee Byars (1932–1997) has been fabricated by Italian gilders and realised for the first time for a public space, standing triumphant in the quieter canal side of the Guidecca. Byars' vision of his twenty metre Tower was as a glorious light between heaven and earth, uniting the world. In 2017 it seems to parody, a tawdry high rise, a monument to power, hubris and indifference.

THE INGRATE

Hasan Manzar

At the age of 22, I travelled to those regions of the world that I had read about, and heard about since childhood; how strange and novel their ways of life were! That included the people of Pacific Islands, extreme north and extreme south of India, the inhabitants of thick African jungles and gypsies from Alaska to Siberia.

I had been reading that somewhere women fought the wars. Not with their mouth, but with arms, legs and weapons. I used to fantasise about their men sitting at home and waiting for their women's return in the evenings.

Margaret Mead and her team, after devoting a lifetime in those islands, discovered that where women were the warriors, men took care of the children; to what extent? That was not clear.

In some places, the families consumed the body of their dead, in others vultures and jackals did. The head of the family among Eskimos transferred near-death loved ones to a custom-made igloo at a distance, constructed with large ice blocks replicating the original house of the dying. A furry animal skin served as the deathbed. The entrance to the igloo would then be sealed and everyone returned to his or her home. They would come back on a particular day, when they were confident that the dying was dead. Just to make sure.

The relentless curiosity behind my wanderlust also sought small details, which travellers and anthropologists forgot to note down. For instance, what was done to the dead-body in that doorless igloo? Did they eat it themselves or did it become food for bears and wolves after customary rituals, as it happens in our case. Or, did they dig a hole in the thick ice floor and slid it down for seals, etc. so that they could gulp it along with its soul – to save it from wandering aimlessly.

There were places where they would not touch any kind of meat including that of locust. Elsewhere, every kind of flesh was relished and all kinds of monkeys elaborately so. But this was when I had become a tourist. Since it has been mentioned, let me describe it.

First, the monkey is dipped in boiling water in an iron drum. Then it is shaved with the blunt edge of the butcher's chopper before it becomes entitled to be cooked with red chillies and African spices. The next stage is laying it down in the middle of the diners. All eyes ogle the steaming dead body but no one reaches for it – until when? Until the head of the family smashes the head of the monkey and eats out the brain to his heart's content, because he has the sole rights to the whole brain. In other words, in that culture the brain has the same status as it has in those countries where science and technology prevails. After that, everybody pounces on boiled rice – or mashed yam – with the monkey, until the end of the feast, when young and old, men and women get up. Without leaving any traces of the monkey, not even its skin. Like us, they don't waste food.

Wild rodents are savoured with simplicity and contentment; python, or any other healthy snake, with greater relish. One wild mouse with rice or mashed cassava could feed two or three, and was often roasted on fire where its tail disappeared in the process of cooking – depriving all the others.

*

This variegation of the world tempted me to see it, although during that period these words about my penchant did not come to mind. Later on, not fortresses, palaces, cathedrals, temples, pagodas, tombs and skyscrapers, or theatres, stores overflowing with expensive goods bathed in spectacular lighting appealed to me. And those bazaars with narrow streets not at all, where overdone women came out on balconies every evening. I was never interested in all this. For me, the humble village mosque still holds more attraction than the marble and redbrick worship places built by kings.

Long ago, when I buried myself in my favourite books and wondered about how human life in different places went on, restiveness spurred me, which I could not clearly identify.

In Tibet, Brahmaputra flows a thousand or two thousand feet below in the Himalayan valleys. On both sides of the ascending hills of the valley, people have constructed homes in the rocks. The outer structures extending from the caves are perched as if floating in the air. How did people live in them? They must be celebrating weddings, births and funerals. How was it possible? I wanted to go and see for myself. I was not aware of the word 'tourism' then.

As I grew older, my mind started warning me: 'If you get caught in this whirl, you will lose your life. Get married, become a family man. Lead a respectable life; you may even end up in politics one day!' After all, I was a rising sun of a land-owning family.

I wouldn't blame the one I loved, who had initiated then confessed her love, of ditching me. We both were of same age. What happened is that she grew up faster, and left for her in-laws to spend her life with someone else; sobbing? I don't know. For those few days, I disappeared. She never turned to ask, 'How are you? Do you ever miss me?'

I could never bring myself to spend my life with anyone else.

However, a new world of attractions started opening up; that of thousand shades of people's devotion, of worries, fear, daring and rituals to win over the gods. Sometimes, after committing a sinful act, one went to the centre of the village for a life offering for one's redemption. An adultery committed during the day was a 'ram', during night a 'rooster'. Many acts are not as bad at night as they are when committed during the day. Its nature's concession for man – a discount!

I should have mentioned this incident earlier, but I forgot. I was very small, so much so that I still slept with my mother. However, I listened intently to women's gossips.

One night, when mother and father were talking at a normal voice, I heard a strange story about a woman. I had never seen that woman, and neither had my parents I suspect, because there was no mention of 'so-and-so's mother, or so-and-so's daughter-in-law'. She must have been an outsider, but what she had done was known all over. She did not have children, which wasn't unusual. Some had, some didn't. But my mind was bursting with curiosity even then. Once I asked my mother in the presence of women.

'How come, those who have husbands have children and those who don't have husbands don't have children?'

The ceremonies of; engagement; the adorning of yellow dress few days before wedding; the wedding occasion itself; the birth of a child; and the routine of quarrels between husbands and wives was a constant theme – always in the air!

'She left no stone unturned in order to get pregnant.' Mother was saying about that woman. She spared no doctor, tomb, amulet or recitation of Koranic verses by young mothers who had delivered within the first year of marriage. Above all, she gathered the grain from pigeon feed that people brought to the Mecca mosque courtyard and which came with the broom while sweeping. Father was saying that she grounded and ate the bread she made from that leftover pigeon-feed for ten days.

'Her husband thrashed her frequently. Sometimes he threw her out of the house at night and locked the door.' I started crying when I heard this and was scared too. I wondered how scared the poor woman must have been on the street at night, all alone. Stray dogs must have surrounded and barked at her, the way I was caught among them once and was rescued by other pedestrians.

'One day when her husband wasn't home, she took a bath with buckets full of water. Without drying herself, she went and sat on the holy book - naked!' said father while mother muttered words seeking forgiveness from the Almighty. That scared me even more.

'Who could have taught her that kind of satanic ritual?'

When the husband returned in the evening, he had to knock on the door for a long time. Eventually, he broke it down, because she wouldn't open it. There was no one inside. When he entered the room, he found a scared saw staring at him. He shooed it away and it ran out as soon as he stepped away from the entrance. No one could grab it.

'God is forgiving. She was innocent.' Mother repeated these words as she wept.

'There was soaked open book on a book-rest placed on a wooden platform.'

'Please, say no more, for God's sake!' Mother pleaded.

I think, that night I slept hugging mother more tightly than ever before. For years I could not get the thought out of my mind that every saw seen in the sweepers' neighbourhood was once a woman.

I fantasised that the Pacific islands overflow with wonders. You find a new shape of human being anywhere you go. I believe the animals there too live and behave in ways that would leave our tigers, monkeys, bears and hyenas dumbfounded.

Jim Corbett, who spent major part of his life in Himalayan jungles and wrote books about them, mentioned a tribe in one of his books, who lived in a novel way. I don't remember the details but that the men worked in the fields and orchards and women looked after the home. Men made the rocky land fit for cultivation. They ploughed, spread seeds and watered the crops. And probably also brought water home. Chopping firewood and delivering it home was also one of his responsibilities. When the women announced that food was ready, the unfortunate man would bring two utensils and wait outside the door. He would do the same thing even when he was inside the house; pick up his empty dishes and stand outside the door for food. The woman would put food in the dishes and he would sit at the doorstep to eat. Then he would gargle; drink water which she had poured while hovering over him, carefully, so that the utensils did not clatter. The manner of feeding was the same, probably during lightning or torrential rains.

He would go back to work after the meal. If times favoured, he would go inside and lie down on the bare cot. To call him man-of-the-house would be as foolish as calling a beggar a bard. The woman wouldn't be surprised if she found him in her bed at night, nor he would be surprised to find her in his cot.

Corbett might have tolerated this strange way of life a couple of times, then questioned: why so? Why don't you eat with your wife and children? How can she eat inside the house while you sit outside like a beggar or a hired hand!

'We are beggars and servants after all.' Someone quipped.

That is when a sane man revealed the story behind it.

Generations earlier, all the men were killed in a battle. Only women were left. Why would men from other casts marry them? Even though, she was willing to accommodate him at her home. That is when they decided to tie the knot with their employee farmers, who obeyed as a command from the mistress.

'We all belong to a lower cast, including me, and when summoned we come to the door to receive our food from the mistress. We do, however, have the permission to spend the night inside the house.'

Those days, Margaret Mead, Beach & Ford, Kipling, Corbett, Anderson, they all tempted me to get out of home and see the world. Go and verify if what they have written was true. Why go on living in the same place with eternally same ceremonies for death, marriage and religious festivals; like watching an old movie released every year for a few days; in which every scene has been seen a hundred times. The film would conclude on tragedy or repentance followed by an embrace!

The food consisted of the same fare: beef or mutton, vegetables or lentils, bread or rice. My heart and mind craved novelty. My mind could offer only one option to forget Zardozi; to leave home. Who knows how many tribes I would discover that even Margaret Mead and Corbett had not met? I did find novelty. Not on every step of my journey though, but after wandering hundreds of miles and confronting sky high lashing waves in small and large boats.

I can see that place where a priest was being buried, upright, in salt, inside a square well. That is, bags full of salt were heaped around him until the hole was full. They explained that others were submitted to the river.

'Don't you burn them?' I asked.

'There is no firewood. Our cooking is also done on dry leaves and grass.'

My question remained unanswered: why salt? And where does the salt come from? Just like Margaret Mead and her team did not explain what those warrior women in the Pacific islands did when there was no war to fight. Did she become a woman or remained as a man?

For instance, I read that in New Guinea, when the hair begin to sprout on the upper lip of a boy i.e. he approaches adolescence, a grownup man introduces him to having sex with a woman by subjecting him to sodomy. A grown-up man introduces him to sex life but the training to it is the homosexual way with the trainee playing the passive role. It is not concealed from men; however, it is assumed that women remain unaware of this moment of manhood for the boy. This form of education probably continues for a year, and is considered normal part of life and believed that the boy acquired strength. There is another tradition linked to this one. The boy is fed lemons to prevent him from becoming pregnant! In a year's time he qualifies to teach new young boys that lesson until he himself acquires a wife. Neither the society shows any remorse or the women object to this practice. But, as usual, I could not overlook the question as to what does an adolescent girl had to go through in that society? Perhaps I have not been able to find out. Perhaps the men in that society were kept in the dark about coming of age for women, just like the women were kept ignorant about the boys. Perhaps the men just pretended not to know. I think instead of lemon, the girl might have been fed with pineapple. My curiosity in this other side of the gender divide remained.

I have also rowed in a flat tin bottomed boat to a place where a woman, after day long warring, returns home to cook dinner for her son out in the square. The food always consisted of boiled rice and dates. That habitation was surrounded by such disorderly streams that each one seemed to flow in a direction of its own choice; while concealing mud and stone pikes here and there under their surface.

More than a hundred years earlier, the young and old of that region fought the cartridge rifles of the British with their long barreled guns that used square pellets and gunpowder – till the end. They loved their land so much. When they exhausted their pellets and last pinch of gunpowder, and the enemy was too far for hand to hand combat, they all turned in the direction of Ka'ba and touched the ground with their forehead.

'Who is the woman who did the cooking?' No one could tell. 'Don't the dogs and crows eat that food?' They all shook their heads in unison. They all walked along with me as if anticipating some gain. The women peeped from doors. Probably I was the first stranger to come there.

Near a dilapidated mosque, there were some caved-in graves too. A clay dish was placed on a sill. I asked the youth walking shoulder to shoulder with me.

'Is this the dish in which food for the returning soldier is placed?'

He responded with gestures that it could be. The crows sitting on a tree branch were quietly staring at me. I felt that the dish wasn't empty, but the crows showed little interest. Before arriving there, I had heard that on the last day of the battle when the remaining fighters prostrated, the vultures on the surrounding trees had fled away and were never seen there again. I moved on with an incomplete story. I could not find what happened to that food? Perhaps they expected me to eat that food on

behalf of the soldier who never came back. His return would amount to
the return of all of them.

I saw a lot more. I went to Chile and Argentina. I went to the Congo
basin, the thick forests on the banks of Aravadi, Andaman, wandered
through countless Pacific islands. I went wherever my resources and
youthful fervor took me. Every unique custom and novelty was preserved
in my mind and is still there. Except for one region, which I want to forget
and which buried my desire to see the world – forever.

It was a vast region. In a way, it was snatched away from the desert by
nature, because a wide river flowed right through its middle and the
tributaries had cultivated miles of jungles. Rain and floods left behind lakes
full of fish and blind dolphins. Small clusters of population, interlinked
tribes, were scattered all over. There were thickly populated towns, but as
I have mentioned, I was interested in the villages, or those forest dwellers
that had their own language. It seemed the dialect changed every ten or
twenty miles, and so did their social rituals; if they had any.

I infiltrated a tribe who was neither interested in any kind of agriculture
or animal farming. As if they were living in paradise and not on earth
where food came to them without effort. They were neither quarrelsome
nor worrier like. They just sat around the entire day, like the Arapesh of
New Guinea; silent men and women lazing here and there. But, they cared
for each other, were kind to the children and incase of illness they would
carry the patient for miles to the far flung town healer.

However, another tribe had a completely different way of life. It was a
small tribe spread over a large area. They all belonged to one cast. Being
located at the basin of that wide river, they had plenty of water but did
little cultivation themselves than their employees, who also were of the
same cast. Since the land was fertile, they said it needed very little labour.
They also had places of worship, along with tombs and shrines of
prominence for people of status, or those supposed to have a direct link
with God. Only the dead deserved such honour. As in the case of Egyptian
pyramids, this treatment was not likely to be bestowed on every dead.

These people were cordial. However, in spite of being one tribe and cast,
they were hopelessly divided in different families. It was a taboo for a girl
from one family to be enamoured by a boy from another. And the boy, who

was categorised as belonging to another village, if found lurking around the house of a girl, was struck by as if a heavenly curse within no time.

They considered themselves better than the rest of the world. Their world was limited to the territory between the barren lands and the river. They would extol love, but always be ready to annihilate each other. Something like Margaret Mead's Mondugamurs and like those mentioned by Richard Burton; but the latter were eunuchs – 'Agha'.

Passing through these tribes, I came to a community about which few others knew, or shrank from talking about it. In a way they were isolated from the world. Only one shopkeeper agreed to reply to my question.

'They have taught a wrong lesson to the whole world.'

'What lesson?' he responded by turning away to a customer talking about tobacco prices; pretending as if I wasn't there.

The men in that community did farming and lived a regular life outside home. In case of war, they fought themselves. Their women did not bring guns and swords to fight. There was nothing alarming about them except that the women stayed at home and kept the men away in jungle, farm or whatever, where men lived and performed all manly chores. It was a community where women brought up their male child away from home in the jungle. His marriage and demise also happened outdoors. The anthropologist in me was intrigued by this news.

I assumed that among the buildings, shops and teahouses, there would be a hotel for me to stay. A 'hotel' was the name given to the teahouses; a small tin-roofed room, shutter-less and with brick platform on which water and milk remained steaming. Close by, men sat on benches quietly, or bragging. I wanted to stay there for a week or so, if I could find a place to stay. I wasn't going to live in the jungle like other men. The gadflies and fleas would have turned me into a skeleton overnight! Not to mention the snakes. I didn't enquire about lodging facilities, and none of the women on the street agreed to offer me a place in her home. What was all this? Some form of family-planning to control the population?

I wandered to a group of a dozen men sitting under the shadow of a tree. They were sitting on the ground with a kind of rope which strapped their bent knees to their stomach. The rope was their twisted shawl I found out later. They were muttering words like 'lawyer', 'judge', and 'detention'; as if they were all stuck in litigation. I shook hands with all of them and sat down and extended my packet of cigarettes towards them. In return they took out their cigarettes or cheroot. I had savoured Burmese cheroots and cigars from the West Indies, so I didn't see any danger trying out their variety of smoke. The first puff sent me into a coughing spasm. They were spitting out behind their backs. They were curious about me and I was interested in them. They anted to know who I was and how did I get there. More importantly, why? Because only they must be going to other villages and towns for their needs and only a lost soul like me could have ventured to their abode.

I put forward my questions apprehensively, the gist of which was: why was their life different from other tribes and since how long? They laughed and looked into each other's eyes for quite a while. I became uncomfortable and regretful about my questions.

I offered them my cigarettes again. Without accepting them, a shrewd old man.

'You won't understand, because there is nothing to understand.' He continued, 'What you consider a jungle is the home. And what you call home is the jungle.' Adding with bitterness, 'Women's jungle.'

Shifting in his place, another man said, 'We are all same. We live where we were born. We were born in the jungle and have always been here. The women were born at home and live there. The only difference is that we don't stop them from coming to the jungle, but they do not allow us to cross the threshold of the home.'

'If we feel the need of a woman, we can't go there.' A young man said with a chuckle. 'But when the woman needs a man, she comes willingly and lies down with her man; out of others view, of course, not in front of them. That is the bone of contention between us.'

'They don't want to live with the men, that is all.' The old man stood up dusting his cloths. The others followed suite and dispersed in the fields.

I could conclude only one thing from the meeting; either such issues were of no interest to them, or too painful to talk about.

I had with me baked potatoes, roasted chickpeas and parched rice. My mind was working against my wishes. What is all this? Where have I landed; where men are afraid of women!

I could see people working in the fields at a distance. A man had climbed a tree and was chopping its branches. Two men were busy making objects from split wood. At another spot a metal worker was beating the bottom of a cauldron overturned on burning fire. A man was sitting under a shed smoking *chilam* — a waterpipe. All of them were away from the built area, as if they were lepers. No one was interested in me, not even the occasional passerby.

I washed my hands, feet and face at a narrow stream, sprayed salt on the baked potatoes and planned to leave that place before nightfall. I was going to take away along with me the unsolved riddle of the locality. It would be better to bury it in my mind. Otherwise I would have only rice and chickpeas in the company of hefty mosquitoes for the night.

Suddenly, as if nature took pity on me as I lied dozing on the grass. I saw a girl of about eight trying to wake me up.

'*Baba*, mother is calling you.' I imagined that would be an elderly woman.

'Me? Your mother?' she replied in affirmative to both questions. I gathered my belongings and followed her.

I don't think I was happy, but rather afraid of a disaster she might inflict on me. All the women of this tribe struck me like those from New Guinea who left their men at home to look after the children while they got hold of cane spears and iron prongs to fight the enemy. Would this mother assign me to baby sit? It would be better if she would order me to stand outside her door to dish out some food for me.

On first sight the woman looked old, but I changed my mind quickly as an inner voice said, 'She is ageless.' She opened the door and sat down in a cane armchair, right there. I stood two steps below under the sun. The little girl who had fetched me, stood behind what could have been her mother, grandmother or whatever. There were other women around, in doorways, windows and walking past me, but they had no interest in me. The one who had summoned me, neither asked me in or offered anything to eat or drink.

Our conversation came to the subject for which I had come. She asked nothing about my family or was interested whether I had children or not, nor in what I did. She was interested to know what had I come to see. 'Who told you to come here? Nobody comes here.'

I had to muster enough courage to reply. 'I have come to see this strange world where women stay at home and men in the jungle. As to who sent me; this did, who keeps me exploring strange things.' I pointed my right forefinger to my temple. 'I heard from people in far flung cities....'

'That there is such a tribe where women do not want to stay with men.' She completed my sentence. 'It has not always been like this.' She closed her eyes and shook her head. Her face reflected her timeworn age. She ordered her daughter, granddaughter or whatever, in her tongue who brought some sort of a drink which I gulped in single breath. At that moment she looked like an ever young woman.

'Repeat your question,' she said.

I replied obediently that I was interested in travelling to various countries to see how their way of life was different than others. She mumbled a long sound without opening her lips, picked the cigarette packet from her lap extending it towards me with a jerk. I thanked her and gave her mine, 'Keep it.'

She lit her cigarette and, as if, exploded. Her low voice ended, the softness her expression vanished and was replaced by hatred peeping through her mask of wrinkles. The girl nodded her head on every word, so did other women who had gathered around.

'Because we hate them; the old, young and the very young; all of them. We give birth but we see them as baby snakes. That is our faith.'

'How about nursing babies, they would be staying at home, right?'

'Even nursing babies. Since a few years there is no woman has delivered a single baby at home, therefore, there is no question of keeping him at home.' She said it like announcing a verdict in a court.

I found myself unable to articulate my question. 'And the baby girl?' I was afraid she might end this interview.

'A baby girl is shown to the sun, whenever it rises, and then brought home.'

'And a boy is left there even if he is devoured by a snake or scorpion?'

'The place of delivery is sealed from all sides. That is where he is brought up.'

'And his needs?'

'His feeding, toilet, bathing and changing all are handled by the mother over there, not at home.'

After an awkward silence, I asked with a suppressed smile, 'If a man and woman warm up to each other, what then?' They all tried to conceal their smiles.

'She can go to her man at night, or even during the day.'

'Her man?'

'Yes. She retains only one man.'

I wanted to ask what if he wishes to exceed the one spouse rule! But it would have been like touching a beehive, so I said instead.

'Is this how it has always been?'

'No.'

'Then how did it happen so. Who started it?'

All the women present looked at her anxiously. She held the arm of a middle aged woman turning her towards me.

'Her young daughter was shot dead by the father.'

'Why?'

'Because she was adamant to choose her own husband, whereas the father had already promised his friend who was older than himself! Like an empty pot in the house for him to implant what he wished to propagate, if he is man enough.' She went on, 'Then he went to the police station, placed the gun in front of the officer and said uprightly, "I have shot my daughter, because she was promiscuous and shamelessly confessed of having given her heart to another man".'

The officer was son of the same soil, he respectfully asked him to sit down. When he returned home, gun in hand, all the men and boys were awe struck as if a hero had returned from war.

The elders were wondering, and the children followed suit. 'What will happen to '*kavvi*' (female crow)? Will she be taken to be put in the ground?' Only the mother and sisters were weeping, out of men's sight. Only the grandmother spoke out.

'That has been going on forever, whether you weep or kill yourself.'

Then she called a young woman by name. She came forward and started crying. Two women in the crowd blurted in unison, 'But she had long forgotten how to cry!'

The old woman gently stroked the young witness's head saying, 'Her old, shrivelled mother-in-law was shot dead by her own son (this young woman's husband), because she admonished him for drunkenness and his losing all family assets in gambling. She advised him to get hold of himself.'

'How will you face God after you die?' she said to her son.

'You will answer Him for me,' he had replied.

When she fell, he blurted out, 'She is not even good enough to be earning a few pennies, what would she do by staying alive anyway.'

The young woman started sobbing saying, 'I couldn't even save her…' and walked out.

It looked like one witness at a time was being presented to the court which constituted of one person; the old woman sitting in cane armchair. She was the prosecutor, defence, judge and the executioner. It was hard for me to tell her age. I saw a strange thing on her face; simultaneous expression of conflicting emotions. Motherly affection accompanied with outrage of a victim; love and indignation. To me she looked maiden, as well as elderly. I am using 'elderly' for her – old woman.

'Her daughter, mother of three one of them still being breastfed, was killed by her husband through his brother. The brother who was known for having a camel sitting in his head. This halfwit swore on the holy book in front of the village elders to have seen his sister-in-law with another man in the sunflower fields.'

'Seen doing what?'

'Breastfeeding! There was no one around.' Everyone laughed, including the judge.

'Her child?' asked the judge.

'No. That man.' They laughed again. When they finished laughing, the judge asked.

'Why did you not kill the man?'

'My brother didn't tell me to.'

'But he was there?' asked the judge.

'I don't think so.' Replied the dimwit, and the defence lawyer added, 'He probably ran away.' The judge admitted the argument. No one bothered to ask what the fault of the killed woman was.

'The truth was that the man had a chronic disease in his groins and genitalia, no woman let him come near her because of his repulsive ailment. When his secret was revealed he accused the woman for making it with another man. So killing her became a matter of honour for him. The woman went into shock when she heard this and told her mother that her days were numbered.' Several other women told her to run away.

'With who? Where? I don't know anyone outside this village.'

'Wherever.' They replied.

'When it comes to killing a woman, the men keep their promise. They don't back out from it. The honour issue is considered a bigger crime than burning a ready harvest in animosity. Crops can bloom again, but a violated honour can never be resurrected. He didn't do it himself, instead had it done by the brother who had a camel sitting in his brain, "Consider it done." The brother had said because his advances were repulsed by his brother's wife earlier.'

'I felled her in one shot!' he announced victoriously after the deed had been done.

'Then?'

'Everybody started calling the dead woman *kavvi* (she-crow-sinner), as the tradition goes.' Said the old woman, as she hugged the other woman.

'What is that?'

'A woman who brings dishonour to her man.' Replied one of the women present.

'The woman who dies at the hands of her father, uncle, brother or son is referred to as "*kavvi*", as if that was the name given to her at birth.'

'She should be called the wife of black crow.' I said out of irritation.

'Who is that?'

'The wife of cuckoo, who has a sweet voice.' Their faces lit up.

'She doesn't receive a funeral prayer nor has a grave. Some tender hearted people bury her out of pity while earning frowns from the rest. That is why no one from the family of the deceased accompanies the funeral procession.' The woman continued.

'Bloody cowards!' I said. 'But why don't they keep the children at home, what is the fault of those poor creatures?'

'When her mother was widowed, the brothers of the deceased refused her a place at home or to look after her; she was from different a cast... What then?' the old woman gently pulled a young woman while she spoke.

'My mother's son was adopted by his grandfather. My two sisters died in childhood. Later, my mother married my father, secretly. Who would have saved her from other men if she had remained single? He was a labourer laying railway tracks. My father spoke another language, but was very hard working and pious. Mother worked as a labourer at the same site. That is where they first met.'

'They were madly in love with each other. It would be wrong to call it dog like faithfulness,' said the old woman, 'and they moved here.'

'When I was 12 and my brother 10, my mother's elder son came looking for her. Mother was very happy to see her son after a long time and prayed for all those who returned her son all grown up. Father was happy too, and so were both us kids. We had meals together. Mother didn't let me make the bread; she wanted to do it herself for her son. I remember she cooked special vegetables and applied ghee to the bread. After the meal he said "You made me search for you all over the world mother." 'I missed you every day, son. I prayed for your wellbeing before going to sleep,' she reached out to hug him. He held her hand and said, 'I have come here to settle an old debt. No one is willing to give his daughter's hand in marriage until I do so. I am 28. They call me a shameless son of a *kavvi*."

'Mother was startled as if she heard that name for the first time. "As long as he doesn't restore the honour of the tribe, he can go to the sluts; we have nothing to do with him".'

The old woman shook her head saying slowly, 'He doesn't marry anyone from the whorehouse, but wants the one he fancies to remain faithful to him so that no other man could touch her. And if she didn't obey, he would throw acid on her face justifying it as a matter of honour.' There was silence for a while.

'What happened then?' The old woman addressed the younger one.

'Mother tried to free her hand sensing danger.'

'I had been hearing this silently since I was 18. Grandpa was dead. Uncles said what they could do. They had young daughters but were not willing to marry any of them with me. When I asked them what they wanted me to do, my eldest uncle said, "Go and find that she-crow and kill her, him too she is living with shamelessly. Then you can choose any of my nieces for your wife." I have been looking for you since that day. Mother freed herself from his grip and ran to the door in terror. My father leapt to grab the bamboo with sharp sickle affixed at one end, but before he could reach for it that murderer shot my mother – his mother – and then shot father – my father. No one had seen the gun or where it came from before that. Before mine and my brother's turn, neighbours barged in and he ran away shooting in the air. He must have earned his woman.' She wailed.

'Have you heard? If feeding and bringing up a snake is a kindness; not keeping him away is foolishness.' Added the old woman.

'Keeping him away forever? Is he never allowed inside the house?' I asked.

'He can come inside the house — after his death.' Interjected another woman at a queue from the old woman.

'How is that?'

'He is readied for burial outside in the jungle then carried by the women to the house. So that he knows that was the home he was kicked out from.' The old woman and I chuckled together.

The crowd inside had thinned out. The women were in their own respective dwellings where smoke was rising. One could make out from women's comments that it was meal time, more importantly; it was time to send food to their men. Even my exhausted brain could figure out that they were not coming to collect their food or eat at the threshold of the house. Little girls and women would carry the food to the brink of the farms where the men would collect. I had watched old men and boys leaving firewood and farm produce when the old woman presented them one by one.

'Doesn't a woman ever tell her son to shoot his father?' I asked.

'He is her husband. If he is killed, her fields would become barren. Her world would come to an end.'

'Doesn't the marriage of the man become barren when he has his wife killed?'

She gave me a kind of look which seemed to ask, 'How old are you?'

'There is nothing auspicious in marriage for a man. He merely acquires a wife.'

It was dusk and I was famished. Far off, where the sky met the earth, there was still enough redness that if I started walking I could make it to somewhere where men and women lived together; and women were not under constant threat of being killed any moment. Even after a night of lovemaking, she could not be sure what would come over him in the morning, which drives him to shoot the body he cherished. I could still make it to a place where a nursing mother did not carry the fear in her heart of being shot dead by those little hands of her son she kissed, one day. And not even bother to bury her afterwards. A place, where a growing girl playfully teasing her brother was not fearful of one day being shot by him.

Disorganised thoughts floated in my mind like wool pecks under sunlight beams. My mind grumbled, 'A female never feels completely safe with her male. Like a cat about her mate after laying kittens.' Since childhood, I had been listening to cat cries following her wailing to protect the kittens through the night.

The old woman was lying down with her eyes closed. I, imagining that she might be tired, thought I should leave. I stood up shaking of dust from my cloths and hands, pulled out chickpeas and roasted rice. Before eating I considered sharing my goodies with that ageless old woman sitting in the wicker armchair who had shown me so many weeping faces. She gestured to stop me from approaching her, and came to the threshold to receive the peas and rice. I chucked some into my mouth and said.

'One last question.'

'You want to know how they got rid of them.'

'Where were their guns and axes from which, not only the young women but grandmothers also, pleaded mercy; for they knew that females could live only as long as they were not accused of tarnishing family honour.'

'Ha!' she busted like a balloon, 'My father was enemy of such ignorance and traditions, which made everybody his enemy. He was spending his remaining days hiding in the jungle where his life would have been in danger if my mother had not guarded him with a gun in her hand. She was a woman of the mountains. All the men drink all kinds of wines; made from dates, barley, sugarcane and, if available, human blood. The more tired they are the more they drink and hang their guns, axes and swords on the walls.'

'On that night, women decided they had spent long enough living under constant fear and could bear no longer, took out the sting of the scorpions.'

As the men staggered out of drunken slumber, they were told, 'Today onwards you are the crow. Women are not crows. That is your world; this is ours.' The woman who declared this first pointed to the jungle and then to the homes. 'You probably know that a quail which loses a fight never faces the defeater again.'

My head dropped with shame. To humour myself I thought: 'You are lucky not to have been born here for you would have to spend all your nights with mosquitoes!'

The old woman was saying, 'The man has never acknowledged the effort, sacrifice, carrying him in her womb, labour pains, nursing and fighting off death day and night; nor rewarded her. A crisis or a difficult moment not only transforms his thinking, but also, as if his brain loses all emotions; as if suddenly all blood is drained out in an instant. At that moment mother is not a mother, daughter is not a daughter and sister is not a sister. And a few days on he is back to his usual self to the extent that if a father brings a new wife for himself the son starts addressing her as "mom". The murderer once again becomes the beloved of all.'

'Someone who has murdered his wife can even find people who would agree to marry their daughter with him!' I said. My question cum statement awakened the same kind of hatred in the old woman as was ignited in me.

A while later I said in a jest, 'And when he loses his head again, every woman appears a slut, for whom the only solution he has is – *shoot*!'

Translated by Imtiaz Piracha

DREAM OF THE FUTURE

Muddasir Ramzan

Sindbad, Hayy bin Yaqzan, Odysseus, Azad, Amir Hamza, Robinson Crusoe, Gulliver, Hatim Tai, Don Quixote, Peter Pan; such characters took him to an expedition – on a journey to the future:

An attractive handmade wall-hanging, richly embroidered in silicon-silk, a masterpiece adorned with a map of the United Kashmir, showing the bloodshot coloured Kashmir transforming into emerald and then sapphire, enveloping the front wall of the embassy of United Kashmir in New York, smugly stares pervasive as if it hides a thousand secrets. The beautiful Vale now enjoys close alliances with its two neighbouring powers, which once controlled it for more than a century. The lay-humans, who fought not with India and Pakistan, but with their circumstances and their representatives, chose to use their energy and support from both the countries to improve themselves. Their intellects, which were caught in the debacle of freedom, made their way to administer their prosperity. Their grown-intellect then changed the future of their land. The description inscribed on the masterpiece below – *To the President of USA, for initiating a process that made the United Kashmir possible* – reflects it as a symbol for the history of Kashmir.

***

Ibrahim was born in early 1970s to a local established contractor. Unlike his two elder brothers he wasn't interested in joining school, despite every effort made by his parents and relatives. For some five years, after his admission in a local school, he was forced to attend classes; but finally when his family and teachers understood that he didn't have education in his fate, they stopped convincing him. He was considered a disgrace to his well-to-do family, not less than an outcast. In the streets, where he mostly spent his time, he was lured by the freedom of the near to the ground youngsters of his town, who in turn desired to belong to a family like his. All the youngsters of the town, who were wasting time in different activities in the streets and the mountain peaks, were shown a direction to earn money in a newly built carpet-centre in their neighbourhood by the government, where they could learn the craft of weaving carpets, become artisans and support their families. When he had nothing to do he too joined the centre and turned into an artisan – a carpet weaver.

His parents and relatives, and the people of his town, were very proud of his other two brothers when they became administrative officers. However, they could only feel sorry for him. He was articulated as an example in the underprivileged families: where the parents want their children to aim high, they try to make them believe that money isn't an a-priori necessity to do well in life; and how the impotent will ruin the life of even those who have everything available. Ibrahim's brothers, who were pronounced as the replicas of success, bought land and constructed a big house in a posh colony of Srinagar and left their town along with their parents. Ibrahim too was asked, rather requested, to live with the rest of his family but he thought of himself as a mismatch and decided to stay alone in their ancestral house, which made it easy for him to celebrate his love with a girl of his neighbouring town. He was living what he thought was an ideal life – cooking, eating, wooing his girlfriend, sleeping, and working occasionally in the fields. He would visit his parents only when he was short of money, where his mother would feed his belly with his favourite foods and his father would feed his pockets.

But his ideal life didn't last for long, it concluded when the family of his supposed girlfriend found her a groom who was doing some government job. He was completely broken when the brother of his beloved beat him and humiliated him. He realised his worth, which was nothing more than dust. His days were hardly passing now. He moved for a time being to live with his parents, but he realised he was only a guest there and he couldn't heal. Now he was regularly travelling back and forth, from his town to Srinagar. One day he found a chance to gather courage to tell his mother about his beloved and he requested her to convince his father, so that he could do something and get them married. Soon when she informed her husband about Ibrahim's love for a girl, the wrath of his father fell upon him. Insulted, he swore not to visit his parents again and went to live with his uncles back in the town. In the 1990s when the youngsters in Kashmir were crossing borders to get training and guns to fight against Indian oppression, disappointed and to give meaning to his life he too contacted an undercover agent of a group of freedom fighters. He crossed the LoC (Line of Control) to grow into a freedom fighter.

***

He didn't want to mock the people of the other side for their backwardness, but he couldn't hold his laughter when he was told: *look this is called thermos, in it tea remains warm.You only have samovars, right? Here you'll find modern gadgets you could only dream of in your home.* He realised that the grass was no greener on this other side. *For them we are backward and for us it is them, and the rest of the world see all of us as the marginalised, the Others*! When he finished his training in *Azad* (Free) Kashmir, he was sent back to his homeland. After few months of his hiding and playing with the security forces in the villages he got a chance to replace someone of his group who was despatched to Srinagar. One dark night he went to meet his family with his other two companions. The crying of his parents, while looking at him, wasn't because they had missed him, but for all the trouble they were facing for him. In fact they were happy to see him, but they were against the idea of militancy. They made him understand its negative impacts and shared the troubles they faced from the government and from the troops. But he didn't want to hear that and he left.

He received a bullet in his left ankle while his two companions got killed in an ambush-attack by Indian soldiers. He somehow managed to reach his parents' house, they transported him to a doctor, their relative, in a far-off town who treated him well and hid him for months in a sort of hideout in his house. While he was recovering, he accepted the fact that the gun was no solution to his nation's problems and then with the support and influence of his family he was able to protect his life from both sides,

Kashmiri militants and Indian soldiers, but his family's power couldn't save him from spending a few years in a district jail.

While in jail he was taught how to read and write Urdu and English. There he got interested in books; also he was able to revive and hone his weaving skills. After his release, his family made him live with them in Srinagar where he cherished the books of his elder brother's personal library. He was a changed man now. Known all over as a *surrendered-militant*, he resumed his work and began making carpets. Thinking of himself as a failure in comparison with his brothers made him sacrifice the pleasures of life, like marriage. To achieve something in his life he worked hard to make new designs and set an example in the carpet world. He started making wall-hangings which portrayed the culture and common life of Kashmir. His carpets – he was himself creating new designs of carpets – served as prototypes all over Kashmir. Finally his creative nature sculpted his world, he was able to have his own carpet house where he made carpets in his own models; he had his looms in almost every village of Kashmir. His popularity arose when he was contacted by carpet experts all over the world. His carpets were valuable possessions in carpet showrooms worldwide especially in Delhi, Dubai, London and New York. After all his struggle and experience and his distant dreams, before his untimely death, he was able to create that masterpiece in which he imagined the future of his homeland.

THREE POEMS

Carole Smith

Reflections on a Memoir

In the book, the terrorists I feared
are freedom fighters. The daily killings
were unavoidable. Children mutilated
by grenades are air-brushed out.
Spite-driven betrayal of neighbours
is never even touched on.

This is the island deep in kindness,
deep in cruelty, where I grew up;
but the greeting 'Go towards the Good'
did not bless my friend shot in the back,
or her sister reeling in pain, pursued
by gunmen down a sunlit shopping street.

The foreign minister's much praised memoir
tells less than half the story.
There was no war even,
only a necessary struggle for power;
and sixty years on there is still no war,
yet still no peace.

Finistere

Air vibrates to engine throbs
as, one by one, sardine boats
sweep from the harbour mouth
past jagged rocks, deep into night.

Beyond a luminous sea, clouds
tumble around a sinking sun.

On a rocky island near to shore
a fifth-century Irish priest
sought refuge.

Tonight, watching the horizon melt,
I am aware of worlds beyond,
where Grecian marble lies uncut
and even Celtic saints are young.

It is hard to leave this place
where time and the world
   ebb and flow.

Rainforest

Last night a tiger roared by the salt lick;
in daylight I see only cicadas and butterflies.
Climbing to the waterfall, I yearn to shed
my western skin, blend with the rainforest,
the cycle of decay and rebirth.

At a pool formed by crashing torrents

my guide kicks off her shoes and dives
cleaving through a glittering surface,
unhindered by hijab, trousers and her shirt.
I paddle gingerly, jeans rolled up.

'Come and swim,' she calls from underneath
tumbling water which frames her like a neriad.
Once, yes; now I simply listen to the symphony
of insects and absorb her primal joy.

THREE POEMS

Omair Bhat

Sabiha

In the spacious sitting-room my friend sits
facing me, one small foot visible beneath her
silver-threaded sari. Sipping Darjeeling tea,
we discuss the pilgrimage to Mecca
of Lady Zainab Cobbold. Outside it is raining.
Steely clouds shut out the light,
oily puddles form along the road.

Each gesture of my friend's slim hand
emphasises her words: the age-old pattern
of the Kashmir rug lies between us,
Kufic script, gold-framed, on the wall behind.
Her serene face transforms in exaltation
as she tells me of her own Hajj:
a lifetime's dream and, *alhamdullilah*, it came true.

'On the pilgrimage we are equal before God,
and we journey from the four corners of the earth.'
Her carefully chosen words and air of breeding
make me want to call her Sayyidah, Lady.
I picture moon-splashed deserts; in the morning
grape-blue sky. As the sun rises
waves of gold shimmer on the sand.

She smiles, then lightly laughs:
'I was the guest of a Saudi princess
in a tent with air-conditioning,
electric lights, a refrigerator.
Each of us escorted by a servant.'
Outside the window leaves rustle in the rain
as I travel with her to the sun-stricken land.

I can smell the cooking, sense the movement;
hear the deep, resonant call of the Muezzin,
picture the many and glorious gates to the Mosque,
see the pilgrims tread the hallowed ground.
Mecca, in a valley imprisoned by stony hills,
savage deserts, green oases, holy cities;
sand grouse, flamingos, jasmine, lilies.

I see my friend's slight form circling
the canopied Ka'bah, gesturing with her hands
as she repeats the prayers. I smell
Attar of roses distilled from blooms at Taif.
I am with her beneath the setting sun
as the desert sands turn mauve and pink,
finally to sleep beneath a starlit sky.

Night has closed in outside. It is late: I say
goodbye, step into the tight cold London air
taking with me the warmth of the sun.
My thoughts circle around the joy,
the fulfilment gifted to my friend
by these sacred rites, so generously shared
with a mind much differently atuned.

Preservation

She plucked snow
(from bare almond trees
in the courtyard)

and sometimes, absently,
picking rain drops
from the window sill, in haste,

a heap under her feet, I asked her
What are you contriving winter
for, mother?

She said to me, quietly,
seasons fight wars each day now
so who, for instance, knows

when salt of summer will replace
snow on my tongue, and
instead of water in the channels

in the turmoil of winter
blood of summer will flow
like spilled gasoline? but, like seeds

of rue from autumn,
we will have winter, washed in rosewater,
for more than two decades.

We don't fear death anymore

When we die, in our country, we suddenly find
ourselves transformed into roses and poems.
We become beginnings of an end.
We whirl in mad wind and come on the
other side of the earth. We unfetter
light from the heavy chains of smog.
We unravel mysteries of darkness.
At our homes, in small gatherings,
we become occasional mentions
in conversation we are no more part of.
We remain however centric
to the conversations we are part of
no more as us but as milestones
of distant cities.
We become writings on the wall.
We become reminders of Sundays.
We become shuddering sighs.
We become salt of tears.
Our names, etched on our gravestones,
are vouched upon by mothers.
We become revered. We become
vision of seers. We are
dreamed of and deciphered.
We inhabit rustle of autumn.
We fly with pigeons.
We never really go away.
We never vanish.
In our absences we stay on,
possessed by the disease of hope,
as fragmented memories.

REVIEWS

RETURN TO FUTURE

Hassan Mahamdallie

A bank of seventeen small video screens mounted on pegs grow out of the gallery wall like mushroom spores. Each screen projects a talking head: man, woman, young, old, black, brown, white, all musing on the future. Their future, their family's future, their nation's future, the future of the planet, my future, your future, our future.

The kaleidoscopic installation is named *Conversation Piece* and is made from 300 interviews conducted at the turn of the millennium across five continents, by futurist Dr Maya Van Leemput and photographer Bram Goots, who work together under their organisation *Agence Future*. Each participant, turned into a talking head, was asked about their ideas, images and feelings about personal, local and global futures. Some are very academic and erudite, some are passionate, some reflective.

One older man references sci-fi writer Ray Bradbury and how he lifted 'the veil' on future possibilities. A black woman states 'a man who doesn't think of the future is already dead'. Another interviewee warns, 'If we're not thinking about the future we're going to get a future we don't want.' An elderly white-haired guy says we need to use foresight in the same way as we use hindsight. A Navajo elder talks of how his ancestors communed with the spirits; conjuring up visions of futures. A young Australian man interviewed on the street hopes that twenty years hence 'the best thing that happens to me isn't limited by my mindset now', while a woman wearing glasses muses that maybe humankind needs 'a catastrophe to bring us closer to nature'.

But the one I relate to most is the woman sitting on a sofa somewhere, who, in the moment, struggles to articulate any kind of future, and ends up saying 'I'm going to pass on that'. That would be me, I reckon.

I have to admit to being somewhat obsessed by the past. One of my favourite quotes from Marx is: 'Men make their own history, but they do not make it as they please; they do not make it under self-selected circumstances, but under circumstances existing already, given and transmitted from the past. The tradition of all dead generations weighs like a nightmare on the brains of the living.' I know Marx is also talking about the future, but 'learning from the past', or hindsight, as a way of shaping the future is something that has been drummed into me. It is only recently that I realised that there was even such a thing as Future Studies, so my trip to 'A Temporary Futures Institute' occupying a floor of the Museum of Contemporary Art (M HKA), Antwerp, Belgium, acted as a crash-course in this stream of thought and academic enquiry. The 'futures institute' – which one might also describe as a multi-media arts exhibition+ was a curated imaginative play on the concept that future possibilities are infinite, but that not all are possible, and most are probably not even desirable.

A Temporary Futures Institute. Museum of Contemporary Art (M HKA), Antwerp, Belgium. Curated by Anders Kreugar and Maya Van Leemput. 28 April – 11 September 2017

The work of a dozen or so contributors were grouped under four categories first articulated by the father of Futures Studies, Jim Dator, who in 1971 founded the Hawaii Research Center for Futures Studies at the University of Hawaii at Manoa. Dator recently wrote:

Many people consider 'the future' to be a time and place lying somewhere 'ahead' of us towards which we are tending. Some people even seem to assume that 'the future' somehow pre-exists, and that we are able, or should be able, to 'predict' what it will be like. Our long experience in the futures field has convinced us that it is not possible to predict the future. Rather, it is possible, and necessary, to 'forecast' and 'experience' logical, theory-based, *images* of 'alternative futures', and to use our analysis of them to envision, invent, and move towards the creation of 'preferred futures', continually re-examining our preferences on the basis of experiences with new and old images of alternative futures.

Many years ago, we concluded that all of the millions, indeed billions, of images of the futures that are in people's minds and actions are specific versions of four generic images of the futures. We eventually labelled them Grow, Collapse/New Beginnings, Discipline and Transform.

So the M KHA 'futures institute' is organised into Dator's established categories of Continued Growth, Collapse, Discipline and Transformation. Continued Growth is the future most often sold to us by politicians and the powerful, Collapse is perhaps its antithesis – the hope of the powerless that it will all 'go west', but that something good may sprout in its ruins. Discipline is the desire for curbs and rules, articulated from the top down or the bottom up, by which we might avoid catastrophe and collapse, such as financial regulation or ecological preservation. Lastly, Transformation contains both utopias and dystopias – both the dream that a better world is possible and the nightmare of the future domination of technology over humans.

Although the contribution of Goots and Van Leemput (who co-curated the temporary institute along with Anders Kreugar) is under the Continued Growth section, their work acts as an introduction to the whole Futures concept. Along with the *Conversations* video installation, which demonstrated convincingly that the future is a fundamental human preoccupation, they exhibited a piece titled *A Timeline in Four Layers* to remind us of the eclectic history behind Futures Studies. Wooden posts with names and brief descriptors on the top were placed on the floor, taking us through the history of human thought from the Sumerian Epic of Gilgamesh, the Oracle of Delphi, Kong Qiu a.k.a. Confucius ('study the past if you would divine the future'), Nostradamus, Ibn Khaldun, through to William Morris, HG Wells, Mary Shelley, Fritz Lang, then Ridley Scott, CERN and Philip K Dick (*Do Androids Dream of Electric Sheep?*) and the TV series *Black Mirror*.

There were also some blank blocks to signify past-future-dreams-that-never-were and also a block labelled the RAND Corporation (Research and Development), which I had previously understood to be the only entity looking at Futures (and not in a good way) on behalf of the USA all-powerful Industrial-Military Complex; involved in secret weapons development, Cold War strategising and War Game Theory. So, I was glad to see that more benign forces have been and are 'in the field of play'.

Amongst the Continued Growth section was a six-screen video installation by Lithuanian Darius Ziura, who has, since 2001 returned every three years to his home village of Gustoniai, making one-minute silent video portraits of all its inhabitants, of which in 2001 there were under a hundred souls. So we witness continuity of sorts as we see the

Agence Futures Timeline and Conversation Piece
Photo: Bram Goots

same person get older in front of us, interspersed with blank screens to signify the departed, the not-yet-born and could-have-beens. It made for a mesmerising visual compression of time versus mortality.

The 'Collapse' section combined a heaviness of subject area and a lightness of touch. It comprised of Michel Auder, a veteran filmmaker who was part of the artists' set around Andy Warhol's Factory, renowned visual artist Simryn Gill from Singapore/Malaysia/Australia and the Centre for Postnormal Policy and Futures Studies, whose Director, Ziauddin Sardar, edits this journal.

I loved Michel Auder's work, partly because of his connection to Warhol's 1960s New York City studio, around which various seminal figures gathered, including Lou Reed, Nico, the Velvet Underground, Edie Sedgwick, Anita Pallenberg, Gerard Malanga and various exotic personalities such as Candy Darling, International Velvet and Viva Superstar (Janet Hoffmann), who married Auder, some of whom appear in his exhibited silent film *1967*.

However, it is his 1993 film *Voyage to the Center of the Phone Lines* that really keyed into the futures/collapse theme for me. The film strings together grainy boring 'holiday snaps' to illustrate a bizarre, scary and hilarious set of cordless and wireless telephone conversations between unnamed, unknown people. In one, a separated couple angrily discuss various scenarios about how to keep their teenage daughter 'under control'. The estranged couples' world has collapsed, his business has folded, she can't earn a living or get any alimony from him, their only link to each other being their rebellious and unpredictable daughter and her unsuitable boyfriend. 'I'll wave my fuckin' gun in his face. What do you want me to do!' shouts the father down the phone to his ex-wife. 'I went there [to the boyfriend's house] with a fuckin' bat last time.' 'So. I'm just forewarning you…I'm going to beat the shit out of her [the daughter] if she lies to me again.' Unfortunately, it doesn't seem like much hope will spring from this collapse – even the younger daughter, off phone, is flexing her teen-muscles: 'Whatever!' we hear her say in response to a command from her down-the-phone-line father.

From family collapse to economic collapse – and onto the work of visual artist Simryn Gill. Most striking were her large black and white photo prints entitled *My Own Private Anghor 2007–2009*. Gill is of Indian descent, was born in Singapore, raised in Malaysia, and is now based in Sydney. *My Own Private Anghor* collection depicts a housing estate in Port Dickson, Malaysia that financially collapsed in the 1980s and then began slowly to collapse back into the landscape from which it arose. Gill concentrates on how the process of decay was accelerated by local thieves, or strippers, who stole the aluminium frames from the windows, leaving glass panes resting on bare walls, in which we see reflected the inside and outside environment. As one art reviewer wrote:

> The complex was built in the 1980s, but never occupied. Over time looters have stripped the site of saleable metals. Surfaces have eroded. Dried leaves pile up on the floors and vines creep through the window openings.

> Gill's pictures, largely of abandoned domestic interiors, speak of both promise and ruin, of palpable economic collapse. They are documents, but resonate like meditations, deep drives into form, light, presence and absence.

> Bare windowpanes propped against the walls serve as a compositional through-line. One or more appear in every image, a tinted, shadowing or reflective frame within each frame. The panes serve as architectural foils or rhymes,

effectively flattening the space and echoing, for instance, the dark void of a nearby doorway.

The installation by the Centre for Postnormal Policy and Futures Studies represents a kind of dissident intervention in the exhibition. Although it clearly draws on Futures Studies (the co-curator being John A Sweeny, who was a researcher at Jim Dator's Center for Future Studies), it has, for instance, its own categories of Contradiction, Complexity and Chaos. The Postnormal concept is key. It is more explicit and perhaps less discursive than many of the exhibits that make up this Futures collection. As the curators write:

Simryn Gil potato prints and photographs in the 'Collapse' scenario
Photo: Bram Goots

Postnormal Times is a call to arms. An invitation to challenge our assumptions and biases about the contemporary world and possibilities for the future. It demands that we interrogate our sense of what is and is not 'normal'…In normal times, we have confidence in our facts and values, and we can take our time in making correct and appropriate decisions. In PNT, there is a sense of urgency, and the future feels like a runaway train barrelling into the unknown.

This is all a bit of a rude awakening to be confronted with halfway through the exhibition. The installation embodies the contradiction of wanting to express an impatient urgency with the necessity to patiently explain. The exhibit comprises screens that explain key concepts of Postnormal Times, including the 'menagerie of Postnormal Potentialities': Black Elephants (widely predicted events that are downplayed), Black Swans ('outliers' that appear 'out of the blue') and Black Jellyfish (normal interconnected phenomena that escalate into systematic instability or chaos). At the centre of the exhibit is a board game by which one is invited to trace a future narrative using choices of future phenomena and human collective values. You are then invited to input your journey onto a template. Comments included:

- I like strange and unusual behaviour when it is executed with integrity. Automatic systems should urgently take this into account.
- Let's see how creative and weird things can get. Why not? Of course, things could go horribly wrong, but…such is life in postnormal times!
- I didn't even know that augmented body hacking was possible. For me, this is a total black swan. I can only guess that we will need to use the value of acceptance to navigate this complex issue.
- There will be no future. With love.

The 'Discipline' grouping of exhibits provided some wry humour, based on the present-day notion that someone else, whether it be a government, a corporation, a lobby group or an individual knows better than me, what is best for me. This seems to me to be the strange outcome of consumer choice and individualism, combined with the attempts to regulate the chaos of the globalised free-market economy. I think it's what right-wing economists call 'nudge theory' – defined on Wikipedia (probably an example in itself) as 'a concept in behavioural science, political theory and economics which proposes positive reinforcement and indirect suggestions

Centre for Postnormal Policy and Futures Studies, 'Postnormal Times 2017'

to try to achieve non-forced compliance to influence the motives, incentives and decision making of groups and individuals'.

Thus Mei-Mei Song, a Futures educator from Taipei played with a future technology pricing system in an interactive exhibit titled *Shopping in the Future*. I was welcomed to 2037. In front of me were five 'products': a work permit, a Virtual Reality Travel Package, a third-hand tunic, a bowl of rice and a water capsule. You waved your hand over the product and an app immediately computed whether or not you could have access to the product, depending on your resources and past history. I was informed that I couldn't afford the 'sumptuous water from the Scheldt River condensed into a capsule' and was advised instead to 'consider water supply from more basic sources'. Such is life in 2037 (2017).

I also liked Song's posters from 2037 advertising a 'Wild day or night with the number one Hologram Band: Beyond Signals' being simultaneously streamed across time-zones on 26 July, 2037 along with the venue listing including Vienna, Italy; Latvia, Northern Russian Resistance; London, Scotland; Seattle, United States of Liberal and Houston, District 2 of America.

Although Stuart Candy's exhibit was tagged under the Transformation section, it had some kinship with Mei-Mei Song's work. Candy had 'invented' for us a NurturePod, complete with advertising copy, branded wrapping and a price in Euros (cut-price at €789). The pod had a lifelike infant snuggled in it, was plastic and womb-shaped and rocked gently as if suspended in amniotic fluid. On the baby's face was a VR mask and it was clutching a VR control in each of its chubby hands. The contraption was sold to us as 'Augmented Infancy' and a 'Programmable para-parenting pod', and the amusing but awful underlying question behind it was 'can this be that far away?' As the commentary accompanying Candy's exhibit said: 'It takes the idea of transformation in a near future to a doubtful extreme just like so many tech-optimist advocates of transformation do'.

And then I read Stuart Candy's biography: a professional futurist and experience designer, Stuart Candy is currently the William Bronson and Grayce Slovet Mitchell visiting professor at the School of the Art Institute of Chicago and faculty member of the world's first foresight and design program at OCAD University, Toronto. Etc. Etc.

Blimey! It was at that point during my tour of the exhibition that I came to appreciate that, notwithstanding a cautionary scepticism at academia's self-regard, there are a fair few clever and creative people out there looking into the future(s). But ordinarily we know little of who they are or what they do.

In my view 'A Temporary Futures Institute' was an attempt to encourage the viewer to take a leap not so much into the unknown but dive into a pool of possibilities. The implicit invitation, or challenge, was then to track back from this and that future, either desired or dreaded, back into our present. The Postnormal element was perhaps the bridge; those analytical stepping-stones that we need to link our present with desirable and undesirable futures. But somewhere in there, and very much present in the Antwerp exhibition, is the role of the dream, the vision or the

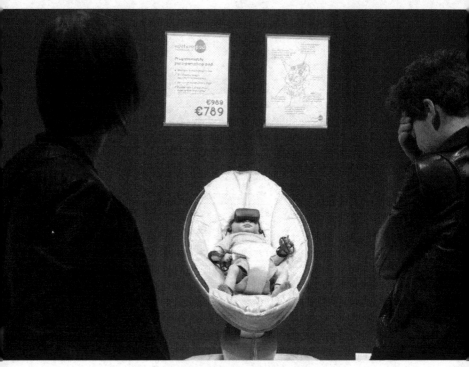

Stuart Candy, Nurture Pod
Photo: Bram Goots

imagination that is fundamental to humankind. This is something of great interest to me. In his seminal paper, 'Welcome to Postnormal Times', Ziauddin Sardar has written:

> The most important ingredients for coping with postnormal times…are imagination and creativity. Why? Because we have no other way of dealing with complexity, contradictions and chaos. Imagination is the main tool, indeed I would suggest the only tool, which takes us from simple reasoned analysis to higher synthesis.

I think he is onto something here. A pity we drum it out of our children at an early age before thrusting them into adulthood and telling them 'it's over to you now'.

STALKERS OF ANXIETY

C Scott Jordan

A new distinct shadow is emerging within contemporary American film. This new other does not have a proper face so it cannot be furnished with appropriate make up, accent and other character tropes. This other is abstract and as such not easy to pin down. It is anxiety-inspiring, and often wrapped in, enigma.

How did Donald J. Trump get elected President of the United States? It is a question that is being asked by conservative and liberal alike. Republicans and Democrats are all left in a sort of awe at the very phenomenon. Numerous questions arise. What happened to the good old rural, blue collar citizens on whose back the wealth of this nation was created? How can citizens make political choices that are against their interest? How have they come to see the federal government as the arch enemy out to get them? How come the rural folks have elected candidates who refuse to regulate the pollution of the lands and waters essential towards clean drinking and fish supplies which are the staples of their economy? These are obvious, natural questions but the answers are complex and call into question the entire history of American democracy. We can point to large demographics. We can say with some confidence that everyday rural, blue collar citizen is forced to sacrifice health for wealth and ineffective government for freedom. In the ignorance of these uncertainties and artificial dichotomies, a deep anxiety rules the hearts of these people. Then, there is the anxiety on the other side: those who are concerned with the rise of populism in America. This accumulated anxiety has a distinctively postnormal feel to it. It is through postnormal times that this new movement in film can be identified and studied.

The films that capture the anxiety of these tumultuous times are still being written. But the atmosphere of anxiety surrounding American life is now beginning to filter in Hollywood and is slowly being represented through film in varying ways. Within the last year there have been a few films that have begun to shed light on the absurdity that permeated the air of American life during the rise of Donald Trump and other alt-right movements. Riddled with uncertainty the films present characters with relatively high intelligences faced with insurmountable challenges that are bordering on the utterly ridiculous. This produces an improbability that cannot be shaken over the course of a feature length film. On top of this our narrators are horrendously subjective and often untrustworthy. Indeed, even when the main character is our narrator, and sometimes the hero, they cannot even trust themselves. After all, often times the hero and narrator are living in different realities, different times, even if these two roles are contained within the same character. Then again, this is a post-Truth world. Truth is dead or at least stripped of its innocence. The combination of the settings' uncertainty and the ignorance (either recognised or hidden) creates an anxiety felt by both characters and audience. Watch Starz' *American Gods* and see what I mean.

In this anxiety, we see another fatality, the death of genre. These films feel like a horror film, but over the movement of the plot one is left unsure of whether one is watching a horror film, or a comedy, or a tragedy, or a romance. The traditional narrative of genre is blended beyond the recognition of its constituent definitions. The dominant theme is anxiety which is often played out with the revelation this postnormal movement in film has best been played out with the more rural, blue collar characters. In the steadfast held values of these protagonists, there is a real life or death struggle to overcome the conflict postnormal films present.

Of course, the representation of the rural, blue collar citizen in American film has a long history. It is worth noting how it has changed. I would argue that this change has occurred in three distinctive movements.

The earliest representations, during the 1920s through to the 1960s, come in the form of personas that are the Salt of the Earth. These are the little men, the heroes who overcome corruption or society issues to rise above, take on the authority or the norm, and make America great for the first time. These are the Atticus Finches (*To Kill a Mockingbird*, 1962), Jefferson Smiths (*Mr. Smith Goes to Washington,* 1939), and Tom Joads (*Grapes of Wrath*, 1940) of the world. They were not always the most intelligent or most noble, but they stuck to their beliefs and eventually win the day. Often based on classic American novels, these characters led America to world dominance and gave birth to the idea of the American dream. The Salt of the Earth person understood that value is created through hard work and that it is no bad thing to exit stage left to an uplifting musical number. Luckily, the presence of non-whites or the socially 'irregular' isn't necessary in order to save the day in pre-1960s America.

In the face of the turbulence of the 1960s and 1970s, the rural, blue collar hero was abandoned. Often they were made out to be the backwards, lost, and hopelessly uneducated. They are the racist side character, incapable of proper grammatical communication, and fall victim to their own idiocy. Sometimes their fates are tragic, other times they can be written off as innocent in the light of their own ignorance. They are the Ugly Idiot American, often depicted as overweight, wearing hats and denim, and incapable of higher thought or arithmetic. The Ugly Idiot American is dangerous like Lee Harvey Oswald (*JFK*, 1991), Private Leonard Lawrence (*Full Metal Jacket,* 1987), and the back-country family of *Deliverance* (1972). The Ugly Idiot American can be the dopey hero such as *Forrest Gump* (1994) or Bobby Boucher (*The Waterboy*, 1998). Often times the Ugly Idiot American sits in the background, biding their time for a good laugh or to devise a reckless plan. They usually only have hyphenated names or nick names reminding us of the regions of the US they come from like Tex. They are Maj. King Kong (*Dr. Strangelove*, 1964), Cletus (television's *The Simpsons*), or a variety of roles played by such character actors as Clifton James (often credited as the Dopey Sheriff). They are derogatory caricatures so much so that they have even led many Americans to hide their southern accent out of fear of being judged as less intelligent for having it. This period of representation still exists today as a tool of comedy that has only been made more powerful in the aftermath of certain politicians and reality television stars.

The newest phase of rural, blue collar representation builds upon the prior two by adding humility and integrity to the character. These are the Comeback Kids. They can simply take pride in the identity they have had thrust upon them. This is easily seen in Chris Kyle (*American Sniper*, 2014), where the identity is owned and pursuit of heroism unfettered. This can also be witnessed in a pragmatic owning of the identity while refusing its weaknesses. This is most readily observed in Frank Underwood (*House of Cards*, 2013). This phase of rural, blue collar representation is being used in postnormal films and they give us a deeper insight into the anxiety of the age and fresh take on such phenomenon as the election of Donald Trump and the rise of the alt-right political movement.

Two recent films do a wonderful job of setting the stage for the feeling of these new postnormal times in American cinema. In opposite, yet complementing ways, these two cinematic screenings tell classic and deeply American stories through this emerging lens giving the audience a new, yet essential position to prepare for the futures ahead. The cinematography is key in both to establishing a sense of the eerie and a majestic uncertainty. Through vast landscape shots and focus on the setting, the central roles are minimalised before the titanic space surrounding them. This diminishes the character's trust for their situations and highlights, for the audience, the uselessness of their preordained world views. Clear navigation towards the character's resolutions is as muddled as the distinction of genre in these films.

The first film is Robert Egger's *The Witch* (2015). *The Witch* is, as it subtly suggests, a New England Folktale following a freshly outcast family in 1700s New England as they build their new life, centralised around a fundamentalist form of Christianity, beyond the society of their former English immigrant colonisers. Following the disappearance of one of the family's children, a grief stricken mother, a strong and passionate father, and four children lost between pubescence, superstition, and religious conviction struggle to hold together against the supernatural forces haunting them in the surrounding wood. Their firm beliefs and moral structure is taken to its limits as their understanding of the world, good, evil, and each other are all called into question. Interfamilial white lies mix with inexplicable happenings that are evaluated with wayward superstition and unshakable religious conviction. In the end the truth is almost as unbelievable as the ridiculous conclusions provided by the family's not-so-common sense. They are rapidly and hopelessly consumed by a postnormal storm.

First, the Father, the patriarchal pillar of wisdom, tells us he is allowing his family to fall into exile due to the village's incorrect views on the Bible. We the audience must trust that he knows best. We want to trust him as the pinnacle of truth as within a few frames we see that he has provided a small estate for the family and they appear to be thriving. Then the youngest child disappears under the eldest child's watch. The Father is certain it was the work of a wild animal. Then we find out the Father has stolen the Mother's priceless heirloom cup and sold it for provisions so the family may survive the coming winter. But stealing is wrong. This also means this perfect home he has created has flaws. The crops aren't taking to the land. He is also secretly teaching his son how to hunt, taking him into the woods against the Mother's wishes. The son and the daughter go out looking for their lost brother and only the daughter returns. The Mother, having appeared to have lost another child turns to blaming the foul play on Satan himself. The Father allows his daughter to be blamed for the missing cup and the son's knowledge of the woods when he knows it is his fault that led the boy on the fool's errand. The suspicion that they are being stalked by a witch is quickly taken as a viable possibility and the Father, once our rock, now is left uncertain as to whether or not his own daughter has given herself to Satan and become the witch that haunts them.

The second film is Denis Villeneuve's *Arrival* (2016). While *The Witch* is the classical form of American story, *Arrival* takes on the more futuristic sci-fi aspect. In America's infancy its greatest fear was the agents of Satan and repression, as America became a super power, its antagonists had to take on other-worldly, extraterrestrial embodiment. *Arrival* begins with the original greatest threat: Aliens have appeared from somewhere and they must want something. Worst of all, we do not know how powerful they are and they could potentially destroy us all with little to no effort. Traditionally in alien encounter movies English is taken as the intergalactic language of choice. *Arrival* turns this class-act idiotic Western assumption and a linguist becomes our film's hero. This film is steeped in uncertainty as the world waits for one linguist to save us from our ignorance. Meanwhile the military and humanity itself stands ready to act before they attack us. At its heart it is a classic encounter with the other story. Our hero, Louise, who cannot count on the alien language having any similarities to any Earth forms of communication (that which she has dedicated her life to studying), must try to communicate nevertheless. Her colleague attempts to offer her mathematical truth, but even this, removed from the living and subjective, can offer no solace. She must defeat her own mental bias and break out of her way of thinking to save the world from its ignorance-driven actions.

The first shots of this film are quite different from *The Witch* in that we find the characters trapped in small rooms. This gives a sense of claustrophobia which is gradually expanded. First we move up to a large lecture hall but are given the point of view of a screen. Suddenly the watchers have become the watched as the audience sees a room of students and the teacher, our hero, look on as the news reveals that we are not alone in the universe. This shot gives the American audience a remembrance of where they were and how they felt on September 11, 2001. Steeped in uncertainty, we are brought to a large expanse. An open land of rolling hills and centred in it, the alien space craft. A large metallic concave essence. Audience and characters are all belittled before the massive metal contact lens looking craft as seemingly miniature helicopters fly by it.

Finally, the telling of this story lends to the ignorance felt while viewing this film. We are hearing a love letter to the hero's daughter. The letter is written with the knowledge that a great tragedy is going to occur, but we cannot tell if the letter is a flashback or an afterthought of the alien conundrum before us – the audience. At moments we see our hero struggle with both memory and intuition, left in pain as she breaks beyond her all too human linear progressive timeline of thought. Hers and our perspective is taken beyond the confines of time.

Beyond the cinematography and flexible truth of both *The Witch* and *Arrival*, the musical score ties the bow on this postnormal package deal. The musical editing gives one the illusion that no score exists, though when one looks back they are almost certain they heard bass beats or even the scratches of stringed instruments. In fact, both films blend natural sounds (although enhanced even to the point of hyperbole) with very subtle musical accompaniment. This blend is refined with a sharp emphasis on sound effects from footsteps, to crunching, knocking, and even the handling of various items. There is no safety in the ignorance and uncertainty surrounding these films. The audience can expect no comfort from an elaborate plot and feeling driving musical score either.

In the past two years several films such as *The Witch* and *Arrival* have given the definitive feeling of the postnormal, the anxiety that things are not as they should be, that nothing seems to be normal anymore. But they are unable to come to grips with this anxiety and continue to linger on the dangerous presumption that the normal is still out there. *A Cure for Wellness*

(2016) is a great example of this. When a partner of a major financial firm in New York City sends a letter saying he will not be returning from the European spa he vacationed to, a young, up and coming stock broker is forced to visit the spa and bring him home. When he arrives at the spa he notices various strange happenings that reveal a hidden past to the castle the spa was built into and the disappearance of several patients. At times this film feels like the next great psychological thriller moving from twist to twist until the final reveal, but at other times it feels like the old Hammer exploitative horror films of the 1960s and 1970s. At the same time a narrative delving into greed, excesses of neo-liberal economics and the stresses of the fast paced modern world tries to elicit a message of warning. In the end, a definite antagonist, an ultimate evil is revealed and vanquished. The day is saved and everything can return to normal, or so the audience thinks.

Two other ground-breaking horror films came out earlier in 2017 that invoke a similar feeling. *Get Out* (2017) and *Split* (2016). Both of these films take a deep social issue, racism in America and mental illness not being considered worthy of actual medical study, respectively, and exaggerate the circumstances to deliver a thought provoking product. The problem arises again, like in *A Cure for Wellness*, when the heroes face their antagonists and come out on top. Evil is vanquished. The day is saved.

The hero goes home. The audience go home. The issue, be that corporate greed, mental illness, racism, xenophobia, economic inequality, terrorism, they all still exist. Worst: all these heroes make it to the credits not through creative means, but by remaining within their own world views and with the tools conveniently left for them. There is an insatiable desire to find and locate the causes of all our troubles elsewhere. There is no awareness the system we have created, the paradigms we established and work within, are the problem. Postnormal Times is not engaged and thus the turbulent state of the system is in no way appreciated.

Oddly enough, it is in the rural, blue collar characters of recent American cinema that truly postnormal film meets true postnormal heroes. The first example of this new representation of the rural/blue collar character who rises to become a postnormal hero comes from last year's best picture nominee, *Manchester by the Sea* (2016). In the film, Casey Affleck delivers a best actor nominating portrayal of Lee Chandler, a down and out day labourer who is suddenly given custody of his teenage nephew after the death of his brother. Lee is a man numb to emotion due to a horrifyingly tragic past and now must face the death of his brother, the pain of his old home town, and the uncertain future of his friends and family. In the film's beginning Lee is freed from the past, floating along in the present as a maintenance man with no future prospects and without passion for life. Upon Lee's return to his hometown, everything is familiar, yet unrecognisable. Things that were taken for granted have evaporated, truth now seems to come at random, and the ignorance discovered in uncertainty forces Lee out of himself. Whereas Lee is a dead character at the film's opening, a shell waiting for his last sunrise, he is now in charge of a young life filled with potential, faced by his ex-wife and the horrifying secret they hold, he must live again. Most importantly he must get creative and think for others for the first time since his leaving his home. In the end, we see through flashback Lee, his brother, and his nephew as young boys fishing and joking in a safe and familiar world. Now they have to navigate the treacherous waters of life and the New England bay area they call home.

Similar sentiments can be found in *Buster's Mal Heart* (2016), where we follow Buster through the two worlds he lives within. In the first, he is the family man, over worked, under paid, and under respected by superiors and his in-laws struggling to give his wife and daughter a better life. In the second he is a nomadic frequent radio prophet moving between empty vacation homes hiding from the cops and preaching the coming death of society with Y2K approaching. The first Buster is responsible, loving, and dedicated to life. The second is reckless, disrespectful of other's property, and free from the cares of the modern fast paced world. These two worlds are brought together by the appearance of the strange character known as the Last Free Man and a dream sequence where the two Busters are lost at sea in a small boat. As the Last Free Man eventually leads the first Buster down a destructive path, the first Buster works to kill the 'free' and prophetic second Buster in the boat. By the film's conclusion both Busters are destroyed yet the audience is unsure if either actually existed. Was this film all just a massive glitch in the matrix, could this all be the fleeting thoughts of a man lost at sea? We must watch the film through both Busters but can never trust either and both must take uncharacteristic steps to evade their utter destruction.

Lastly, I want to draw attention to *Logan* (2017). Now this may seem a strange pick as the superhero films seem to have more to do with a denial (and potential postnormal lag inducing effect) of the modern world fraught with issues. *Logan* takes the superhero flick and pivots it in a new direction. Here we see a deconstruction of the costumed white knight and perhaps the closest thing to a reconstruction of the hero that postnormal times will allow. Logan awakes to his car being vandalised near the Mexican border in the south of the United States. In traditional superhero narration, the bad guys would be stopped and somehow someone would be saved, everyone lives happily ever after. Instead Logan brutally murders his would be attackers and no one is safe, including Logan himself who suffers a severe amount of injury from the encounter. This world is done with the Mutants who were once heroes as Logan is one of the last of his kind. Done with his days as the Wolverine, he only wishes to help the only man who ever helped him in his past, Professor X, now unable to control his vast powers, and live out the rest of their days away from the sick and dying future they find themselves in. Suddenly a young girl needs the Wolverine one last time. Followed by a dangerous corporation, Logan, this young girl, and Professor X must run north to get her to safety. All along the way, the old way of doing things only ends in tragedy and Logan must even face a clone of himself, reminiscent of the old powerful Wolverine as his healing ability has faded with time. Logan's old challenge has been to find the right balance between man and animal to prevail in a world that hates and needs him. Now Logan must find a new place for himself and the future of mutant kind, in the form of lost children, in a dying world, in legend, and deeply troubling postnormal times.

The fate of all of these heroes is great tragedy. But each makes piercing strides against the thick and often impossibly navigable ignorance of populism floating in a sea of uncertainty. Each hero must face destruction to be recreated in a new creative way that enables him to navigate the complexity, chaos, and contradiction at the foundation of postnormal times. The rural/blue collar character, the basic block of populism, makes an ideal candidate for this heroic endeavour. These characters are steadfast in their beliefs and suffer the most when the greater forces of the world around them fail. Their ideals create profound conflict as the lines between good and evil, right and wrong, and whether to act or not are blurred or one's eyes can no longer be trusted. These heroes have the endurance to face almost certain defeat and destruction in the face of postnormal times. As the film moves quickly to represent the conundrum in the social and political nature of American life, as truth is dead and lies, corruption, and tyranny move beyond the regular to become law and the new normal, they are the sacrificial lambs who will redeem their representation in the history of American film by exploiting the stereotypes and contradictions in their characterisation.

NAME YOUR INNOVATION

Shanon Shah

How much do the multitude of Muslims and non-Muslims hate the Islamic State (IS), formerly known as the Islamic State in Iraq and Syria (ISIS) or the Islamic State in Iraq and the Levant (ISIL)? Let us count the ways. This militant Sunni movement established its so-called Caliphate in 2014, headed by Abu Bakr al-Baghdadi, which promoted the wanton killing of Shi'ah Muslims, enslavement of the Yazidis (a religious minority), beheadings of foreign aid workers and journalists, and gruesome punishments for disobedient Muslims living under its jurisdiction. It also claimed responsibility for massacres on civilians around the globe as part of its *jihad*, or holy struggle.

From much of the Western media's coverage, though, one would be forgiven for thinking that IS's ideology was embraced, at least tacitly, by the majority of Muslims. 'Where are the mainstream Muslims condemning these atrocities?' – a leitmotif made popular by the terrorist attacks of 11 September 2001 – has remained a staple question in public debates about IS. Well, one prominent response was the Open Letter to Baghdadi (which can be accessed at: http://www.lettertobaghdadi.com), released in September 2014 and signed by several conservative Islamic scholars, lawmakers and community leaders. (These included the former and current Grand Muftis of Egypt, Ali Gomaa and Shawki Allam, Hamza Yusuf, founder and Director of Zaytuna College in the US, and Abu Ammaar Yasir Qadhi, Professor of Islamic Studies at Rhodes College, also in the US).

Jan-Peter Hartung, *A System of Life: Mawdudi and the Ideologisation of Islam*, Hurst, London, 2013.

The lengthy letter used sophisticated arguments from within the Islamic canon to refute IS's excesses and its basis for authority. The signatories blasted IS for its reintroduction of slavery, its persecution of the Yazidis, its wanton killing of innocents, and its widespread use of torture, among other atrocities. The underlying argument behind this litany of criticisms, however, was that a Muslim was only allowed to issue a *fatwa* (legal opinion) after fulfilling specific requirements in knowledge and by deferring to established Islamic authority. Muslims are not allowed to 'cherry-pick' from the Qur'an to derive legal rulings without considering the Qur'an and *hadith* (recorded traditions of the Prophet Muhammad) in their entirety. Therefore, according to the signatories, the fundamental problem with IS was that it was issuing religious edicts that bypassed the authority of the *ulama* (religious scholars). IS were basically doing 1950s free-jazz improv on the scriptures, with dire consequences. Or, if you like, this was a nightmare version of the 'Star-Spangled Banner' by Jimmy Hendrix – the 'Squiggly Black Standard'?

Amongst jihadi groups, IS are indeed unique in that instead of fighting to restore the Caliphate, they claim they have *already* established it. But if we're talking about bypassing the ulama or playing fast and loose with Islamic conceptions of the state, then IS is hardly exceptional. These characteristics, among others, were central to the thinking of twentieth century Islamist journalist and philosopher, Abul A'la Maududi (1903-1979), founder of the Jamaat-e-Islami.

Born in Aurangabad, India, he was the youngest son of Ahmad Hasan, a lawyer by profession. On his mother's side, Maududi was related to Sayyid Ahmad Khan, the nineteenth-century Islamist modernist thinker. Maududi grew up amid the rise of anti-colonialism in British India and the dissolution of the Ottoman Empire after the First World War. At 15, Maududi became a journalist and wrote about concerns shared by numerous other Indo-Muslim writers. Amid the rising tensions between Hindus and Muslims and increasingly aggressive Hindu communalist propaganda, Maududi's stance began to harden and his activism became explicitly and exclusively Muslim. Although he was initially influenced by the Indian Caliphate Movement, he eventually became disillusioned with its leader, Abul Kalam Azad, who struck an alliance with Mahatma Gandhi and joined the Indian Congress Party – Maududi blamed Congress for what he saw as the betrayal of Islam in India.

Yet neither did he support the secessionism of Muhammad Ali Jinnah, the founding father of Pakistan. Maududi's project was more ambitious. Instead of fighting for one independent Muslim nation-state that would exist amongst several others, Maududi was committed to upholding Islam as an 'all-encompassing system of life'. He was interested in establishing *the* Islamic state par excellence.

According to Jan-Peter Hartung's excellent study of Maududi's ideas, to do this, Maududi drew upon existing concepts within the Islamic tradition and improvised on them. For example, the concept of *jahiliyya* – the period and state of affairs in pre-Islamic Arabia – existed since the earliest days of Islam. Although reformers such as Ibn Wahhab (1703–1792) and Ibn Taymiyyah (1263–1328) defined it as a state of moral decay that continued to persist among some Muslims, historical understandings of jahiliyyah were not that monolithic. Maududi, however, jazzed up the meaning of jahiliyyah – to him, it meant 'sheer ignorance', 'polytheism' and 'monasticism' and included Sufism, Shiism and Western ideologies. Maududi effectively equated jahiliyyah (ignorance) with *kufr* (denial or disbelief).

Maududi also raised the stakes on several other aspects of Islamic tradition. The concept of *tajdid* (renewal), for example, describes movements within Islam that have aimed to correct or purify the divine message over the centuries after the Prophet Muhammad's death. Conceptions of tajdid went hand in hand with some degree of pessimism about Islamic history that was common amongst Muslims from time to time. Maududi, however, contended that *everything* went downhill after the introduction of dynastic rule under the Umayyads in the seventh century. To him, Islamic history was basically nearly fourteen centuries worth of wrong turns and dead ends. And according to Maududi, the *mujaddids* (renewers) of each generation were ineffective because their efforts were piecemeal and did not extract the essence of the Qur'an. Along similar lines, Maududi was also stingingly anti-ulama and anti-monarchy. (And so are IS, who are virulently opposed to the Saudi monarchy and the Wahhabi ulama who support the regime.)

This does not mean, however, that there is a linear trajectory between Maududi and groups like IS. In fact, Maududi's writings do not appear prominently in IS propaganda. But this is why Hartung's 'history of ideas' approach is so much more valuable in helping us to understand how and why some notions survive, thrive and mutate, but not others.

Most crucially, Maududi developed his thinking not only amidst the political and intellectual upheaval in colonial India. New political ideologies were also reshaping the future of the West. Fascism and Communism, in particular, were proving to be threats to the Western European status quo. Through the intertwining networks of colonial and anti-colonial movements, these ideologies made their way to the rest of the world, including the Indian subcontinent. And although Maududi took great pains to distinguish his Islamism from both these ideologies, he could only do this after carefully – albeit selectively – engaging with and critiquing them.

It is not enough, however, to say that Maududi's ideas were also influenced by the Western ideologies he purportedly dismissed. Hartung contends that all modern political ideologies are based on the 'dominant matrix' of Darwinism, hence their vision of society's linear progress from the 'backward' or 'uncivilised' to the 'enlightened' and 'refined'. In effect, Maududi created a linear, Darwinist model of Islamic government, in which there was no turning back. The destiny of humankind depended upon its ability to escape jahiliyya and steadily evolve into an Islamic 'theo-democracy' (*ilahi jumhuri hukumat* – Maududi's neologism).

Maududi's thought was able to flourish partly because the cultural and political environment in colonial India provided fertile ground for the widespread dissemination of intellectual ideas. Publicly-recited poetry was immensely popular and was a major mode of transmission of anti-colonial views amongst large sections of the population. The emotive poems of the poet-philosopher-politician Muhammad Iqbal, for instance, demonstrate how such ideas were successfully spread beyond the literate establishment. According to Hartung, in the Middle East and North Africa the reformist agenda was a more top-down affair. Muhammad Abduh (1849-1905), the Egyptian jurist and religious scholar, viewed reform as something to be spearheaded by experts. Even the means of communicating reformist thought in Egypt – religious treatises and journals – were effectively focused upon literate and educated elites. In this sense, Maududi's theological project had far greater populist appeal in the Subcontinent.

Here, Hartung's 'history of ideas' approach does not permit Maududi to be reduced to a mere Islamist. There's a difference between Maududi's conscious, deliberate Islamist project and the spread of his ideas beyond the usual Islamist circles. As an illustration, look at the way he read the Qur'an as someone who had an explicitly political and evolutionist approach to Islam. According to Maududi, the Qur'an contained an eternal and unchangeable message which was revealed within a particular context. In fact, the linguistic codes that transported the divine message varied *within* the Qur'an, depending on the period and occasion of revelation. This is how Maududi explained the difference between the earlier, more universal Qur'anic revelations in Makkah and the later, more specific, legalistic verses revealed in Madinah. But guess what? This methodology shares a lot with that of Nasr Hamid Abu Zayd (1943-2010), the Egyptian linguist and liberal Qur'anic scholar who was declared an apostate by the Egyptian shari'ah court in 1995.

Perhaps this comparison between Maududi and Abu Zayd is where the most problematic elements of Maududi's thought become clear. In his vision, the ideological purity of the Islamic state meant that only Muslims could become its citizens. Citizenship could never be granted towards non-Muslims – the Islamic state simply had no room for them. Maududi came to this conclusion despite the copious amount of jurisprudence and historical examples of coexistence between Muslims and people of other faiths.

More chilling are the implications of this for Maududi's definition of apostasy. His starting point was a peculiarly linear reading of verse 256 from Surah Al-Baqarah (the Chapter of the Cow) in the Qur'an: 'There is no compulsion in religion. The right direction is from now on distinct from error....'

According to Maududi:

> No compulsion is there in religion [*la ikraha fi'l-din*] means that we do not compel anyone to come into our religion. And this is truly our practice. However, we initially warn whoever would come and go back that this door is not open to come and go. Therefore anyone who comes should decide before coming that there is no going back. Otherwise he should kindly not come.

The implication is clear – anyone is free to enter the Islamic state, but no one can leave. A bit like Hotel California. The Islamic state is thus tasked with applying the death penalty for apostasy, which Maududi defined as disloyalty to God *and* towards the community of believers.

Maududi's position on women, elaborated in his book *Parda* (1939), was equally problematic. Women were meant to 'remain in their houses' and obey men as their custodians (*qawwam*). It was also the Islamic state's duty to impose strict gender segregation. Ironically, Maududi did not justify this position based upon a rigorous reading of core Islamic texts. Instead, he arrived at these conclusions by relying upon anti-feminist Western literature that painted a picture of moral decay when women were supposedly allowed to roam freely in society. If anything, these sources reflected the patriarchal underpinnings of Victorian and post-Victorian sexual morality. Among the gems consulted by Maududi were George Ryley Scott's *A History of Prostitution* (1936), Cyril E.M. Joad's *Guide to Modern Wickedness* (1939) and Edith Belle Lowry's *Herself: Talks with Women Concerning Themselves* (1911). Maududi's position on women is thus emphatically not an example of free-jazz improv. It's not even the equivalent of a bad cover version of a classic. This is more like Alvin and the Chipmunks covering Milli Vanilli and passing it off as Michael Jackson's *Thriller*.

Internal contradictions and inconsistencies notwithstanding, Maududi's ideas took root in South Asia and travelled elsewhere, too. Hartung argues that one environment where they germinated well was, ironically, Egypt, via the efforts of Sayyid Qutb (1906-1966), the leading ideologist of the Muslim Brotherhood in the 1950s and 1960s.

The thing is, Qutb played jazz, too. For starters, he adapted Maududi's conceptualisation of jahiliyya and made it even more total. For Maududi, the concept of jahiliyya was a means to elaborate what he meant by Islam as a 'total system'. Qutb shifted the emphasis onto jahiliyya as something to be fought and vanquished, turning it into something that was much more useable for aspiring militants.

As with Maududi, the development of Qutb's thought has much to do with his particular context of oppression. Qutb's imprisonment and torture by the pan-Arabist and socialist regime of Gamal Abdel Nasser (1918-1970) meant that he endured a different order of oppression, compared with Maududi's struggle against colonial rule, escalating Hindu-Muslim conflict and intra-Muslim rivalry. This is what significantly contributed to Qutb's revision of the concept of jahiliyya and, eventually, *takfir* (excommunication) and jihad. Qutb was released from prison in 1964 but was rearrested in 1965 on charges of trying to overthrow the government and attempting to assassinate Nasser. In 1966, he was executed by hanging.

Maududi, on the other hand, succumbed to poor health – he had a lifelong kidney ailment which worsened later in life and he also developed heart problems. He went to the United States for treatment and was hospitalised in Buffalo, New York, where his son worked as a physician. He died in Buffalo in 1979 but is buried in Lahore. That same year, he became the first recipient of the Saudi Arabian King Faisal International Award for his service to Islam. In other words, at the end of his life, the anti-Western, anti-colonial Maududi's life depended upon medical treatment in the infidel land of the US. Not only that, as an anti-monarchist and anti-ulama ideologue, Maududi ended his life being feted by the Saudi kingdom.

This gap between Maududi's actual legacy and his initial ideals can also be seen in the movement he founded in 1941 – the Jamaat-e-Islami (JI). By 1942, JI faced its first serious factional dispute when its leadership split into those who were pro-Maududi and those who supported his long-term foe, Amin Ahsan Islahi. And although Maududi had opposed the creation of the state of Pakistan, he gradually accepted its existence as a conduit for gradual Islamisation. The Jamaat thus split into two independent organisations following the partition of India – Jamaat-e-Islami Pakistan (JI-P) and Jamaat-e-Islami Hind (JI-H).

Within Pakistan, Maududi continued providing an aura of charismatic authority for the movement. Although it was regularly repressed by the Pakistani government from the 1940s to the 1960s, JI-P could claim significant success during the military rule of General Muhammad Zia-ul-Haq, when it inspired his Islamisation policies. During the Bangladesh Liberation War, JI-P opposed the independence of Bangladesh and supported the Pakistan Army. The new JI-B became a marginal movement immediately after the independence of Bangladesh but, in the proceeding decades, it worked its way through strategic political alliances. In 2001, it achieved impressive electoral success, winning seventeen parliamentary seats as part of a coalition led by Khaleda Zia's Bangladesh Nationalist Party. Until today, however, the role of the JI in the Liberation War remains controversial and deeply divisive, as explored in issue 23 of *Critical Muslim*, 'Bangladesh'.

In India, the JI-H went down a different path. The leadership decided to participate in elections in 1962 but was banned between 1975 and 1977 under Indira Gandhi's emergency rule. After Maududi's death, JI-H became even more autonomous and pragmatic. After the rise of the right-wing Hindutva Bharatiya Janata Party (BJP) and its electoral victory in 1998, JI-H became ardent defenders of secular democracy in India.

The movement that was envisioned by Maududi to uphold Islam as a total 'system of life' thus had no choice but to fragment and make concessions to the nation-state. In India, particularly, the stance of JI-H now appears almost antithetical to Maududi's founding vision.

How do we evaluate Maududi's legacy then? Did it fail? Was Maududi's vision of an Islamic state unworkable at best and hypocritical at worst? Hartung is more generous than that. To him, the fact that Maududi could influence so many different groups within the Islamist spectrum is proof of the 'enormous richness of his ideological outline'. The fact that Maududi's grand theory-building and political project has not come to pass can also be interpreted in his favour. Contemporary Islamists, Hartung argues, do not feel the need to 'reinvent the wheel' after Maududi's extraordinary exertions – they simply want to continue where Maududi left off.

Maududi's legacy also shows us how unproductive it is to go down the rabbit hole of what constitutes 'authentic' Islam and the quest to quash 'cherry-picked' interpretations. Maududi was a religious improviser extraordinaire – and look at the following he cultivated. He imbued traditional concepts like jahiliyya and *khilafat* (caliphate) with new meanings, and conjured entirely new ones like 'theo-democracy'. This should be a huge relief especially for progressive Muslims, who – like IS – are often accused by the status quo of 'cherry-picking' or 'changing the meaning of the Qur'an' when they advocate gender equality or full equality for sexual minorities. We are all playing jazz.

This is not to claim that Islam is now a free-for-all. There are urgent discussions to be had about what the Islamic position should be on issues such as injustice, violence and environmental degradation. And so, as flawed as it was, the Open Letter to Baghdadi was an important intervention.

Perhaps the problem with Maududi was not that he improvised on particular Islamic concepts, but the ends to which he put his improvisations. Killing apostates and denying women equal rights as citizens are just not okay, no matter what theological justification one reaches for. And maybe this was his biggest blind spot – Maududi might have gone to great lengths to envision an Islamic state that would protect Muslims from external aggressors, but his vision did not address the nasty possibility of yesterday's liberators turning into tomorrow's oppressors.

TRANSFIGURATIONS

Alia Masood

It was with some excitement that I opened the first page of Sarvat Hasin's debut novel and prepared to become fully immersed in a mesmerising story of four sisters, their devotion to their mother, fondness for a father largely absent as a result of war, and their friendship with a young boy who lives across the road. My anticipation was further piqued because the tale is rooted in Karachi, a city in which I spent the early part of my childhood and to which I feel inextricably linked by family connections and an accumulation of memories. What's more, the blurb on the jacket compares *This Wide Night* to a novel for which I hold particular affection.

Anyone who has read *Little Women* by Louisa May Alcott will immediately grasp that this was a 'remake', due to the many parallels between the two books. The synergy ranges from the fact that both novels are set during a time of fighting and upheaval: Alcott's covered the American Civil War in the late 1800s whilst Hasin's is set during the India-Pakistan struggles of the 1970s, culminating in the creation of Bangladesh. Both works of fiction also explore similar themes, such as domesticity, work, and the constraints placed on women in society, reflected in the conflict between the accepted way of raising females and a more progressive approach which focuses on encouraging girls to think beyond their personal and societal limitations.

Sarvat Hasin, *This Wide Night*, Penguin Random House India, Delhi, 2016

Writing a story so closely identified with what is undoubtedly a much-loved literary heavyweight may not necessarily weaken a writer's work if it is read as an homage. I am reminded of the Bollywood films that are based on classic works of English Literature such as *Bride and Prejudice*, Gurinder Chadha's Indian take on Jane Austen's *Pride and Prejudice*, although this cross-over story was not received well by critics or the film-going audience. Hasin's book is perhaps also an attempt to write a version of a classic novel that is re-made from a South Asian perspective, a seductive and melancholy read that becomes grimly weighted and ethereal with every turn of the page.

A childhood spent in Karachi, Pakistan, and my teenage and adult years in London, delivered me the opportunity to broaden my literary space and identify with a diversity of stories whether they resurrect life in late 1800s America or are suffused with emotions, sounds and smells, all of which bring back memories of my young self. For this reason, the idea that *This Wide Night* is inspired by *Little Women*, a novel that whispers so very deeply to my heart, generated an initial thrill. However, upon reading the opening chapter I realised it is not merely referencing, but very closely following sequences from the book, and it was at that moment that the novel lost its shine for me. Those who have not read *Little Women* may well have an entirely different experience of reading Hasin's work, but for me this prior knowledge detracted somewhat.

Although not original, the book is well-written in places, depicting the trials and tribulations of tough, feisty and empowered young women with the solitary male on the outside. Hasin's writing is at times lucid, cleverly worded and steeped in emotion. Her description of places is truly evocative but this is all a little diluted by the nagging fact that this is a form of adaptation and the parallels lessen the rich storytelling capacity of the author. I expected so much because, like its source, this book was supposed to give voice to women but instead is told from a man's perspective. A male protagonist providing the medium through which the story of a female is conveyed is hardly a crime, and can be a worthy exercise if it means it offers another lens on a life, but for a large chunk of the story that lens is missing.

The character of Laurie is secondary in *Little Women*, to the role of the four sisters, yet Hasin very much places Jimmy (Laurie's doppelganger) at the heart of her story. The blurb declares that Jimmy will never be able to penetrate the inner circle of the women, but instead he locates himself at the centre of the periphery. Automatically, one wonders what direction this is heading if the theme is about the outer and internal struggles of this female group, yet articulated by a man. I kept imagining that perhaps Hasin had a subversive agenda here, whereby the narration is deliberately designed to make the reader move away from drawing too many parallels with *Little Women*, and possibly even think that here is a book which will present Laurie's point of view. But, as the story continued, I felt increasingly unsure of this theory.

As Laurie's story, though entwined with that of the girls, was not overall important in *Little Women*, he proved relatively endearing, even with all his flaws. Yet, Hasin places Jimmy as the narrator and everything is central to him, despite the implication that he occupies the margins. His shortcomings are magnified and I couldn't help but find this anti-hero difficult to like. I must confess I was never all that interested in Laurie, and so would never have been particularly enamoured by Jimmy either but what I found here was that it was all about him, and his perspective, and his vision of the sisters. During the part of the story where he is not even present among the sisters, having travelled to London, the author abruptly switches to third person narrative. This could have been a clever device to emphasise the narrator's incompleteness or disconnection when the sisters are absent from his life but really it didn't work for me.

Jimmy travelled to London in the 1970s and at this junction I was bursting for the trajectory to explore so much more. There were many young single men from the Indian sub-continent who had arrived in the UK at that time and were building lives and networks. The novel could have touched on their experiences, and struggles to integrate whilst maintaining their national identity. How lonely their existence must have felt at times, and how different it is now for those who are second and third generation living in the UK who have family and community to provide us with the support base that our forefathers felt lacking. Hasin's depiction of London is much to be admired but it is her sculpting of characters that falls short. I knew of some men of my father's generation who met and married English women but the relationship between the protagonist and the English woman in the novel is achingly one-dimensional and rather perpetuates the stereotype of the sexual lasciviousness of the white woman. This feeling of how to keep or manage different identities and what that means and how that would change and impact on him just doesn't arise. The narration itself is not located in any particular time. There is the odd clue that this was not narrated at the same time the events took place, but we don't know if he is looking back at events forty years later or less or more.

This Wide Night would have benefited greatly from one final very thorough edit. The writing could have been far more polished had the occasional spelling mistake and some awkward sentences been sorted out. This of course is down to the role of the editor, rather than the author, during the course of the publishing process. The prose has moments of beauty, and with an edit it would have flowed to perfection. The way it is written, so disturbingly close to the original story, coupled with the lack of editing, the confusing time-line all impinge upon the novel's success and could prevent it from going the full distance. This is a shame as the author obviously has an abundance of good stories in her.

I also felt that the character of the mother, evidently based on Mrs March, to be inadequately crafted to the extent that we learn so little about her. The author stopped short of delving deep enough to uncover why the mother's fate is so closely tied to the girls' eventual unravelling. Why did they feel such strong morbid despair? This wasn't touched on. The Captain, however, is depicted brilliantly, his words and his presence even when he is not there, take precedence. Again, though, if drawing parallels with Alcott's work, the girls' father, though very important to the girls and loved by them, is often away and clearly not the central figure. Here, the Captain is not meant to be at the epicentre of the emotional wellbeing of the family, but because the mother's character is sparsely drawn, he becomes so. The mother was the one who kept the girls together, as a unit, who celebrated them and gave them the space and freedom to not be forced to conform to society's expectations. But she is very much a secondary character hovering in the shadows even though we find how profoundly her daughters are connected to her. She is a leader of this group of autonomous women but this doesn't come across. There is very little sense of her presence. This would not matter if the story was not wound so tightly around her by the end.

Repeatedly the novel's landscape triumphs over the detail of those characters who inhabit it. The sense of war and suffering, of families fearful of the way in which their lives are being turned upside down is a victory of the written form.

> It was the time, too, for the city to fall apart. We could feels the seams coming undone even before the military came in. These were the years that would be written down in history as bloodstained and dirty but it didn't happen all at once, instead it crept slowly upon us.

It remains for the storyline to feel a poor runner-up. The explanation for why Leila goes to Paris instead of Ayesha is similar to *Little Women*. When Jimmy refers to his wife in the novel's opening paragraphs, the omission of a name provides a sense that it was most likely to be Leila, the youngest sister, modelled on *Little Women's* Amy March, who is the artist. In *Little Women*, the role of the 'professor' was as a complementary love interest to the protagonist, Jo, who he eventually marries. Meg's story as the eldest sister is largely about domesticity and the pressure to find a partner first. Hasin somewhat blends these two story arcs by having Maria, the eldest sister in *This Wide Night*, marry a professor.

The only glaring difference between the two novels is the ending. There were so many developments to the plot that you knew were coming and anticipated would happen, but in terms of continuity I found that I had expected something would occur but in logical terms did not know why. Personally, I feel that if I had not read *Little Women* I would have found it very confusing. Maybe the author is experimenting with a subversive agenda to illustrate that as a society we will never be able to penetrate the lives of these sisters and will remain the outsider. Clearly, this novel is about strong independent female characters but the result is disappointing. The ending is contrasting and you can see where the author attempted to change things and introduce an element of darkness, as a homage to *Virgin Suicides* (again noted in the book's blurb). However, this only serves to create a surreal conclusion that no one expects. It could be argued this is indeed a fabulous twist but for me it made little sense. Lurches in continuity continued to confuse. At times the narrative conveyed an immediacy. So at the end Jimmy receives an urgent phone call in the middle of the night, he rushes out, not even waiting for his *dada* to finish getting dressed. And yet it is also mentioned that he had bought cigars and presents for his wife but if he had left in such a panic he would not have had time to gather these.

Louisa May Alcott was pushing for a revolutionary educational agenda, having come from a liberal background and seeking to challenge traditional family roles. Hasin's agenda is unclear. But she is clearly a promising writer. I look forward to her next offering.

ET CETERA

ON POPULISM

Merryl Wyn Davies

In times such as these – Brexit, Trump, Macron being the most notable headlines – it seems appropriate to reconsider the complacent authority vested in the old adage 'vox populi, vox Dei', the concept that the voice of the people is the voice of God. We live in confusing times when the popular will is leading the democratic spirit a merry dance. Personally, I have long been a sceptic about the voice of the people – an eternally pliant ambiguity wrapped in a quandary of perennial vacillation, qualities never part of my idea of the divine.

How has the voice of the people, the popular will, come to be invested with the dignity of articulating the voice of God? The idea has roots in Biblical and Qur'anic tradition, becoming part of the interpretive repertoire of all the monotheistic religions. The Qur'an is unequivocal in placing its message in the hands of 'the people' (al nas). The focus is equally strong in the Christian Protestant traditions from which came the declarative investiture of 'We the People' with constitutional independence. The people are called to take responsibility for implementing the good news of divine guidance. The optimistic idea that the majority of the people will ultimately do the right thing and elect to follow the path of righteousness easily elides into the self-confident, and effortlessly self-serving assertion that those who claim allegiance to the revealed truth are the equivalent of that truth. The only problem with this correlation is history: high on aspiration; pity about the track record of performance. Not that reality has ever dented popular invocation of the rhetoric or assumption of the mantle of righteousness.

The familiar Latin formulation 'vox populi, vox Dei' indicates that the idea itself goes way back in time. Its origin is telling. The popularity of the formula arises from people getting the wrong end of the stick. As usual we are dealing with no innocent oversight. Taking the phrase out of context permits the venerable strategy of calculated inversion of meaning and intent for maximum latitude, the ideological elbow room to cause mayhem. The aphorism is credited to Alcuin of York (c 735-804) a scholar, clergy, poet and teacher remembered as 'the most leaned man anywhere to be found'. Alcuin was therefore an impeccable authority for what has proved a most useful idea – so long as what the monk actually argued is considered irrelevant. Keep the 'vox populi, vox Dei' as it easily trips off the tongue, conveniently forget the 'tumultuositas vulgi semper insaniae proxima sit' that followed: 'the tumult of the crowd is always close to madness'. Far from dignifying the popular will with divine authority Alcuin was advising his pupil the Emperor Charlemagne to beware and never listen to the urgings and enthusiasms of the cheering mob.

It would be fair to say subsequent history makes Alcuin the origin of the two faces of the popular will. On the one hand his most favoured words emboldened and empowered the idea of democracy which is reasoned, dignified humanity wearing its Sunday best raiment striving for what is right and proper. On the other hand the popular will carries with it its nemesis, an evil twin exactly in the sense of Alcuin's cautionary warning: populism, the ability of the mob to be stirred and manipulated to no good end. Two theories and down the Ages one perplexing question: how on earth does one distinguish one from the other? What constitutes the voice of the people? How is it to be heard and known? On what occasions should the voice be heeded and when is it not only politic but proper to ignore the urgings of the crowd? I am afraid this is not a question on which either history or current practise is decided.

Must we always live with ambiguity, in a quandary of which way to turn? This is no new problem. In 1327 Walter Reynolds then Archbishop of Canterbury preached a sermon on vox populi, vox Dei. The purpose of the sermon was to give warrant to popular acclamation by the mob for the investiture of Edward III as king usurping the place of his still living father Edward II. Alas this was no early stirring of a nascent democratic spirit, a sort of popularly elected monarchy, rather a neat ploy to find spurious rationale for a political upheaval bishops and barons had been seeking to bring about for some time. Rather than assume responsibility for deposing a king the elites neatly shifted the blame to the will of the people the better to get their own way. Popular enthusiasm for the new young king had been fed by endless rumour, which history still cannot verify, filtered and circulated to the masses about the personal peccadillos and proclivities of Edward II. One might call that populism in action.

Populism always implies the idea of manipulation of the emotions and passions of the crowd. The harangue of the demagogue looms misdirecting the ignorant multitudes and clearly no good can come of it. What is necessary is for the voice of the people to be properly audited so that it can be accurately assessed and heard with clarity. What could be better than to present the people with the issues and reasoned argument on the choices they offer? Then all one need do is arrange for a regularised recording of the individual decisions of the populace and obviously the opinion that gets the most support is the legitimate will of the people. Ah, isn't democracy wonderful.

In theory, of course democracy delivers. But there's many who slip between ballot box and governance. Democracy, the rule of the popular will, is no self-evident system: it can be and is constituted in a variety of ways and there's the rub. Remember the warning of Francis Pym. Pym was Foreign Secretary in Margaret Thatcher's government that had just prosecuted the highly jingoistic, successful and popular 1982 Falklands War. The following year Thatcher called a general election and a thumping landslide victory was expected. While appearing on a television programme during the election campaign Pym stated 'Landslides don't on the whole produce successful governments.' Elective dictatorship, the untrammelled exercise of unquestioned governing power by an overwhelming elected majority was what he was understood to mean. Give Thatcher and her ideological cohort too much power and they would ride roughshod over all dissent from within their own ranks let alone anywhere else. Pym was right. Election over huge majority in Parliament secured, Pym was unceremoniously sacked and his so called Wet, or moderate, wing of the Conservative Party was equally redundant. It took years of behind the scenes plotting for the Wets to oust the pestiferous Leaderene Mrs Thatcher. By that time swathes of Britain and the lives of large numbers of ordinary people had been laid waste in search of the ideological purity of market forces.

There are many ways of making democracy into elective dictatorship. It is of course the stock in trade of innumerable nations. Robert Mugabe regularly tops the polls by hounding, intimidating and generally manipulating the mechanics of elections. It was the defining feature of the eastern bloc countries who presented the electorate with no choice and then trumpeted 99 per cent majorities. Totalitarians of every stripe utilise the window dressing of democratic consultation of the will of the people. But, as we have seen in the case of the Mother of Parliaments, the people are just as capable of thrusting dictatorship on themselves.

Democracy is about constituting and institutionalising a system of representation that, hopefully, accurately reflects the voice of the people. It is not only the Mother of Parliaments that can frustrate this aspiration and deliver a democracy deficit at the behest of the people. Consider that other bastion and standard bearer for the virtues of democracy the Congress of the United States. An increasing number of constituencies of the House of Representatives have been so gerrymandered, carved, twisted and constrained as to make them effective one party zones. And that is exactly how they operate. In growing numbers of seats just one name appears unopposed on the ballot paper offering the electorate no choice. Or make that offering the electorate the choice of endorsing the single candidate or simply not participating. Indeed in American elections despite all the hype and bluster about the foundational importance and shining example of the democratic spirit the winner usually is apathy, non-participation. Those who do not vote are a higher percentage of the populace than support any other individual candidate. The people they say: 'who cares', 'whatever'; surely this is not anyone's idea of the voice of the divine. And then there is the bizarre institution of the Electoral College which means no American votes directly for any candidate for President of the most powerful country on earth. The founding fathers of the American constitution were especially enamoured of democratic libertarian rhetoric but shared a sceptical view of the popular will, a pronounced horror of populism. The Electoral College was their means to restrain populist tendencies. In two recent elections, 2000 and 2016, the winner of the popular vote has failed to gain a plurality in the Electoral College handing victory to George W Bush and Donald J Trump respectively. It should be added that for a country so proud of being democratic America is in parts highly activist in restraining and preventing citizens from acquiring and exercising the vote. There are regular purges of what are claimed to be errant voter rolls that suspiciously disenfranchise bona fide citizens, impediments to voter registration and laws withholding the franchise from certain citizens such as ex-convicts. Winston Churchill is famous for repeating the aphorism that democracy is the worst form of government except for all other forms – but there are times when the most vaunted exemplars seem determined to join the herd of other lesser forms of consulting the popular will.

If apathy and chicanery rule, how is the real voice of the people to be known? Politicians have devised an answer for that: referendums. The simple ploy is to appeal directly to the entire electorate, skipping all the complexities and distractions of the selection of representative intermediaries and just get the people to answer the question. One single question, focus attention folks and tell us what you think. Sounds easy. Does that really reflect the Brexit experience? The question on such a convoluted and complex issue is considerably more difficult, it turns out. As for reasoned debate was it populist stirring of base xenophobia or democracy at its purest? And when the resulting vote is so closely divided between yes or no what action has actually been mandated? Does democracy come down to the tyranny of a marginal minority to ignore the wishes and opinions of a sizeable minority? Does one referendum require another to clarify precisely what the voice of the people said or will say in light of the original result? Does repeating the question until it generates the result you want make referenda the perfect instrument of populist manipulation or concerned striving for true democracy?

There can be no doubt that in this day and age the people demand to be heard. Something must be done and people want things to change. The voice of the people is volatile. Such is the mould breaking mood that within one year a virtually unknown politician can conjure into existence a movement, morph it into a political party and end by presiding over a government with a secure legislative majority: the Macron effect. Is that populism or just democratic swings and roundabouts?

Beyond the confines of the First World hearing the voice of the people reveals a game of whispers which becomes vox Dei only when endorsed as a matter of political expediency by the counsels of other nations, the great powers. In country after country people taking to the streets to make their voice heard is populist cacophony, background noise unless and until it is determined to be genuine democratic stirring of legitimate conscience. Think of any number of popular uprisings – Georgia, Ukraine, Thailand, and of course the big one the Arab Spring – and the routine is clear. People spill onto the streets, occupy a central place, protest, argue, issue demands, declare principles in a welter of democratic activism in its most innocent and nascent form. People risk their lives and livelihoods for the sacred trust of articulating the cry for justice, freedom and proper representation of their wishes. It is populism in search of democracy. Its fate in each instance is most likely to be determined by outside forces. Tahrir Square was hailed in the West as a beautiful moment until Egyptians actually got a democratic election. Suddenly the popular will in the main voted for a party shaped by religion which was not at all the choice required of them by western powers. How swiftly was old style repressive dictatorship reinstituted with foreign assistance to become just the very thing required to displace the voice of the people. Whether it is populist uprising or free and fair democratic procedure for much of the world the voice of the people is inchoate background noise waiting to be told whether it can have any say at all.

One is not supposed to be quite so disparaging of democracy. As the misuse of Alcuin's words have proved over the course of time the will of the people has acquired an aura of sanctity. Reform is always possible, admission of minor flaws acceptable, major scepticism, however, is not popular in polite society. The suggestion that populism and democracy can be indistinguishable because they are but flickers in the eye of the beholder – a questionable conclusion that smacks of having very little confidence in the rational maturity of the general public. I think it is time to explain my position. My concern is that distinguishing the will of the people by hearing the voice of the people is getting harder and harder. The distinction between populism and democracy resting as it does on manipulation by elites is not perishing from the earth but making a major assault on our consciousness, thanks to the ample tools servicing our information age. People are being given the headline news that their views matters while what matters to people is becoming ever more difficult to discern among the welter of forums and media available through which to broadcast and disseminate information.

In the age of rolling 24-hour news and the plethora of social media platforms as well as opinion polls and surveys on every subject under the sun it is suggested that popular opinion otherwise known as the will of the people can be known. Really? Recall Brexit, Trump and the teary eyed Theresa May on election night. If 'vox populi' were to be 'vox Dei' then surely the polls should tell us so, except that they don't. Reflecting the views of people in the street is the most basic technique of modern journalism it is the ever popular vox pop, our portal into the greater arena of 'vox populi'. And for me this is where it all goes wrong.

I know a thing or two about vox popping. I cut my milk teeth as a cub reporter on this stratagem. It is a tawdry imposter for real respect for popular opinion. Vox pops are cheap, and random, as most news outlets will acknowledge. What they are less ready to admit is that they are self-serving because they are convenient substitutes for genuine inquiry. What they serve is the desire for quick and cheap ways to fill column inches and air time. What they deliver is a false sense of the importance of ordinary people and the pretentious bluster that even though random they are telling us something worth knowing about what ordinary people think is important.

Whenever instructed to vox pop, I, the eager cub reporter on a local weekly newspaper, would duly answer 'yes Sir, back in five minutes.' Our newsroom, situated in the centre of the town, backed onto the bus station. Thus for the expenditure of no travel expenses or meal allowances or any other devious journalistic money making device the job could be done with minimal effort or time. At a bus station an ever changing cross section of the local population could be found conveniently foregathered at any time of day loitering without intent, the perfect captive opinion fodder. Being a local paper one was accompanied by a photographer – people like to see their picture in the paper. We would accost whomsoever we wished and demand their opinion on what was deemed the burning question of the week. While I took down the response in best shorthand, the photograph would be taken then the name of the respondent (and never forget to ask their age!). Four or five such brief encounters and the job was done and it was back to the office before anyone had noticed one's absence.

What could possibly be wrong with such basic human encounters? Let me tell you getting people's opinions can be like pulling teeth. Thus it was that I learnt the skills of the trade, the subtle ploys of asking questions that fed people the answers I desired. It was always considered desirable to have a range of opinions to demonstrate the free thinking of the populace at large therefore the same question would not suffice for everyone, variation had to be introduced to induce differential outcomes. When as so often people would answer 'yes' and pause interminably or 'no' as their attention drifted away one merely had to write the question in answer form to accommodate with proximal accuracy what had transpired in the conversation. As my familiarity with the format grew along with my familiarity with the mindset of the local populace I gradually realised how easy it was to manipulate popular commentary, how hard to discover what it is people really think, or indeed think about. And then came the fateful day. I approached a gentleman: 'Sir, can I ask what is your opinion of…' I cannot remember the precise nature of the inquiry. I have never forgotten the reply: 'Oh, I don't 'ave opinions'. There it is, the root of my scepticism. I have met a man honest enough to own up to a condition more common than anyone would like to acknowledge. Sometimes people just do not care about the things we think they should, sometimes they feel unequal to drawing conclusions on subjects that seem remote, complex or difficult; more often than we would care to admit they simply do not have opinions.

Ever since that day I have been deeply scarred by the knowledge that one should never set one's hope too high when it comes to people. They are ever open to populist manipulation within or without the guise of democratic consultation. Never expect that your own considered rational and sensible view on any subject will necessarily be shared by the public at large. Always remember there will always be people who should not have the opinions they do but democracy means we have to respect them anyway. Never forget there are those who have no opinions at all and democracy means empowering them for whatever its worth, they too have the right to put a mark somewhere for something for whatever their opinionless fancy should be at the time. No, not exactly vox Dei, just the world we live in.

TEN POPULIST MOMENTS

There are many unexamined assumptions about populism that don't stand up to scrutiny. Many journalists and academics discuss it as if it were some kind of ideology, like liberalism or conservatism. Others go further and regard populism as an inherent feature of right-wing politics. In the wake of Brexit and Trump, populism is increasingly referred to as though it were a new feature of political culture. These assumptions belie ideological biases rather than empirical fact.

It would be more fruitful to start by regarding populism as a form of politics that juxtaposes a morally virtuous people (the 'us' or 'we') against a corrupt elite ('them'). The definition of 'us' and 'them' can shift depending on the particular populist's ideological leanings. For example, the corrupt 'they' could be the liberal media, supreme court judges, bankers or leaders who are soft on immigration. As such, populism is a political strategy. It's a way for political hopefuls to cast themselves as outsiders seeking mass support from 'the people' to challenge a status quo that is portrayed as deeply unjust – a perception that could be completely spot on or pure deception.

What's more, these hopefuls often choose when they want to turn the populist dial up or down. For example, Argentina's Juan Domingo Perón was not a populist all of the time during his first stint as president from 1946 to 1955. In fact, it can be argued that Perón employed populist tactics only for the three years before he was elected president up until 1949. After that, the post-war economic crises disrupted his populist efforts and Perón had to maintain political power through more authoritarian measures.

Bearing this in mind, here is a List of ten populist moments that can balance the current Brexit- and Trump-dominated headlines.

1. The People's Party (United States) (1892-6)

Not all successful populist movements rely on larger-than-life leaders, nor do they need to result in majoritarian victories. Established in 1891, the People's Party was an agrarian-populist political party in the United States of America. It was even known as the Populist Party – not to be confused with the American Populist Party, a minor political party founded in 2009 and which advocates 'classical liberalism'. The People's Party was built upon a coalition of poor, white cotton farmers in the South (mostly from North Carolina, Alabama and Texas), and wheat farmers in the Plains states (mostly Kansas and Nebraska). The party was highly critical of capitalism, especially the banking and railroad industries, and allied itself with the labour movement. It did remarkably well in the 1892 presidential election, with its candidates James B Weaver and James G Field winning 8.5 per cent of the popular vote and carrying five states – Colorado, Idaho, Kansas, Nevada and North Dakota. It also won an impressive ten per cent of the vote in the 1894 House of Representatives elections. Between 1892 and 1896, the People's Party was a major force in left-wing politics in the US. In 1896, it merged with the Democratic Party, but a remnant of the party remained until 1908.

2. Luiz Inácio Lula da Silva (2006)

Da Silva, known simply as Lula, is a founding member of Brazil's leftist Workers Party (PT). He ran for president three times unsuccessfully – in 1989, 1994 and 1998. In 2002, the Brazilian Real fell by 33 per cent amid jitters in the financial markets that he was poised to win the presidency. Nine years later, after two terms, Lula left office with an approval rating of 87 per cent. His administration saw tens of millions of Brazilians escaping poverty through his policies, including the successful Bolsa Familia (Family Allowance) and Fome Zero (Zero Hunger) programmes. That Lula remained so popular throughout his time in power is remarkable, but his most populist moment came in 2006. Dogged by allegations of corruption against the PT, Lula embarked on a successful coalition of interests between the private sector and the labour movement – a strategy that was dubbed Lulism by his aide, André Singer. Lula's legacy, however, has been marked by controversy. His hand-picked successor, Dilma Rousseff, was impeached by the Senate in 2016. In 2017, the still-popular Lula was sentenced to nine years and six months in prison for corruption and money-laundering. His eligibility to contest in the 2018 elections depends on the outcome of his appeal against the court ruling.

3. Tony Blair (1997)

The first day of May 1997 was like a new dawn – optimism filled the air. Tony Blair and the British Labour Party won a resounding victory in one of the greatest general election victories of the twentieth century, overturning eighteen years of Conservative government. The morning after the night before, the iconic image of Cherie Blair answering the door of Number Ten in her nightie and bedhead to receive a bouquet of congratulatory flowers summed up a new era. But Blair's firm couching at the centre end of centre-left politics won as many critics as it did admirers. More left-leaning Labour stalwarts bristled at his New Labour 'Third Way' project that straddled capitalism and socialism-lite. One also cannot mention Blair without referencing the 2003 invasion of Iraq, the consequences of which reverberate to this day. Ironically, the popular protests against Blair's involvement in the war foreshadowed the fall of New Labour in the 2010 elections. Sadly, Blair's aggressive foreign policy and his obsession with his legacy eclipsed many of the positive policy implementations achieved during his time in government. Regardless of what his detractors say, though, Blair did uphold investment in social services, the National Health Service and the championing of equality and diversity. Unfortunately, his reputation as a populist hero will always be tarnished, rightly or wrongly, by his disastrous decision on Iraq.

4. Syriza and Podemos (2014-5)

While the rest of Europe appeared to be lurching to the right on a wave of populist sentiment during the past decade, the Mediterranean seemed to be bucking the trend. Countries rendered a husk of their former selves by the post-2008 implosion of their economies were still floundering in financial wilderness. This was exacerbated by crippling debts and intense pressure from the refugee crisis that disproportionately affected them. Yet it was the far-left movements that made impressive political breakthroughs in Greece (with Syriza), Spain (with Podemos) and, to a lesser extent, in Italy (with newcomers Senso Comune). Syriza swept into government in 2015 and Podemos began its meteoric rise in 2014. These far-left populist movements have not yet delivered the utopia that had been hoped for, as illustrated by Syriza's failed attempt to challenge some of the EU's more pro-establishment policies. But they show that there continues to be an alternative to the status quo.

5. Emmanuel Macron (2017)

After the populist upsets of Brexit and Trump, the world's attention turned to the French election of May 2017 with much trepidation. Marine Le Pen, leader of the far-right Front National, must have felt she was tantalisingly close to being handed the reins of power. Anti-Muslim and anti-immigration sentiment captured the public imagination and the result seemed like anyone's guess. Late in the election rounds, however, a former banker, Emmanuel Macron, began to emerge as a serious contender. Could he possibly upset the latest in populist upsets by preventing a Front National win? It turned out he could. Macron became the acceptable centre-left candidate in opposition to Le Pen's far-right populism and won comfortably. Yet for many, he was a compromise candidate. According to them, his win was, if anything, a defeat for populism – including, arguably, of the far-left variety led by Jean-Luc Mélenchon. A 'Frexit' had been averted and things would carry on as before. Le Pen bemoaned the victory of the 'continuity candidate' while those on the left made no secret that they had held their noses to vote for Macron whom they felt offered no new solutions to France's problems. The rest of the world, however, temporarily breathed a sigh of relief.

6. Evo Morales (2006)

In 2005, Evo Morales became Bolivia's first president to come from the indigenous majority since the country declared independence in 1825. As the charismatic leader of the coca growers' union, he emerged from the social movements that had forced the country's two previous presidents from office. Within a year of taking office, he renationalised Bolivia's oil and gas industries, which helped to increase the country's public investments and boosted its foreign reserves. Poverty soon went down by 25 per cent – extreme poverty dropped by 43 per cent. He also drove the rewriting of the constitution which redefined Bolivia as a 'multi-ethnic and pluri-cultural' nation. Since being re-elected in 2009, however, it appears that Evo, as he is popularly known, has had to deal with increasing public disgruntlement. In February 2016, he narrowly lost a referendum that would have allowed him to stand for a fourth term in office. Internationally, Bolivia's relations with the US have cooled since Evo assumed the presidency. He forged close links with other left-wing Latin American leaders, including Venezuela's Chavez and Fidel and Raul Castro from Cuba. In 2013, he expelled the US Agency for International Aid, accusing it of conspiring against the Bolivian people and in 2014, he branded US President Barack Obama an 'imperialist' at the UN General Assembly. Evo has achieved a great deal during his presidency, but questions remain about his ability to address corruption and Bolivia's overdependence on fossil fuels.

7. Barack Obama (2008 and 2012)

Poor Hilary Clinton. Denied a chance to become the first woman president of the US by a populist opponent. Twice. The second time, when she was trumped by Trump in 2016, is still fresh in many people's minds. The first time, she was pipped to the post during the Democrats' primaries by one Barack Hussein Obama. Yes, in 2008, Obama was often described as a populist presidential candidate – in a good way by some left-wing commentators. Others dismissed his campaign as empty, pie-in-the-sky fantasy. Once in office, he became more pragmatic – at least until he had to run for re-election in 2012, which involved fending off the right-wing populist Tea Party movement and barely disguised racist attacks on his background. And this is why, according to him, he is the real populist – not Trump. In the heat of the 2016 presidential campaign, Obama said, without referring directly to the Trump campaign, 'They don't suddenly become a populist because they say something controversial in order to win votes…. That's not the measure of populism. That's nativism, or xenophobia, or worse. Or it's just cynicism.'

8. Joko Widodo (2014)

Joko Widodo's victory at the 2014 Indonesian presidential elections was hailed as a breakthrough for the country's evolving democracy, after decades of military dictatorship that ended in 1998. For one thing, Jokowi, as he is popularly known, was a local politician who made it good nationally – he was the Governor of Jakarta before running for the presidency. More captivating for the public was his journey from small-town carpenter to president of the world's largest Muslim country. And even more remarkable was that Jokowi's opponent also ran on a populist platform. Prabowo Subianto, the wealthy son-in-law of former dictator Suharto, engaged in a campaign that was xenophobic, anti-elite, pro-poor and dripping with anger. Jokowi's populism, however, was non-confrontational, inclusive and technocratic – he primarily focused on the improvement of public services. It's a bit like the Indonesian Obama going against the Indonesian Trump and winning. Since securing the presidency, however, Jokowi has had to contend with the old elites trying to regain influence and has himself been sliding into authoritarianism. A wildly successful populist campaign has yet to translate into a populist or even popular administration.

9. Aung San Suu Kyi (post-2015)

Could one of the world's most famous former political prisoners and pro-democracy icons be turning into a populist? If we're thinking of populism as a political strategy that can be used at particular moments in time, it's not unthinkable. Ever since she was placed under house arrest by the Burmese military junta from 1989 to 2010, Aung San Suu Kyi proved to be extremely popular but was arguably not a populist. Her party, the National League for Democracy (NLD), boycotted the 2010 elections, resulting in victory for the military-backed Union Solidarity and Development Party. But in the 2012 by-elections, the NLD won 43 out of 45 seats and Suu Kyi became an MP. The NLD won a landslide victory in the 2015 elections, taking 86 per cent in the Assembly of the Union. Constitutionally, Suu Kyi was unable to become prime minister – her husband and children are foreign citizens – but she assumed the newly created role of State Counsellor, which is akin to Prime Minister. Since coming to power, however, 'The Lady' has turned out to be a nasty piece of work. She has remained silent over numerous human rights issues, including the imprisonment of student activists, the exploitation of workers and has strenuously denied the very existence of horrific persecution of the Rohingya minority. The line between political pragmatism and populism is a fine one.

10. The Scottish Nationalist Party (2015)

If we define populism as a strategy employed by political outsiders – whether on the right or left – to challenge the status quo, then it would fit the SNP circa 2015 like a glove. The 2014 referendum for Scottish independence was a nail-biter. The narrowness of the vote – 44.7 per cent in favour of independence and 55.3 per cent against – made unionists uncomfortable and emboldened pro-independence supporters. The post-referendum momentum continued and resulted in a previously unthinkable landslide for the SNP in Scotland in the 2015 general election. The party's number of seats in the UK parliament went from six to 56 overnight – that's more than an eightfold gain. But cracks began to show after the 2016 EU referendum and the rise of the Labour Party's Jeremy Corbyn. The SNP could no longer bank on its self-styled progressive, inclusive brand of nationalism. Even unionism didn't seem like such a bad thing anymore to some Scottish voters, post-Brexit and post-Trump. The party still emerged victorious in the 2017 snap elections, winning 35 out of 59 seats. For now, the SNP's brand of populist nationalism seems to be running out of steam.

CITATIONS

Introduction: Fibs and Fibbers by Ziauddin Sardar

On various definitions and approaches to populism, see Cass Mudde and Cristóbal Rovira Kaltwasser, *Populism: A Very Short Introduction*: (Oxford University Press, 2017);
Bart Bonikowski, 'Three Lessons of Contemporary Populism in Europe and the United States'. *Brown Journal of World Affairs* 23, no. 1 (2016): 9–24, and Robert S Jansen, 'Populist Mobilization: A New Theoretical Approach to Populism'. *Sociological Theory* 29, no. 2 (2011): 75–96.

The post-truth titles include: Matthew d'Ancona, *Post-Truth: The War on Truth and How to Fight it* (Ebury Press, London, 2017); Evan Davis, *Post-Truth: Why We Have Reached Peak Bullshit and What to do About it* (Little Brown, London, 2017); James Bell, *Post-Truth: How Bullshit Conquered the World* (Biteback, London, 2017); Daniel Levitin, *Weaponised Lies: How to Think Critically in the Post-Truth Era* (Penguin, 2017); and Ari Rabin-Havt and Media Matters, *Lies Incorporated: The World of Post-Truth Politics* (Anchor Books, New York, 2017). See also the wonderful short philosophical treatise by Harry G Frankfurt, *On Bullshit* (Princeton University Press, 2005).

Other works mentioned include: Bertram Gross, *Friendly Fascism: The New Face of Power in America* (Black Rose Books, Montreal, 1980); Joe Earle, Cahal Moral and Zach Ward-Perkins, *The Econocray: On the Perils of Leaving Economics to the Experts* (Penguin, 2017); Paul Wilmott and David Orrel, *The Money Formula: Dodgy Finance, Pseudo Science and Howe Mathematicians Took*

Over the Markets (Wiley, London, 2017); and Cathy ONeil, *Weapons of Math Destruction* (Allan Lane, London, 2016).

The quote by Ibram X Kendi is from *New York* magazine, August 21-September 3, 2017, p32; Jon Snow, 'In fractured Britain the media are part of a distant elite', *The Guardian* 24 August 2017. The Didier Eribon quote is from *Returning to Reims,* Semiotext(E), translated by Michael Lucey, Los Angles, 2013; original French edition published by Librairie Artheme Fayard, Paris, 2009. P222.

On the corruption at the BBC, see: http://novaramedia.com/2016/06/12/the-fantastic-corruption-of-the-broadcasting-british-class/ and http://novaramedia.com/2015/10/02/bbc-reforms-5-reasons-to-fight-for-the-uks-most-reactionary-institution/

On postmodernism, see Jean-Francois Lyotard, *The Postmodern Condition: A Report on Knowledge* (Manchester University Press, 1984; original French edition, editions de Minuit, Paris, 1979) and Ziauddin Sardar, *Postmodernism and the Other: The New Imperialism of Western Culture* (Pluto, London, 1998). See also: 'What Just Happened', in *The Postnormal Times Reader* edited by Ziauddin Sardar (Centre for Postnormal Policy and Futures Studies, 2017)

The Netherworld by Ashis Nandy

The importance of Gustave Le Bon's *The Crowd: A Study of the Popular Mind* (New York: Macmillan, 1896; available in digitcal forms in various places), for any student of populism can be gauged from its impact on a wide range of those influenced by it—from Benito Mussolini and Vladimir Lenin to Sigmund Freud and Wilhelm Reich. On utopias and total politics, see Ashis Nandy, 'Idealism, Ideology and Total Politics', *Outlook*, Independence Day Issue, 11 August 2017. On lynching in India, see for instance, Rupa Subramanya, 'Has India Become a "Lynchistan"?', ORF (Observer Research Foundation), http://www.orfonline.org/expert-speaks, 1 July 2017. Other works mentioned: Pankaj Mishra, *Age of Anger: A History of the Present* (New Delhi: Penguin Books, 2017); David Riesman, Nathan Glazer and Reuel Denney, *The Lonely Crowd: A Study of the Changing American Character*

(New Haven, Conn:Yale University Press, 1950); Wilhelm Reich, *The Mass Psychology of Fascism* (New York: Farrar, Strauss and Giroux, 1980); and Woody Allen (Writer and Director), *Zelig* (Produced by Warner Bros and Orion Pictures, 1983).

Back Home to a Darker Age by Abdelwahab El-Affendi

A copy of the report of the Runnymede Commission on Antisemitism, A Very Light Sleeper:The Persistence and Dangers of Antisemitism (London: Runnymede Trust, 1994) can be downloaded from here: http://www. runnymedetrust.org/companies/17/74/Islamophobia-A-Challenge-for-Us-All.html.The quote is from p9.

On Tony Blair, see: 'Tony Blair's speech to the Foreign Policy Centre', *The Guardian*, 21 March 2006; 'Tony Blair wanted $35 m to build UAE brand and influence', *The Daily Telegraph*, 9 July 2016.

Matti Bunzl quotes are from 'Between Anti-Semitism and Islamophobia: Some Thoughts on the New Europe,' *American Ethnologist* 32, no. 4 (2005), pp. 499. 499-500, 501-503, and 503-507. Other quotes are from: Bernard Lewis, 'The Roots of Muslim Rage', *The Atlantic Monthly*, 266: 3, September, 1990, pp. 47-60;The Jens Rydgren quotes are from 'Is extreme right-wing populism contagious? Explaining the emergence of a new party family', *European Journal of Political Research* 44: 413–437, 2005, pp. 426-429; Cas Mudde 'Europe's Populist Surge A Long Time in the Making', *Foreign Affairs*, 95: 6, November/December, 2016, pp. 25-30; Daniele Albertazzi and Duncan McDonnell, eds., *Twenty-First Century Populism:The Spectre of Western European Democracy*, Basingstoke: Palgrave Macmillan, 2008, p. 3; and Paris Aslanidis, 'Is Populism an Ideology? A Refutation and a New Perspective', *Political Studies*, 2016, Vol. 64(1S) 88–104, p96 and pp96-99

See also: Paul Berman, *Terror and Liberalism*, New York: W W Norton, 2003; J P Zúquete, (2008) 'The European extreme-right and Islam: New directions?', *Journal of Political Ideologies*, 13 (3), 321-344; Sheri Berman, 'Populism Is Not Fascism, But It Could Be a Harbinger', *Foreign Affairs*, 95:

6, November/December, 2016, pp. 39-44; Wajahat Ali *et. al.*, *Fear, Inc.: The Roots of the Islamophobia Network in America*, Washington, DC: Center for American Progress Action Fund, August 2011; Michael Kazin, 'Trump and American Populism: Old Whine, New Bottles', *Foreign Affairs*, 95: 6, November/December, 2016, pp. 17-24 and 18-20; Samuel Huntington, *The Clash of Civilizations*, Simon and Schuster, New York, 1996; and Abdelwahab El-Affendi, ed., *Genocidal Nightmares: Narratives of Insecurity and the structure of Mass Atrocities*, Bloomsbury Academic, London, 2015

Loss of World by Richard Appignanesi

David Kilcullen's quotes are from his book, *Blood Year: Islamic State and the Failures of the War on Terror*, C. Hurst & Co, London 2016, appearing with Kilcullen's interview by Toby Hamden in *The Sunday Times*, News Review, 7 February 2016, p.8. Ayman al Zawahiri quotes is from Laura Mansfield, *His Own Words: A Translation of the Writings of Dr. Ayman al Zawahiri*, TLG Publications, USA, 2006, p.127. The Baader Meinhof quotes are taken from Stefan Aust, *The Baader Meinhof Complex*, The Bodley Head, London, 2008, p.397.

Alain Badiou citations are from 'Philosophy and the 'war on terrorism' Section 8, in *Infinite Thought: Truth and the Return to Philosophy*, translated and edited by Oliver Feltham and Justin Clemens, Continuum, New York, 2005, p.111.

The Manifesto quotes are from Karl Marx and Friedrich Engels, *The Communist Manifesto*, translated Samuel Moore (1888), with an Introduction by A.J.P. Taylor, Penguin Books, 1967, for this and the following quotes, pp. 80 – 84.

Paolo Pasolini quotes are from: Pier Paolo Pasolini, 'My 'Accattone' on TV after the genocide', in *Lutheran Letters*, translated Stuart Hood, Carcanet New Press, Manchester, 1983, pp.100 – 105, et passim; 'A Lutheran Letter to Italo Calvino', in *Lutheran Letters*, op. cit., p.118; 'Unhappy Youths', in *Lutheran Letters*, op. cit., p.16; 'Profezie', in *Ali dagli ocche azzurri*, (1965), translated Giuliana Porucca, Garzanti, 1996; and Enzo

Siciliano's biography *Pasolini*, translated John Shepley, Random House, New York, 1982, pp.361 – 362.

For Badiou's dialogue contributions, see op. cit., pp. 121 – 122. I invent for Pasolini in his spirit. But see Pasolini, from 'Drugs – a real Italian tragedy', in *Lutheran Letters*, p.59.

See also: Brigadier S.K. Malik, *The Quranic Concept of War*, Foreword by General M. Zia-Ul- Haq, Himalayan Books, New Delhi, reprint 2012.

Three Propositions by Sindre Bangstad

For a recent dissertation on the Progress Party in Norway, see A. R. Jupskås, *Persistence of Populism: The Norwegian Progress Party, 1973-2009*, Unpublished PhD Dissertation in Political Science, University of Oslo, 2015.

For a study of right-wing and far-right populist discourse on Islam and Muslims in Norway, see inter alia S. Bangstad, *Anders Breivik and the Rise of Islamophobia*, Zed Books/University of Chicago Press, 2014; S. Bangstad, 'Eurabia Comes to Norway', *Islam and Christian-Muslim Relations* 24 (3): 369-391; S. Bangstad, 'Islamophobia – What's In A Name? Analysing the discourses of *Stopp Islamiseringen av Norge* (Stop The Islamisation of Norway, SIAN), *Journal of Muslims in Europe* 5 (2) 2016: 1-25.

For the work of Ruth Wodak on right-wing populist discourse, see R. Wodak, *The Politics Of Fear: What Right-Wing Populist Discourses Mean*, Sage Publications, 2015.

My paraphrasing of Lila Abu-Lughod's statement to the effect that theories of what it is to be 'native' must not be confused with 'native' experience is drawn on Lila Abu-Lughod's usage of Pierre Bourdieu in her new afterword to L. Abu-Lughod, *Veiled Sentiments: Honor and Poetry in a Bedouin Society*, 30th Anniversary Edition, University of California Press, 2016, p. 277.

The point that European fascists in the 1920s and 30s rarely came to power on their own account is drawn from Robert O. Paxton's classical *The Anatomy of Fascism*, Vintage Books, 2005.

For political science titles on populism, see J-W. Müller, *What is populism?* Pennsylvania University Press, 2016, C. Mudde and C. R. Rovira Kaltwasser, *Populism – A Very Short Introduction*, Oxford University Press, 2017.

Among ethnographies of right-wing populists in Europe, Douglas R. Holmes' seminal *Integral Europe* stands out. D. Holmes, *Integral Europe: Fast-Capitalism, Multiculturalism, Neofascism*, Princeton University Press, 2000.

Sociological titles on right-wing populism applying ethnographic fieldwork include A. R. Hochschild, *Strangers in their own land: Anger and Mourning on the American Right*, The New Press, 2016 and J. Gest, *The New Minority:White Working Class Politics in an Age of Immigration and Inequality*, Oxford University Press, 2016.

For a central title on the 'crises of inequality', see P. Rosanvallon, *The Society of Equals*. Translated by Arthur Goldhammer. Harvard University Press, 2012.

On the expansion of inequalities across Western liberal democracies under neo-liberalism, see T. Piketty, *Capital in the Twentieth Century*, Harvard University Press, 2014.

On technocratic and cosmopolitan 'frequent travellers', see C. Calhoun, 'The Class Consciousness of Frequent Travelers: Toward a Critique of Actually Existing Cosmopolitanism', *South Atlantic Quarterly* 101 (4): 869-97.

For an article which explores the disenfranchisement of citizens in lower social strata, see A. Mondon, 'Limiting Democratic Horizons

To A Nationalist Reaction: Populism, the Radical Right, And The Working Class', forthcoming.

On Salafi-jihadi extremism, see S. Maher, *Salafi-Jihadism: The History of An Idea*, Hurst & Co., 2016 and on how to understand its attractions, see O. Roy, *Jihad and Death: The Global Appeal of Islamic State*, Hurst & Co., 2017.

Stuart Hall's work on the 'great moving right show' and 'authoritarian populism' can be found in S. Hall, *Selected Political Writings: The Great Moving Right Show and Other Essays*. Edited by S. Davision, D. Featherstone, M. Rustin and B. Schwarz, Duke University Press, 2017.

Populism as critical of elites and claiming that they alone represent the people, see Müller, *What is Populism?* pages 3-4.

Racialised Iranian nationalism, see R. Zia-Ebrahimi, *The Emergence of Iranian Nationalism: Race and the Politics of Dislocation*, Columbia University Press, 2016.

For Norwegian-Iranians active in Norwegian far-right political formations, see S. Bangstad, 'Islamophobia – What's in a Name? Analyzing The Discourses of Stopp Islamiseringen av Norge (Stop The Islamisation of Norway, SIAN), *Journal of Muslims in Europe* 5 (2) 2016: 145-169.

The referent 'the people' as an 'floating signifier', see E. Laclau, *On Populist Reason*, Verso, 2005.

On appeals to different constituencies, see Mudde and Kaltwasser, *Populism – A Very Short Introduction*, page 9.

Nationalism as entailing both inclusion and exclusion, see T. H. Eriksen, *Ethnicity and Nationalism: Anthropological Perspectives*, Pluto Press, 1993.

For Islamophobia as a 'great unifier' among far-right and right-wing populists across Europe, see F. Hafez, 'Shifting borders: Islamophobia as a common ground for building pan-European right-wing unity', *Patterns of Prejudice* 48 (5): 479-499, 2014.

Surveys on attitudes towards minorities in Norway, see HL-Centre, *Antisemitism in Norway? The Attitudes of the Norwegian Population Towards Jews and Other Minorities*, The HL-Centre, 2013.

On Robert Mercer's funding of Trump's media campaign, see J. Mayer, 'Trump's Money Man', *The New Yorker*, March 27, 2017.

For the Progress Party's slashing of taxes, see S. Bangstad, 'The Rise of the Populist Right in Norway', *Boston Review* June 3, 2015.

On the 'culturalization of politics', see W. Brown, *Regulating Aversion: Tolerance in the Age of Identity and Empire*, Princeton University Press, 2006. 'Christianist secularism, see R. Brubaker, 'Between nationalism and civilizationism: the European populist movement in comparative perspective', *Ethnic and Racial Studies* 40 (8) 2017: 1191-1226.

For some of the best studies of religion and populism available to date, see the contributions to N. Marzouki, D. McDonell and O. Roy (eds.), *Saving the People: How Populists Hijack Religion*, Hurst & Co., 2016.

The quote from Rogers Brubaker is from 'Between nationalism and civilizationism', page 1211.

My usage of the term 'politics of presence' is drawn from my own 2015 monograph S. Bangstad, *The Politics of Mediated Presence: Exploring The Voices Of Muslims in Norway's Mediated Public Spheres*, Scandinavian Academic Press, 2015.

The concept of 'conviviality' is drawn from Paul Gilroy's seminal P. Gilroy, *Postcolonial Melancholia*, Columbia University Press, 2005.

The quote from Stuart Hall is from S. Hall, *The Hard Road to Renewal: Thatcherism and the Crisis of the Left*, Verso, 1988, page 273.

Nox Populi by Gordon Blaine Steffey

Our current head of state took the Oval office with his name already a brand; his campaign and election were about 'growing' that 'name brand.' In dissent I have been careful not to use it. Here is a complete list of the works I have used in this article:

Eric Alterman, 'Who are they calling elitist? Why do conservatives continue to feel oppressed by the 'liberal elite'?' *The Nation*, 27 March 2008, https://www.thenation.com/article/who-are-they-calling-elitist/ (Accessed 9 July 2017).

Aristophanes, *Equites*, *Aristophanis Comoediae*, vol. 1, ed. F. W. Hall and W. M. Geldart (Oxford: Oxford University Press, 1922).

Michael Barone, 'How stupid and vicious do elites think 'we' are,' *Washington Examiner*, 25 January 2016, http://www.washingtonexaminer.com/how-stupid-and-vicious-do-elites-think-we-are/article/2581264 (Accessed 10 July 2017).

Lisa Belkin, 'Quayle adviser-for-life hits the campaign trail,' *The New York Times*, 11 September 1988, http://www.nytimes.com/1988/09/11/us/quayle-adviser-for-life-hits-the-campaign-trail.html?mcubz=0 (Accessed 13 July 2017).

Ronald Brownstein, 'The Kaleidoscope Society: America's hurtling change is inverting our oldest national motto,' *The Atlantic*, 1 July 2015, https://www.theatlantic.com/politics/archive/2015/07/the-kaleidoscope-society/432237/ (Accessed 11 July 2017).

Margaret Canovan, 'Taking Politics to the People: Populism as the Ideology of Democracy,' *Democracies and the Populist Challenge*, ed. Y. Mény and Y. Surel (New York: Palgrave, 2002).
Ann Coulter, *¡Adios America! The left's plan to turn our country into a third world hellhole* (Washington, D.C.: Regnery Publishing, 2015).

Beverly Gage, 'How 'elites' became one of the nastiest epithets in American politics,' *The New York Times Magazine*, 3 January 2017, https://www.nytimes.com/2017/01/03/magazine/how-elites-became-one-of-the-nastiest-epithets-in-american-politics.html (Accessed 9 July 2017).

Joshua Green and Sasha Issenberg, 'Trump's data team saw a different America—and they were right,' *Bloomberg Businessweek*, 10 November 2016, https://www.bloomberg.com/news/articles/2016-11-10/trump-s-data-team-saw-a-different-america-and-they-were-right (Accessed 15 July 2017).

Ian Hacking, 'Making Up People.' *London Review of Books* 28 no. 16, 2006: 23-26, https://www.lrb.co.uk/v28/n16/ian-hacking/making-up-people (Accessed 1 July 2017).

Richard Heinisch, 'Success in opposition – failure in government: explaining the performance of right-wing populist parties in public office,' *West European Politics* 26 (3), 2003: 91-130.

Laura Ingraham, *Shut up and sing: How elites from Hollywood, Politics, and the UN are subverting America* (Washington, D.C.: Regnery Publishing Inc., 2003). Emphasis in original.

Ernesto Laclau, 'Populism: What's in a name?' *Populism and the Mirror of Democracy*, ed. Francisco Panizza (London: Verso, 2005).

Michael Lipka, '10 facts about religion in America,' Pew Research Center, 27 August 2015, http://www.pewresearch.org/fact-tank/2015/08/27/10-facts-about-religion-in-america/ (Accessed 10 July 2017).

Friedrich Nietzsche, *The Gay Science*, tr. Walter Kaufmann (New York City: Vintage Books, 1974), 121. Emphasis in original.

Eileen Oginitz, 'Evangelicals Seek Political Clout,' *Chicago Tribune*, 3 January 1980.

Sarah Posner, 'How Donald Trump's new campaign chief created an online haven for white nationalists,' *Mother Jones*, 22 August 2016, http://www.motherjones.com/politics/2016/08/stephen-bannon-donald-trump-alt-right-breitbart-news/ (Accessed 10 July 2017).

Dominic Rushe, 'Top US coal boss Robert Murray: Trump "can't bring mining jobs back,"' *The Guardian*, 27 March 2017, https://www.theguardian.com/environment/2017/mar/27/us-coal-industry-clean-power-plan-donald-trump (Accessed 14 July 2017)

My Demagogue Hero by Barnaby Rogerson

The *Iliad* can be found in various translations. Alexander Pope' s translation is available in Kindle from Amazon. On Cleon of Athens, see Lowell Edmunds, Cleon, 'Knights' and Aristophanes' Politics, University Press of America, 1987. James Fenimore Cooper citation is from *The American Democrat: Hints on the social and civic relations of the United States of America*, published New York 1838, H & E Phinney

Awaam by Raza Ali

There are several biographies of Imran Khan including: Christopher Sandford, *Imran Khan: The Cricketer, The Celebrity, The Politician* (HarperCollins, London, 2009), and *Imran Khan* by Ivo Tennant (Gollanzc, London, 1994). See also by the man himself, *Autobiography of Imran Khan* (Pelham, Neew York, 1983) and *Indus Journey: Personal View of Pakistan* (Chatto & Windus, London, 1990).

On ibn Hanbal, see the classic biography *The Life of Ibn Hanbal by Ibn al-Jawzi*, translated by Michael Cooperson (New York University Press, 2016). Mufti Muneeb's declaration on Qadri can be found in Urdu at: http://www.awaztoday.pk/singlecolumn/30745/Mufti-Muneeb-ur-Rehman/Ashiq-e-Rasool-Mumtaz-Hussain-Qadri-Shaheed-Ka-Suffer-Aakhrat.aspx

Desi Populism by Bhavik Doshi

The works cited include: Benedict Anderson, *Imagined Communities: Reflections on the Origins and Reflections of Nationalism,* Verso, London, revised edition, 2016; Chetan Bhatt, *Hindu Nationalism: Origins, Ideology and Modern Myths*, Berg, Oxford, 2001; and Amnesty International, *State of the World's Human Rights*, London, 2017.

A Brit in the Bible Belt by Sughra Ahmed

The *Daily Mail*'s 'enemies of the people' headline can be found at http://www.dailymail.co.uk/news/article-3903436/Enemies-people-Fury-touch-judges-defied-17-4m-Brexit-voters-trigger-constitutional-crisis.html

The *Independent*'s report on the post-Brexit rise in hate crimes is from http://www.independent.co.uk/news/uk/home-news/racist-hate-crimes-surge-to-record-high-after-brexit-vote-new-figures-reveal-a7829551.html

Timothy Snyder's twenty lessons from the twentieth century is at http://inthesetimes.comarticle/19658/20-lessons-from-the-20th-century-on -how-to-survive-in-trumps-america

Monuments to Hubris by Marjorie Allthorpe- Guyton

David Goodhart quote is from *The Road to Somewhere, The Populist Revolt and the Future of Politics,* Hurst, London, 2017. Alexei Monroe quote is from NSK á Lyons, *Perspektive* 2/2; and Barbara Kruger citation is from *Space Force Construction*, *Art Review* 2017 p2.

See also: Alexei Monroe, *Interrogation Machine-Laibach and NSK*, MIT Press, Massachusetts, 2005; and Susan Strange, *Casino Capitalism*, Blackwell, London 1986, republished Manchester University Press, 2015.

Return to Future by Hassan Mahamdallie

For more information on 'A Temporary Future Institute' see: http:// ensembles.mhka.be/events/temporary-futures-center -l-internationale

The Marx quote is from *The Eighteenth Brumaire of Louis Bonaparte. 1852.* The review of Simryn Gill's spare and stunning photographs of decay, by Leah Ollman, appeared in *Los Angeles Times* 12 June 2014, and can be accessed at: http://www.latimes.com/entertainment/ arts/la-et-cm-simryn-gill-photographs-varola-20140602-story.html The postnormal times quote is taken from M HKA exhibition booklet *Postnormal Times*. The final quote is taken from Ziauddin Sardar, editor, *The Postnormal Times Reader*, Centre for Policy and Futures Studies, 2017, p67.

The List: Ten Populist Moments

Wikipedia has a brief but comprehensive entry on the People's Party (United States) at https://en.wikipedia.org/w/index.php?title =People%27s_Party_(United_States)&oldid=787496066.
For background on Lula's legacy and his corruption sentence, see Phillips, Dom. 'Brazil's Ex-President Lula Sentenced to Nearly 10 Years in Prison for Corruption'. *The Guardian*, 12 July 2017. https:// www.theguardian.com/world/2017/jul/12/ brazil-president-lula-convicted-corruption.

To relive Cherie Blair's bedhead, see Denes, Melissa. 'That's Me in the Picture: Cherie Blair, the Morning after Labour's Election Victory, 2 May 1997'. *The Guardian*, 11 May 2015, sec. Art and design. http://www.theguardian.com/artanddesign/2015/may/08/cherie-blair-nightie-downing-street-thats-me-in-the-picture.

For background on Tony Blair's Third Way, see Mellbye, Anne. 'A Brief History of the Third Way'. *The Guardian*, 10 February 2003, http://www.theguardian.com/politics/2003/feb/10/labour.uk1. For more on New Labour, see Parkison, Justin. 'The Rise and Fall of New Labour'. *BBC News*, 3 August 2010, sec. UK Politics. http://www.bbc.co.uk/news/uk-politics-10518842.

The breakdown of votes during the 2016 Spanish General Election can be found on Wikipedia: https://en.wikipedia.org/w/index.php?title=Spanish_general_election,_2016&oldid=791790068. And to revisit Syriza's 2015 electoral victory in pictures, go to 'Greece Election: Syriza Party Wins'. *BBC News*, 20 September 2015. http://www.bbc.co.uk/news/av/world-europe-34309058/greece-election-syriza-party-wins.

On the 2017 French presidential election, see Birnbaum, Michael, and Anthony Faiola. 'With Le Pen Defeat, Europe's Far-Right Surge Stalls'. *Washington Post*, 7 May 2017, https://www.washingtonpost.com/world/europe/in-le-pen-defeat-europes-far-right-wave-crashes-to-a-halt/2017/05/07/e8edfa46-301f-11e7-a335-fa0ae1940305_story.html.

For more on Evo Morales, read his profile at BBC. 'Profile: Bolivia's President Evo Morales'. BBC News, 22 February 2016, sec. Latin America & Caribbean. http://www.bbc.co.uk/news/world-latin-america-12166905.

On Obama's populism in 2008 and 2012, see Erwin-Frank, Jon. 'Why Obama: The Populist'. *The Daily Gazette*, 25 March 2008. http://daily.swarthmore.edu/2008/03/25/why-obama-the-populist/ and

Thrush, Glenn. 'Obama the Reluctant Populist'. *Politico*, 2012. http://www.politico.com/news/stories/0112/71933.html. For his take-down of Donald Trump, see Fabian, Jordan. 'Obama: Trump Isn't a Populist'. *The Hill*, 29 June 2016. http://thehill.com/homenews/administration/286037-obama-trump-isnt-a-populist.

Marcus Mietzner has written on the populism of Joko Widodo at 'Jokowi: Rise of a Polite Populist'. *Inside Indonesia*, 27 April 2014. http://www.insideindonesia.org/jokowi-rise-of-a-polite-populist and 'Reinventing Asian Populism: Jokowi's Rise, Democracy, and Political Contestation in Indonesia'. *East-West Center*, 24 March 2015. http://www.eastwestcenter.org/publications/reinventing-asian-populism-jokowis-rise-democracy-and-political-contestation-in. On Aung San Suu Kyi's more recent political dilemmas, see Baldwin, William. 'Suu Kyi: New Mandela or Old Populist?' *Asean Economist*, 5 January 2016. http://aseaneconomist.com/suu-kyi-new-mandela-or-old-populist/.

For background on the Scottish Nationalist Party's 2015 electoral upset, see BBC. 'Election 2015: SNP Wins 56 of 59 Seats in Scots Landslide'. *BBC News*, 8 May 2015, sec. Election 2015 Scotland. http://www.bbc.co.uk/news/election-2015-scotland-32635871.

CONTRIBUTORS

Sughra Ahmed is Associate Dean at the Office for Religious Life, Stanford University, California ● **Raza Ali** runs a book club for London-based Muslims ● **Marjorie Allthorpe-Guyton** is President of the International Association of Art Critics (AICA), British Section ● **Richard Appignanesi**, former editor of *Third Text*, is a writer and philosopher ● **Sindre Bangstad** is a Research Associate at KIFO (Institute For Church, Religion And Worldview Research), Oslo, Norway ● **Omair Bhat** (b.1995), who lives and writes in Srinagar, India, thinks of himself as something of a poet ● **Merryl Wyn Davies** is a writer based in Merthyr Tydfil, Wales ● **Bhavik Doshi**, a researcher on the Indian diaspora, works in the international development sector ● **Abdelwahab El-Affendi** is Dean of the Faculty of Social Sciences and Humanities at the Doha Institute for Graduate Studies ● **Leyla Jagiella** is a cultural anthropologist ● **Scott Jordan**, a Research Fellow at the Centre for Postnormal Policy and Futures Studies, is a screenwriter and film critic ● **Hassan Mahamdallie** is a playwright and an art critic ● **Alia Masood** is a child protection consultant with a fondness for English Literature ● **Ashis Nandy**, political psychologist and public intellectual, is one of India's foremost philosophers ● **Muddasir Ramzan**, who blogs for the Muslim Institute, lives and writes in Kashmir, India ● **Hasan Manzar**, a Pakistani short story writer and psychiatrist, is celebrating his 83rd birthday ● **Barnaby Rogerson**, writer and publisher, is the author of the widely acclaimed *The Prophet Muhammad: A Biography* ● **Carole Smith** is an English poet and short story writer ● **Shanon Shah** is Deputy Editor of *Critical Muslim* ● **Gordon Blaine Steffey** holds the Barbara Boyle Lemon '57 and William J. Lemon Chair of Religion and Philosophy at Randolph College in Lynchburg, Virginia ● **Eric Walberg**, journalist and writer, is the author of *Postmodern Imperialism: Geopolitics and the Great Game.*